To:

_____

From:

_____

On the occasion of:

_____

LIVING A
MIGHTY
Faith

LIVING A
MIGHTY
Faith

A SIMPLE HEART AND A POWERFUL FAITH

ANGUS BUCHAN

THOMAS NELSON
Since 1798

JANUARY

January 1
THE HEALING POWER OF FORGIVENESS

BE KIND TO ONE ANOTHER, TENDERHEARTED, FORGIVING
ONE ANOTHER, EVEN AS GOD IN CHRIST FORGAVE YOU.
EPHESIANS 4:32

ONE OF the most difficult things in life is to forgive a person who has purposely hurt us. But as we move into a new year, let us remeber that forgiveness allows us to move on and be free. Second Corinthians 2:7 says, "You ought rather to forgive and comfort [one who causes you grief], lest perhaps such a one be swallowed up with too much sorrow."

So let us embrace the freedom of forgiveness in this new year. God has forgiven us so much, and we are called to do the same for those who have hurt us. God sets the example: in 1 John 1:9 we're told very clearly that if we confess our sins we'll be cleansed of all unrighteousness. God is more than happy to meet us where we are.

But in the Bible, we read about what unforgiveness can do. There once was a servant who owed a large amount of money to his master (Matt. 18:21–35). He pleaded with his master to cancel the debt. Graciously, his master did, and the servant went out rejoicing. A little later, a man who owed the servant a small amount of money came to him begging for mercy, but the servant refused. When the master heard of this, he raged, "You wicked servant! I forgave you all that debt because you begged me. Should you not also have had compassion on your fellow servant, just as I had pity on you?" The servant was condemned to repay the whole debt (vv. 32–33). With consequences like these, it's no wonder that forgiveness often benefits us more than the one forgiven.

PRAYER: Father, You offer unconditional forgiveness to all who humble themselves before You. Please help me to offer this same forgiveness to others, so that I too may be forgiven. Amen.

January 2
QUALITY, NOT QUANTITY

SOMEONE WILL SAY, "YOU HAVE FAITH, AND I HAVE
WORKS." SHOW ME YOUR FAITH WITHOUT YOUR WORKS,
AND I WILL SHOW YOU MY FAITH BY MY WORKS.
JAMES 2:18

YOU'LL SEE it in your local bargain store: mass production and demand for more and cheap goods have left our culture with a case of quantity over quality. I don't believe this is the way the Lord means us to live. No matter what your business is or where you work, there's a big difference between just doing things and doing things well.

The same thing applies to our relationships. Our children, spouses, friends, and loved ones need our undivided attention for the relationship to flourish. When our children have serious problems to discuss or are in need of godly counsel, they need you to sit down and pay 100 percent attention to them. We need to be able to give a good amount of our undivided time to them so they can unwind and get to the point, which might be hard for them to verbalize. Quantity can be important, but quality is better—and it lasts.

I spoke to a dear friend recently about this and he said to me, "It is like using the rifle as opposed to the shotgun." A rifle will hit the target, whereas a shotgun shoots all over the place, not necessarily making the impact required.

In this busy year, let us be more concerned about hitting the target than just making a general impact. Let us seek direction from the Lord early in the morning so He will direct our paths during the day. This will enable us to become more effective for the kingdom of God in our workplaces and families. If we show our faith by our works, then our works need to be the best we can give of ourselves.

PRAYER: Lord, please keep my daily efforts from becoming scattershot. I pray for the patience to have lasting, quality impact in the places You've put me. Amen.

January 3

WALKING BY FAITH

WE WALK BY FAITH, NOT BY SIGHT.
2 CORINTHIANS 5:7

SOME YEARS ago my eldest son, Andy, and I were growing seed maize during a drought. We had planted the maize by faith, and just enough rain had fallen for it to germinate. But then the land became drier by the day, and the maize started to shrink.

Early one morning, after his quiet time with the Lord, Andy went out to the field, dropped to his knees, and prayed that God would send rain to save the crop. By midday, big, heavy, black clouds full of rain had come up over the horizon, but they didn't come far enough. Andy could see the white sheets of rain coming down everywhere but where we needed them. Excitement became despondency, even anger.

Andy went back to the office and opened up his Bible to the place he had been reading earlier that morning—Ecclesiastes 11:4: "He who observes the wind will not sow, and he who regards the clouds will not reap." God's message could not have been clearer! Andy repented of having a heart of unbelief and asked God to forgive him. Then he carried on working. That night, sure enough, a gentle rain started to fall. The crop was saved.

When we do our very best and leave the rest in His hands, every drought will end with rain.

PRAYER: Dear Lord Jesus, You bless me every day, and yet I still find it difficult to fully trust You. Please help me to walk by faith, no matter the circumstances, always trusting that You will come through for me. Amen.

January 4
LIVING A BALANCED LIFE

HE WHO HAS ENTERED HIS REST HAS HIMSELF ALSO
CEASED FROM HIS WORKS AS GOD DID FROM HIS.
HEBREWS 4:10

AMID THE hustle and bustle of this life, it is critical to take time to step back and evaluate our lives. I see too many young people who are burned-out, and they haven't even lived half their lives!

Considering our long work hours and nonexistent boundaries between work and home life, it's easy to see why so many people become depleted. But in Mark 6:31–32, Jesus said, "'Come aside by yourselves to a deserted place and rest a while.' For there were many coming and going, and they did not even have time to eat. So they departed to a deserted place in the boat by themselves." If Jesus and His disciples needed a time-out, how much more do you and I?

If we lose our balance and become overworked, our judgment becomes dulled and we make irrational decisions. We might say we can't afford to rest, but actually, we can't afford not to. For me, after an intense period of work, I like to saddle my horse and go for a ride into the hills, where I spend time enjoying the quiet and the beauty of God's creation. Whether it's jogging, creating something, working with your hands, or spending time with friends and loved ones, taking time for rest is critical.

It's no good being a "mover and a shaker" for a few years, only to end up totally burned-out. Make sure you keep fresh for yourself, for your family, and for the Lord.

PRAYER: Lord, I know that I often am tired and stressed out.
Help me to appreciate the importance of rest and relaxation and
to take time out to spend in Your beautiful world. Amen.

January 5
LESSONS FOR LIFE

"LET YOUR LIGHT SO SHINE BEFORE MEN, THAT THEY MAY SEE
YOUR GOOD WORKS AND GLORIFY YOUR FATHER IN HEAVEN."
MATTHEW 5:16

A FATHER once wrote a letter about his son's education, saying, "He will have to learn . . . that all men are not just; but teach him . . . that for every scoundrel there is a hero; that for every selfish politician, there is a dedicated leader. If you can, teach him the secret of quiet laughter. Teach him the wonder of books, but also give him quiet time to ponder the eternal, the mystery of birds in the sky, bees in the sun, and the flowers on a green hillside."

The letter continues: "In the school, teach him it is far more honorable to fail than to cheat. Teach him to have faith in his own ideas, even if everyone tells him they are wrong. Teach him to be gentle with gentle people and to be tough with the tough. Try to give my son the strength not to follow the crowd when everyone is getting on the bandwagon. Teach him, if you can, how to laugh when he is sad. Teach him there is no shame in tears. . . . Treat him gently, but do not coddle him, because only the test of fire makes fine steel."

We need men and women such as this man describes, and those who will teach and nurture them. We bear great responsibility to speak the truth in love, and to not be afraid to stand up for righteousness.

PRAYER: Father God, it is tough for young people making their way
through this world today. Help me to be a positive influence on my
young friends, sharing Your love and peace with them. Amen.

January 6
TURN THE OTHER CHEEK

*"I TELL YOU NOT TO RESIST AN EVIL PERSON. BUT WHOEVER SLAPS
YOU ON YOUR RIGHT CHEEK, TURN THE OTHER TO HIM ALSO."*
MATTHEW 5:39

HAS SOMEONE offended you lately? Or caused you to feel hurt or resentful? It may
have been something a family member said, or a comment made about you at work.
Often the guilty party is unaware they've given offense. But when we feel offended
and bear a grudge, we're the ones who suffer, not those who have hurt us.

Let us take a leaf out of the Master's book. On the night He was betrayed, the
Lord Jesus was sitting quietly, having a meal with the disciples, when they began to
argue about who would be the greatest in the kingdom of God.

Can you imagine how that must have made the Lord feel? He must have been
so disappointed. For three years, He had taught them how to love, how to serve,
and that the greatest should try to be the least. He also knew that that very evening
Judas would betray Him for thirty pieces of silver, and that Peter soon would deny
Him three times. Jesus had every reason to be offended by the behavior of His
closest friends. Yet He lovingly served them.

We can so easily become angry and offended by the actions of others. But Jesus
said we should turn the other cheek and lead by example, being gracious and
empathetic, praying for the those who have offended us, and trusting that in time
their attitudes will change.

PRAYER: Dear Lord, I pray that I might think twice before I take offense at
someone's words or actions. Let everything I do be flavored with love. Help
me to turn the other cheek and not to hold grudges against anyone. Amen.

January 7

DECLARE WAR ON WORRY

"WHICH OF YOU BY WORRYING CAN ADD ONE CUBIT TO
HIS STATURE? IF YOU THEN ARE NOT ABLE TO DO THE
LEAST, WHY ARE YOU ANXIOUS FOR THE REST?"
LUKE 12:25–26

WE LIVE in difficult times. Things seem to be falling apart all around the world. It's not surprising we're left feeling insecure and worried. Interestingly, *worry* comes from an Old English word meaning "to strangle." How often do we feel as though we can't breathe or think straight when we worry? Yet our heavenly Father knows our needs even before we ask Him, so we need not be afraid. God is a giver. He wants to bless us, and it gives Him great pleasure to do so. If we work hard and leave the rest to the Lord, we'll see that He is much more capable of looking after our loved ones and our future than anybody else.

A doctor friend told me that many of the patients who come to him suffer from psychosomatic symptoms, or sickness brought on by one's mental attitude. Some of us are already so negative the devil doesn't have any work to do. When the sun rises in the morning, we say, "Here comes the drought!" At midday, when the clouds roll in, we say, "Here comes the flood!" A person with a negative outlook can never be happy, and worrying about things that are out of our control takes all the joy from our hearts. When you worry, put your trust in the Lord, and you'll find your days will go so much better.

PRAYER: Dear Jesus, when I am worrying endlessly about things I can
do nothing about, help me to hand over all my concerns to You, knowing
that You have the best plan for my life. In Jesus' name, amen.

January 8
FULLY RELY ON GOD

GIVE ME NEITHER POVERTY NOR RICHES—FEED ME WITH
THE FOOD ALLOTTED TO ME; LEST I BE FULL AND DENY
YOU, AND SAY, "WHO IS THE LORD?" OR LEST I BE POOR
AND STEAL, AND PROFANE THE NAME OF MY GOD.
PROVERBS 30:8—9

WHAT A blueprint for balancing wealth and humility! It's second nature for people to strive to be self-sufficient. After all, we don't want to be dependent on anyone. We don't want to be a burden, a passenger, or a taker. But know this: God is different. God *wants* us to depend on Him and not on our own ability. When we have everything we need, we tend to forget where our strength comes from. If we have needs that have not yet been met, that's cause for joy because it can keep us close to the Lord.

The danger starts when we put too much trust in ourselves, in our own ability, in our education, in our finances—and not in God. Remember the story of the foolish rich farmer in Luke 12:16–21. He had a bumper crop and thought to himself that he should build bigger barns, then sit back and take it easy. But God said to him, "Fool! This night your soul will be required of you; then whose will those things be which you have provided?" (v. 20).

Let us continue to do the very best we can. But at the end of the day, let us also understand that our future lies firmly in the hands of the Creator of heaven and earth.

PRAYER: Heavenly Father, it is in my nature to want to be self-sufficient.
Please remind me that every blessing comes from You. Help me to trust
in You to walk with me and provide for my needs every day. Amen.

January 9
SHARE YOUR STORY

I WILL MENTION THE LOVINGKINDNESSES OF THE
LORD AND THE PRAISES OF THE LORD, ACCORDING
TO ALL THAT THE LORD HAS BESTOWED ON US.
ISAIAH 63:7

IT'S IMPORTANT for us to share our history with others. As I ride around my farm, every square foot brings back memories, both fond and tragic. I look out at a row of pine trees my late father planted and I remember him as if it were yesterday. The farm doesn't have a single corner that isn't full of love and the presence of God. My retired foreman, Simeon, is still with me on the farm. Often I'll stroll over to Simeon's house on a Sunday afternoon, and we'll sit and reminisce about the early days when we started.

The greatest story of all, though, is the story of the life of our Lord and Savior Jesus Christ. What a story! In the mere thirty-three years He lived on earth, Jesus gave us all we need to know about life and death. His story is summed up in John 3:16: "For God so loved the world that He gave His only begotten Son, that whoever believes in Him should not perish but have everlasting life." Spend time reading the greatest story of all, especially when the going gets tough. And tell your own story to your loved ones. It will bond you together and remind you of God's goodness to you.

PRAYER: Father, I thank You for always being by my side, no
matter what I have gone through. Prompt me to share with others
Your greatness and all You've done in my life. Amen.

January 10

A FATHER'S ROLE

DO NOT PROVOKE YOUR CHILDREN TO WRATH, BUT BRING
THEM UP IN THE TRAINING AND ADMONITION OF THE LORD.
EPHESIANS 6:4

GOD IS very clear about the need for order in the home. Husbands must love their wives as much as Christ loves the church. If necessary, we must be ready to lay down our lives for our families. When men start to honor and love their wives as Christ loves the church, they'll see a different spirit in the home.

The love we speak of consists of putting food on the table, disciplining the children, and rolling up our sleeves to help our wives. Make sure everybody knows that your wife is the most important person in this world to you. I don't know of any woman who would have a problem submitting to her husband if he were prepared to give his life for her and their children, put food on the table, educate their children, and protect her. Problems arise when the man abdicates his responsibility.

Children need to obey their parents, but parents are commanded to support their children rather than antagonize them. When a father starts to encourage his children, all of a sudden those youngsters will blossom. All parents should watch the words they speak. Those words can mean life or death for a child, because words can stay with children for the rest of their lives. Let's make an effort to ensure our homes are disciplined and ordered, yet filled with love.

PRAYER: Dear Jesus, I know that discipline is not pleasant, but is vital
in the long run for so many reasons. Please help me to do my part in
ensuring order in the home by living according to Your Word. Amen.

January 11

A DEADLY FOE

BE STRONG IN THE LORD AND IN THE POWER OF HIS MIGHT.
EPHESIANS 6:10

A BEAUTIFUL proverb says, "We can never see the sunrise by looking to the west." In other words, where we focus is important. Beware of that deadly foe called discouragement!

In *Streams in the Desert*, L. B. Cowman tells the story of an eagle who had been mortally wounded by a hunter: "His eyes still gleamed like a circle of light. Then he slowly turned his head, and gave one more searching and longing look at the sky. . . . The beautiful sky was the home of his heart . . . and now, so far away from home, the eagle lay dying, done to the death, because for once he forgot and flew too low."

The eagle in this story stands for the soul. We are meant to fly high, close to the Lord, soaring in communion with Him. But when we lower our sights and take our eyes off hope, we become vulnerable to discouragement and begin to sink. Like the eagle, we put ourselves in range of being picked off by a rifle shot. Fly in the presence of God, in the "home of our hearts," and discouragement will have no hold over us. Cowman encourages, "Keep the skyward look, my soul; keep the skyward look!"

Let's focus on the Lord's promises and the joy of his presence. Keep your eyes on Him, not on your circumstances, and you will soar.

PRAYER: God, when my soul is discouraged, raise my sights
toward You so that I may fly as I was meant to. Amen.

January 12
OUR CHILDREN NEED ROLE MODELS

THESE WORDS WHICH I COMMAND YOU TODAY SHALL BE IN YOUR
HEART. YOU SHALL TEACH THEM DILIGENTLY TO YOUR CHILDREN,
AND SHALL TALK OF THEM WHEN YOU SIT IN YOUR HOUSE, WHEN YOU
WALK BY THE WAY, WHEN YOU LIE DOWN, AND WHEN YOU RISE UP.
DEUTERONOMY 6:6–7

I LEARNED one very important lesson with my own children many years ago: they'll never do what you tell them to do—they'll only do what *you do*. Like never before, young people are looking for role models. They're not looking for someone to put on a show, but someone who acts out the life of a parent and leader. I never saw my dad mistreat anyone or tell a sordid joke. He was an honorable man who respected those around him. My dad never owed anybody a penny. He was always a well-dressed, well-kept man. And he didn't speak too much—something I still have to learn! But when he did speak, it was always worth hearing. Dad always had time for me, even though he worked up to eighteen hours a day. I was always so proud to be able to walk next to him and see the respect he commanded from others because of who he was, not because of what he said or how "entertaining" he was.

This is the kind of role model our children want us and need us to be. We find the absolute and ultimate role model in Jesus Christ, our Lord and Savior. What an example He was when He walked on this earth! He expects you and me to follow His example and to be good role models for younger generations.

PRAYER: Dear Lord, please help me to follow the example You gave in the Bible, and to offer a consistent role model to every young person I encounter. Amen.

A PERSONAL TESTIMONY

"GO HOME TO YOUR FRIENDS, AND TELL THEM WHAT
GREAT THINGS THE LORD HAS DONE FOR YOU, AND
HOW HE HAS HAD COMPASSION ON YOU."
MARK 5:19

WHEN I was about six years old, I heard the gospel for the first time and prayed the Sinner's Prayer. I spent hours every day talking to the Lord. I used to dream about preaching to thousands of people. I was passionate about preaching, but lacked the qualifications necessary to become a minister. I began drifting from God, going first to Scotland to study agriculture, then to Australia where I rode horses and played rugby. Finally, I met my wife, Jill. I was a successful young man in the eyes of the world by the time we got married, but I was far away from God.

After we had children, we decided to sell our farm, put everything on the back of a big truck, and move from central Africa to South Africa. I bought a piece of overgrown bush and worked seven days a week, eighteen hours a day, to turn it into a successful farm. The Lord started to break me down to the point where I could not sleep at night. It was then that somebody invited us to church. I didn't want to go, but finally, Jill and I went to a Saturday night bring-and-share, then to church the next morning, where I experienced the power of personal testimony for the first time. A lay preacher shared his own story through floods of tears, and I was deeply moved. On that day, February 18, 1979, I made a sincere commitment to the Lord. My life was transformed, and I have never been happier. That's my personal testimony. What is yours? I encourage you to recount it for yourself today, in thanks to God and in preparation to share with those around you.

PRAYER: Lord, thank You for giving me a story to tell. Help
me to share it with those You put in my path. Amen.

January 14
THE DEFENDER OF THE FAITH

THE LORD IS MY ROCK AND MY FORTRESS AND MY DELIVERER;
MY GOD, MY STRENGTH, IN WHOM I WILL TRUST; MY SHIELD
AND THE HORN OF MY SALVATION, MY STRONGHOLD.
PSALM 18:2

JESUS IS the defender of the faith, the Son of the living God. It's so wonderful to know that there is somebody watching over us twenty-four hours a day, seven days a week. His name is Jesus.

So why panic? Why put our hope in our meager reasoning and resources when we have unlimited resources in God? Jesus died for you, and all He wants in return is for you to rely on Him. He alone will supply all your needs (Phil. 4:19). That is what gives us peace. Believers have a peace that others crave. That is why other people come to us, looking for what we've got. There is a joy, a certainty about us that they can't find anywhere else. It is our job to introduce them to our defender.

The Lord not only defends us; He defends Himself. He is far more capable of defending Himself than we are of defending Him to others. Instead, let them be won over by our love and trust in Him. There is only one God, and He is sovereign and supreme. He has never been defeated. We don't have to be concerned about the evil one defeating us. The devil can never beat us while God is with us. We can rely on the promise in 1 John 4:4 that the God who is within us is greater than he who is in the world.

PRAYER: Dear God, thank You for always having Your eye on me. When I become afraid, anxious, or preoccupied with defending either myself or You, please remind me of Your promises to come to my rescue. Amen.

January 15
LIVING TESTIMONIES

WOE IS ME, FOR I AM UNDONE! BECAUSE I AM A MAN OF UNCLEAN
LIPS, AND I DWELL IN THE MIDST OF A PEOPLE OF UNCLEAN
LIPS; FOR MY EYES HAVE SEEN THE KING, THE LORD OF HOSTS.
ISAIAH 6:5

IT IS dreadful to hear someone who proclaims to be a Christian speaking negative words and using bad language. We are living testimonies and ambassadors for Jesus Christ at all times—not just in religious settings. It's up to us to discipline our mouths and be different from those around us.

I once heard a story about a man who worked on the railways. He had a limited vocabulary and tended to use bad language on a regular basis. After he got saved, he promised the Lord he would never swear again. Nobody believed that he could do it. But for weeks on end he never swore or used the Lord's name in vain. That is, until one day his hand got trapped between two carriages. He let out a profane word as his hand was crushed. When the ambulance arrived to take him away, he asked them to wait even though his hand was a mess. He got down on his knees in front of all of his friends and repented. Only after that did he allow the ambulance to take him to the hospital. The crowd was amazed by how seriously he took his promise to God!

People are watching us all the time and listening to what we say. Let us not be known for having unclean lips, but let people always say that we are an encouragement to everyone around us.

PRAYER: Lord, I pray for Your strength and prompting as I
discipline my mouth. Even when I slip, may my repentant heart
honor You and show an example to others! Amen.

January 16
THE MARKETPLACE

"THOSE WHO ARE WELL HAVE NO NEED OF A
PHYSICIAN, BUT THOSE WHO ARE SICK."
LUKE 5:31

THESE DAYS there are more opportunities than ever for us as believers to share our faith and our hope with others. God has told us to go into all the world and preach the gospel. Yet when we do that, we are often put in situations where we can no longer follow social norms. The same thing happened with Jesus, but He went wherever there was a need, ministering to "those who are sick" rather than catering to the well and pleasing the wealthy Pharisees.

Peter Marshall told how he was invited to speak to an audience made up of very wealthy individuals at a champagne breakfast in Washington, DC. Instead of champagne, Marshall asked for fruit juice. The man sitting next to him noticed he was not drinking the fine imported champagne. Curious, the man wanted to know why. Marshall replied by saying that as a minister, many people came to him to seek his counsel. He said that nine times out of ten, the tragedies in these people's lives were related to alcohol abuse. Accordingly, Marshall felt he could not counsel them if he were partaking himself. The rich man went to see Marshall a week later and committed his life to Christ.

It's not always what we say that impresses the world, but how we act when we're in "the marketplace," or going about our daily business. Let us keep preaching the gospel at all costs and, as Saint Francis of Assisi purportedly said, use words only if necessary.

PRAYER: Dear Lord, may my actions honor You as I go about my daily business.
Prompt me to follow You even when I forget others are watching. Amen.

January 17

REDEEMING THE TIME

YOUR EYES SAW MY SUBSTANCE, BEING YET UNFORMED. AND IN
YOUR BOOK THEY ALL WERE WRITTEN, THE DAYS FASHIONED
FOR ME, WHEN AS YET THERE WERE NONE OF THEM.
PSALM 139:16

DO YOU know that Jesus knows exactly how many days you've got left before He calls you home? And that He knew this before you were even born?

Our choices can largely determine our quality of life, but the length of our lives is in God's hands. At my stage of life, my objective is no longer to see how long I can stay on this earth, but to do what I can with the time God has given me—with redeeming that time. How about you? Are you trying your best just to survive, or are you living life to the full?

Jesus said in John 10:10, "I have come that they may have life, and that they may have it more abundantly." *Abundantly* refers to enjoying life, and to the surplus of peace that comes from living with purpose. If it feels as though you're just existing, remember God has given you the gift of your days so you can aim high and use everything at your disposal for His glory.

Job 14:5 reads, "Since his days are determined, the number of his months is with You." In other words, God has put us on this earth for a limited season. We can either waste the time we have left, or we can ask what God wants us to do and work toward it. If God is on your side, then there is nothing that can hold you back.

PRAYER: Dear God, in moments when I feel drained or aimless,
please show me Your purpose for my brief time on earth. Give me
renewed vision and energy for carrying out Your work. Amen.

January 18

WISDOM FROM THE LORD

FOR THE LORD GIVES WISDOM; FROM HIS MOUTH
COME KNOWLEDGE AND UNDERSTANDING.
PROVERBS 2:6

WHENEVER YOU listen to a person's story, remember that there is always another side to it. In fact, there are two more sides. To use legal terms, there's the argument that comes from the plaintiff, and the argument that comes from the defense—and finally, there's the truth. The truth is the only basis of proper justice.

When I speak to a couple about their marriage, I've often found that things seem straightforward after hearing one person's version of events. With experience, though, I've learned to keep quiet and to encourage the other spouse to tell his or her side of the story. Invariably I find that the situation is not as simple as it seemed at first. For harmony, prosperity, and success in your relationships—whether at home or at work—fairness and wisdom are critical.

This is why spending time with God is so important in our day-to-day living. After listening to both sides of every story, we can weigh them and make our assessment based on what God says. He is our rubric for the truth. Even man's wisdom is but foolishness in the eyes of God (1 Cor. 3:19).

When we are faced with a disagreement, let's do our best to understand the whole situation, and then seek the Lord's mind on the matter through prayer and Scripture. After that, we'll be able to make a more confident recommendation or decision that is not based on prejudice or favoritism.

PRAYER: Lord God, please help me to be fair in all my dealings, and
not make rash or unbalanced judgments. Show me Your wisdom,
which surpasses what I could muster on my own. Amen.

January 19
PATIENCE IS A VIRTUE

THE PATIENT IN SPIRIT IS BETTER THAN THE PROUD IN SPIRIT.
ECCLESIASTES 7:8

CHILDREN INVARIABLY grow up with the same tendencies as their parents. The more time we spend in the presence of God our Father, the more we'll become like Him, full of patience and gentleness. In Galatians 5:22, we're told that patience, or "longsuffering," is an important fruit of the Spirit.

I was taught a wonderful lesson in patience as a young man when I went to buy a bull from a great stockman named Cederick Taylor. After I had purchased the bull, we had a cup of tea, then went down to the loading ramp. But the bull wouldn't get onto the truck.

Cederick walked up to the bull and put his hand on the rump of the massive beast, which probably weighed a ton. Then he spoke to him firmly but kindly, saying, "Come on, boy." That bull changed his whole character in an instant because he felt safe in the hands of his breeder, and he walked straight onto the back of the truck. Losing your cool and shouting won't help, but being patient and speaking firmly but gently, with a voice of love, will move mountains.

So often we give an instant response because we are in a hurry. This usually doesn't work. Instead, listen to the voice of your Father, who speaks to you in love and teaches you the meaning of patience.

PRAYER: Dear God, please show me where a dose of Your patience is most needed in my life. When I am tempted to fly off the handle, keep me firm, kind, and patient. Amen.

January 20
HONOR YOUR PARENTS

HONOR YOUR FATHER AND YOUR MOTHER . . . THAT YOUR
DAYS MAY BE LONG, AND THAT IT MAY BE WELL WITH YOU IN
THE LAND WHICH THE LORD YOUR GOD IS GIVING YOU.
DEUTERONOMY 5:16

THE CHILDREN of the isiZulu nation here in South Africa have been brought up to respect their elders and to treat them in a special way, whether it's refraining from speaking until an elder has finished, or holding doors, or offering to carry their load. But sadly, this seems to be breaking down. My faithful *induna* (foreman), Simeon Bhengu, has told me shocking stories about young men waiting for pensioners' day, when the elderly receive their monthly payouts, then forcefully taking the money from elderly grandmothers and grandfathers. This must break the heart of the Father!

Absalom's advisors told him to attack and kill his father, King David. David was so distraught when he had to flee from Absalom that he wrote Psalm 3. There is no note of vindictiveness in this psalm; rather, a sense of sorrow and resignation. There is nothing more heartbreaking than a son who has tried to overthrow his father because he has no respect or love for him.

Paul wrote, "Do not be deceived, God is not mocked; for whatever a man sows, that he will also reap" (Gal. 6:7). Absalom's army was eventually defeated, and Absalom was killed. On the other hand, today's verse from Deuteronomy says respect for your father and mother will bring blessing. If it's possible, go and find your parents or elders who have made a difference in your life. Sit with them and ask for their forgiveness for your transgressions. Then forgive them theirs, because there's no time for fighting or misunderstandings.

PRAYER: Dear Lord, thank You for my parentage and heritage. Please show me ways
to give them respect, and correct me when I'm in danger of neglecting it. Amen.

January 21

WAIT ON THE LORD

THOSE WHO WAIT ON THE LORD SHALL RENEW THEIR STRENGTH;
THEY SHALL MOUNT UP WITH WINGS LIKE EAGLES, THEY SHALL
RUN AND NOT BE WEARY, THEY SHALL WALK AND NOT FAINT.
ISAIAH 40:31

SO MANY people live life in a rush, desperately trying to work enough to hold it all together. But often we forget that if we rest and trust in God, it allows Him to show us the way forward.

When I was a young man I was like a bull in a china shop. I would do a job, but I would not do it properly and would have to go back three or four times in order to get it done right. Now I am older and I don't have the physical strength I once had, so I sit down and size up the job and take note of what needs to be done. Then I do the job once, and hopefully I do it correctly. By doing less, I can accomplish more.

The book of Ecclesiastes says there is a time to work and a time to rest. And by resting, the writer doesn't mean taking a Sunday to shop and run around. Resting on the seventh day isn't just a suggestion from God; it is one of the Ten Commandments. He knows you need to rest so you can go back to work full of fire and zeal for God. If you take time out to wait on the Lord, He will renew your strength and lead you where you need to go.

PRAYER: Lord, thank You for allowing time to rest in the rhythm
of life. Help me to keep that time sacred, and trust that by
doing less You will allow me to accomplish more. Amen.

January 22
GOD'S CALL ON YOUR LIFE

PRAY FOR US TO THE LORD YOUR GOD, FOR ALL THIS REMNANT . . .
THAT THE LORD YOUR GOD MAY SHOW US THE WAY IN WHICH
WE SHOULD WALK AND THE THING WE SHOULD DO.
JEREMIAH 42:2–3

SOME PEOPLE are just born to sail the seas. They are fascinated by the sea from a young age and love spending time on the water. If you ask them what draws them to the sea, they will not really be able to tell you. It is just something in their spirit.

I, on the other hand, like to keep my feet firmly on the ground. I am a man of the land who loves feeling the soil, riding my horse through the fields, and climbing mountains. Something in my spirit draws me to the soil.

God's calling is a similar thing. We might not always understand what God is doing in our lives or what He wants us to do, but that doesn't mean we should stop what we're doing. Pay attention to what your spirit longs for, and follow that call in your spirit. Go climb your mountain or sail your ocean. God will be with you every step of the way, and the Holy Spirit will guide you. Do the thing that gets you up in the morning, and God will honor it. Things will start to make sense the closer you walk with Him.

PRAYER: God, thank You for planting my passions within me. Help me to
follow a path that uses those inner yearnings to honor You. Amen.

January 23

THE BIRDS OF THE AIR

"LOOK AT THE BIRDS OF THE AIR, FOR THEY NEITHER SOW NOR
REAP NOR GATHER INTO BARNS; YET YOUR HEAVENLY FATHER
FEEDS THEM. ARE YOU NOT OF MORE VALUE THAN THEY?"
MATTHEW 6:26

EARLY ONE morning, as the sun touched the peaks of the hills, I looked up at the beautiful clear sky and saw tiny dots. On closer observation, I saw that they were swallows, just returned from Europe. It seemed just yesterday that they were gathering on the telephone lines, getting ready to migrate. And here they were back again.

Looking at the swallows, I was prompted by the Holy Spirit to recall the faithfulness of God. God is trustworthy. He never changes. He is absolutely dependable. We live in an age when things move so fast it seems as if we cannot be certain of anything. We don't know what tomorrow will bring, but God does, and He will take care of us in the future just as He has in the past.

There is a story about a robin and a sparrow sitting on a telephone line watching the busyness of humanity below them. After a while, the robin, puzzled, turned to the sparrow and asked, "Why are these people running all over the place? Why are they so busy? What are they so worried about?" The sparrow replied, "It's probably because they don't know the heavenly Father whom you and I trust."

Christ urged us to take our cue from the birds. They do not worry about tomorrow, because God feeds them and takes care of them. How much more will God take care of you and me?

PRAYER: Dear God, thank You for caring for me and providing
for me as part of Your creation. Help me to remember that
You are the source of everything I need. Amen.

January 24

BE WHO YOU ARE

THEN GOD SAID, "LET US MAKE MAN IN OUR IMAGE,
ACCORDING TO OUR LIKENESS" . . . SO GOD CREATED MAN
IN HIS OWN IMAGE; IN THE IMAGE OF GOD HE CREATED
HIM; MALE AND FEMALE HE CREATED THEM.
GENESIS 1:26—27

IT IS a situation one hears of so often: opposites attract. That is why one often meets a husband and a wife with two different personalities. For example, you might find an extroverted husband who loves the outdoors married to an introverted woman who prefers art and theater. Both benefit from the other's differences. God has made you in His own image, and every single one of us is unique. Out of the billions of people on this earth, there are no two people who have the same fingerprints. Isn't that miraculous?

It saddens me when I see girls with beautiful curly hair trying to make it straight, girls with stunning blonde hair dying it black, or girls with naturally fuller figures trying to lose weight and look thin. The same goes for smaller, leaner men trying to bulk up like body builders, and hefty farm-boy types trying to slim down like marathon runners. Be who you are. If you have brown eyes, praise God for that. If you have curly hair, praise the Lord. If you are outgoing and outspoken, don't change who you are! If you are quiet and reserved, be happy with yourself. Be what God has made you to be, living for His glory, and you will find fulfillment in life.

PRAYER: Dear God, thank You for all the ways You've made
me unique. Help me to accept my traits as a gift from You,
and point out Your unique gifts in others. Amen.

January 25

NEW BEGINNINGS

"I WILL GIVE YOU A NEW HEART AND PUT A NEW SPIRIT
WITHIN YOU; I WILL TAKE THE HEART OF STONE OUT OF
YOUR FLESH AND GIVE YOU A HEART OF FLESH."
EZEKIEL 36:26

RECENTLY I watched a heifer giving birth to a beautiful calf. The freshness of the spring morning, the birds singing, the cool breeze, the trees in leaf—all brought such joy and a sense of newness into my heart.

There is something invigorating and uplifting about the new life and new possibilities that God places all around us. It's like the smell of the parched earth just after a thunderstorm; all is renewed and refreshed. In John 3:3, Jesus said, "Unless one is born again, he cannot see the kingdom of God." Christianity is all about new beginnings. If we are not prepared to make a fresh start each day, putting the mistakes of yesterday behind us, we will never be fully open to the blessings God has in store for us.

We have all experienced good and bad in our lives, but there comes a time to leave the past behind. As Jesus said in Luke 9:62, "No one, having put his hand to the plow, and looking back, is fit for the kingdom of God." Everyone makes mistakes—and while it is easy to get stuck in the past, God invites us to face the future with anticipation, knowing that we are forgiven and that the Lord has given us a fresh start.

PRAYER: Lord God, please help me to learn from my mistakes, but to
let go of them too—accepting forgiveness and the potential of each
new day. Thank You for making me new through Christ. Amen.

January 26
BY THE GRACE OF GOD

HE GIVES MORE GRACE. THEREFORE HE SAYS: "GOD RESISTS
THE PROUD, BUT GIVES GRACE TO THE HUMBLE."
JAMES 4:6

DURING MY quiet time recently, I was reading the book of Job. The part I found most fascinating was when Job questioned God, and the Lord replied, "Now prepare yourself like a man; I will question you, and you shall answer Me" (Job 38:3).

Then the Lord asked Job, "Where were you when I laid the foundations of the earth? Tell Me, if you have understanding" (v. 4). God asked if Job knew the size of the earth or where its foundations were fastened. He asked if Job could make the sun come up in the morning and go down in the evening. He asked Job if an eagle takes flight at his command.

Of course, Job realized he had nothing to say! He repented and sought God's forgiveness. Many of us, especially when we begin to do well at work or in business, start to become arrogant. There's an old saying: "Pride comes before a fall"—and how the mighty do fall.

In Belfast, Northern Ireland, you can still see the huge cranes that were used to build the *Titanic*. One tragedy in that shipwreck was that mankind really did believe they had built a ship that was totally indestructible. Let us be diligent in giving God all the glory and all the praise when we succeed, because we never know when we will be humbled. As we give Him all the glory, we'll enjoy the privilege of His grace.

PRAYER: Lord Jesus, You are all-knowing and sovereign.
Help me to remember my place in the world, and to give You
credit when it is due (which is all the time!). Amen.

January 27

DO THINGS GOD'S WAY

HE HAS SHOWN YOU, O MAN, WHAT IS GOOD; AND WHAT
DOES THE LORD REQUIRE OF YOU BUT TO DO JUSTLY, TO
LOVE MERCY, AND TO WALK HUMBLY WITH YOUR GOD?
MICAH 6:8

ABRAHAM WAS one of the most favored sons of God because he was obedient. He was the man who waited a hundred years before God gave him his heart's desire—a son named Isaac. When Isaac was still young, God tested Abraham, saying He wanted Isaac back. Abraham didn't hesitate and prepared to offer his son as a sacrifice to God. At the last moment, an angel of the Lord told Abraham to spare his son and to use a ram instead (Gen. 21–22).

Like Abraham, let us never compromise when it comes to obeying the Word of God. He knew that no matter the situation, God is good, just, and merciful, and that our correct posture should be one of humility and obedience.

God is always for us, no matter how it may seem. Our obedience is a way of acknowledging that we're in it for the long haul. This isn't a short sprint; it's a long-distance race of trust and devotion.

God favored Abraham. If we invest all our energy and strength in selfish plans and self-preservation, we're going to lose horribly in the end. But if we do things God's way, He will turn the tide.

PRAYER: Lord God, please grow my trust in You today. In the darkest moments, help me to remain obedient to You. Thank You for always having my best interests at heart. Amen.

January 28
OUR FINEST HOUR

THUS SAYS THE LORD OF HOSTS: "LET YOUR HANDS BE
STRONG, YOU WHO HAVE BEEN HEARING IN THESE DAYS THESE
WORDS BY THE MOUTH OF THE PROPHETS, WHO SPOKE IN
THE DAY THE FOUNDATION WAS LAID FOR THE HOUSE OF THE
LORD OF HOSTS, THAT THE TEMPLE MIGHT BE BUILT."
ZECHARIAH 8:9

THE TIME has come for strong hands to do hard work. We have got to be fit—physically and mentally, but mostly spiritually. How do we do that? We get up in the morning and spend time in prayer. We get to know the Word of God. We keep ourselves pure and true in our behaviors and actions, not allowing the devil to distract us.

The house the Lord is speaking about in the scripture above is the physical temple. But the same applies to a person's body—the home of the soul. God is looking for men and women, boys and girls with strong hands and strong hearts who can do the work and harvest the crop of souls. We have got to get on with the job we've been given to win people to Christ. We don't have time to waste. We can't loaf and be lazy today, saying we will come back and serve God tomorrow. The time is now!

So let us work hard and work smart, remembering the importance of the mission set before us. My dear friends, let's keep our hands strong for the building of His kingdom, because Jesus Christ is on His way.

PRAYER: Dear God, please keep me strong and ready
to do whatever You ask of me today. Amen.

January 29

A BURDEN HALVED

A MAN WHO HAS FRIENDS MUST HIMSELF BE FRIENDLY, BUT
THERE IS A FRIEND WHO STICKS CLOSER THAN A BROTHER.
PROVERBS 18:24

SAMUEL JOHNSON supposedly said, "A man, Sir, should keep his friendship in constant repair," and that is very true.

A dear friend of mine used to farm across the fence from me. We would encourage one another in the early mornings while the staff were coming to work. Often it would still be dark. He'd always tell me to take time out to smell the roses.

A good friend will also always tell you the truth. A flatterer—someone who tells you what you want to hear—isn't necessarily a good friend. A good friend will tell you when the price of gas is going up, when your taillight isn't working, or when there's damp in your bathroom. A true friend will bring around a meal when you're sick, fetch your kids from soccer practice, and encourage you when you're down. This is because a friend cares about you and wants the best for you.

One year when I was battling to get our crop in because our tractor had broken down, another neighbor brought his tractors over to our farm and helped us get the crop in on time. He wanted nothing in return, just the simple pleasure of helping me. What an invaluable friend.

Spend time developing friendships—first with the Lord Jesus, then with those He has placed around you. Remember, a burden shared is a burden halved. Work on your friendships just as much as you work on your vegetable garden, your home, or your occupation.

PRAYER: God, thank You for the friends and neighbors You've placed
in my life. Show me how to be a better friend today. Amen.

January 30
SPENDING TIME WITH GOD

"YOU HAVE PERSEVERED AND HAVE PATIENCE, AND
HAVE LABORED FOR MY NAME'S SAKE AND HAVE NOT
BECOME WEARY. NEVERTHELESS I HAVE THIS AGAINST
YOU, THAT YOU HAVE LEFT YOUR FIRST LOVE."
REVELATION 2:3–4

EVERYBODY HAS nightmares. My nightmare is to find myself standing on a platform, about to address thousands of people, and suddenly realizing the Holy Spirit is not with me: Jesus is not on the platform, and I am standing there alone. Without Christ, my efforts are useless. Without Jesus, I can do nothing.

By the middle of 2003, my itinerary was completely booked up until the end of the next year, with invitations to go to India, Scotland, Wales, Ireland, England, and Israel. "Cancel the lot," said the Lord. His instruction was clear. "I want you to spend more time with Me," He said. "I want you to mentor young men." I thought He meant perhaps five or ten men. I was to be pleasantly surprised! I was totally bowled over by the response to our first Mighty Men Conference. Hundreds of men arrived at our farm.

I saw the power of God moving like I'd never seen up until then. The preaching flowed, and the praise and worship, led by my eldest son, Andrew, was amazing. God broke hearts. He dealt with men who confessed their sins, restoring men who were broken and starting His work. Those who attended told me they would be coming back the following year. That was the start of the Mighty Men phenomenon.

Let us take stock and see where we are in our spiritual lives. We might be busy for the Lord, but maintaining our first love for Him is so much more important.

PRAYER: God, I trust You to bring fruit from the things You
tell me to do; keep me following Your will. Amen.

January 31

FAITH IS EVERYTHING

THE APOSTLES SAID TO THE LORD, "INCREASE OUR FAITH."
LUKE 17:5

WITHOUT FAITH we cannot please God. We must believe that He exists and that He rewards those who diligently seek Him (Heb. 11:6).

Sometimes I tell people that God doesn't answer prayer. They usually get very uncomfortable. Then I say that God answers the prayer *of faith*. You see, it is in believing that we receive (Matt. 21:22). It's all about believing—believing that Jesus Christ is the Son of God, believing that He is a miracle worker, and believing that He is the same yesterday, today, and forever (Heb. 13:8). Having faith in God puts Him in the right place: at the forefront of our lives.

"Your faith has made you well," said Jesus to the sick woman (Luke 8:48). She knew that if she could just touch the hem of His garment, she would be healed. A similar thing happened to Bartimaeus, the blind man (Mark 10:46–52). He was determined to make sure that Jesus heard him when He was walking past, so Bartimaeus shouted loudly, making a fool of himself. Eventually Jesus stopped and asked, "What do you want Me to do for you?" When Bartimaeus asked Jesus for his sight, he received it immediately and was healed. Jesus told him, "Your faith has made you well."

How do we increase our faith? We ask God for it, just as the disciples did.

PRAYER: Dear God, please let my faith grow by leaps and bounds. I can never have enough of it. Amen.

FEBRUARY

February 1
DON'T HINDER THE KINGDOM

I HEARD A VOICE SPEAKING TO ME AND SAYING IN THE HEBREW
LANGUAGE, "SAUL, SAUL, WHY ARE YOU PERSECUTING ME? IT IS HARD
FOR YOU TO KICK AGAINST THE GOADS." SO I SAID, "WHO ARE YOU,
LORD?" AND HE SAID, "I AM JESUS, WHOM YOU ARE PERSECUTING."
ACTS 26:14–15

HOW TERRIBLE it is to think that we are doing something good for God, when in reality we are working against Him. That's what could happen when we don't check our motives. You might actually be building something for your glory, while thinking and saying you are doing it for the Lord. But not every good idea is a God idea.

Some people think God wants all of us to be preachers. This is not so. God has anointed some of us to speak, others to serve, others to support, and others to take care of the poor and the needy. For example, my wife is doing what God has called her to do—to take care of the widows and the orphans—all without stepping into the pulpit.

In today's verse, Saul, who was on his way to Damascus, thought that he was doing God a favor by killing Christians. His life was turned upside down when he found out the truth. Like Saul, if you forget about your own program and ambition and start doing what God wants you to do—then your life will be full of opportunities.

Sometimes it takes awhile before we realize this, and it can be a crushing blow after all the work we have put in. But it's always worth it to change to His path. Ask the Lord to confirm that you are following His will, and listen and obey when He answers.

PRAYER: Lord, show me Your will, and help me to do it
no matter what that might mean for me! Amen.

February 2
THE OBEDIENCE GOD REQUIRES

FOR I DESIRE MERCY AND NOT SACRIFICE, AND THE
KNOWLEDGE OF GOD MORE THAN BURNT OFFERINGS.
HOSEA 6:6

OBEDIENCE IS the product of holiness. God wants us to be holy people, but we can only become holy when Jesus is the most important person in our lives. That is why the Word of God says in 1 Samuel 15:22, "To obey is better than sacrifice, and to heed than the fat of rams."

The Lord told me very clearly that He wanted me to preach the undiluted gospel of Jesus Christ and to minister healing to the sick, in obedience to His Word found in Mark 16:15–18: "Go into all the world and preach the gospel to every creature. . . . In My name . . . they will lay hands on the sick, and they will recover." When I pray for the sick and lay hands on them, it is in obedience to His commission and with the expectation that God will raise them up. My motivation is to show the world that Jesus Christ is still the Healer. He is number one.

Knowing Christ makes us want to turn His call into action. My calling would have gone nowhere had I sat around and prayed and worried about it, sending up "sacrifices" and "burnt offerings" instead of acting in obedience, mercy, and the knowledge of God through His Word. What call is God asking you to turn into action today?

PRAYER: Dear Lord, please guide me obey Your call on my life. Help
me to move past thinking and into action as You will it. Amen.

February 3

THE POWER OF FOCUS

"EVERYONE WHO HAS LEFT HOUSES OR BROTHERS OR
SISTERS OR FATHER OR MOTHER OR WIFE OR CHILDREN
OR LANDS, FOR MY NAME'S SAKE, SHALL RECEIVE A
HUNDREDFOLD, AND INHERIT ETERNAL LIFE."
MATTHEW 19:29

MY BROTHER, a pro golfer, once told me this story: During the final of a major competition, a golfer was lining up on the eighteenth hole for a putt that would win the championship. As he was about to nudge the ball toward the hole, a train passed by, giving a long, loud whistle. The golfer made his shot, the ball went into the hole, and he won the competition. The organizers came running over, apologizing profusely for the distraction of the train, but the golfer looked up, confused, and said, "What noise?" He was so focused on the game he hadn't even noticed. If only we could maintain that sort of clear and intense focus in our lives!

In the Bible, the Lord speaks about being distracted by things such as possessions, friends, and difficult circumstances. These things will come, but our focus should be on God—we should keep our "eye on the ball," so to speak. Let's do everything in our power to please the Lord, leaving the rest to His safekeeping.

Don't allow yourself to be misled by foolish accusations or by silly distractions that will keep you from the true purpose of life.

PRAYER: Lord, when I run up against the countless distractions
of each day, please allow me to maintain my focus on
You and on what You've given me to do. Amen.

February 4
DESCEND THE MOUNTAIN

NOW IT CAME TO PASS IN THOSE DAYS THAT HE WENT OUT TO THE
MOUNTAIN TO PRAY, AND CONTINUED ALL NIGHT IN PRAYER TO GOD.
LUKE 6:12

WE ALL love those mountaintop experiences, when God is close and we feel inspired. But it is no good spending all your time on the mountaintop because then you are of no earthly use. You can't spend all your time down in the valley either, because you will dry up and have nothing to say. So, just as Jesus did, you can find the balance between spending time with God first and foremost, and getting back down to where the people are.

You don't need a formal education or to be a preacher in order to serve the Lord. Where are you today? That "valley" is your mission field. You don't need money or skill to spread the gospel. What does it cost to make somebody a cup of tea? What does it take to sit down and write a letter to someone who is lonely? It costs you nothing, and even doing something small means serving the Lord.

It's a mistake to go up the mountain and stay there because that is where you think God is. God is also down in the valley, with His people. He is with you and me. I pray that God would take away all your fear, insecurities, and weariness, and that He would give you the confidence you need to serve Him. May He guide you as you descend the mountain and offer a loving and helping hand to those who need it.

PRAYER: God, thank You for those times of refreshment and
inspiration. Let me take that down into the world and pass it on to
those who need You, rather than keeping it all to myself. Amen.

February 5

COMMANDMENTS FOR LIFE

"FOR GOD SO LOVED THE WORLD THAT HE GAVE HIS
ONLY BEGOTTEN SON, THAT WHOEVER BELIEVES IN HIM
SHOULD NOT PERISH BUT HAVE EVERLASTING LIFE."
JOHN 3:16

WHY DID God give us the Ten Commandments? The Ten Commandments are to keep you and me on a straight line. They won't save us (only Jesus can do that), but they do provide an arrow pointing the way. For me, they give me a moral guide for my day-to-day life, urging me to honor my wife, protect my children, treat my workers with respect, be content with my lot in life, and not to envy others. These precious commandments have led to true happiness and contentment in my life. But first, they are there to show us where we have gone wrong so that we can repent and make things right.

Jesus said that He came to fulfill the law; He did not come to take anything away from the law (Matt. 5:17). If there were no need for the Ten Commandments, there would be no need for Jesus to come to earth. The Lord came to fulfill the Old Testament law and save us from our sin, making it possible for us to live with integrity and obedience. Spending time with the commandments shows us how to get back to the fundamentals. Contrary to popular belief, there is a right way and a wrong way to do things. There are no shortcuts; we always reap what we sow. So be obedient to the commandments. If you go the extra mile and conduct yourself honorably, you will have a bumper crop of blessings.

My prayer for you today is that you would walk in integrity and confidence because of your veneration for God and the guidelines He's put in place for us.

PRAYER: Lord, please give me fresh inspiration every time I look at Your commandments and study Your Word. Keep me on the narrow way. Amen.

February 6
THE VALUE OF MISTAKES

SO SHALL THE KNOWLEDGE OF WISDOM BE TO YOUR
SOUL; IF YOU HAVE FOUND IT, THERE IS A PROSPECT,
AND YOUR HOPE WILL NOT BE CUT OFF.
PROVERBS 24:14

WHY DO we find that business owners are reluctant to take on young, inexperienced people? Because everyone makes mistakes—but people with limited life experience make more. But if we don't allow youngsters to make mistakes, they'll never learn.

Don't be afraid to take a risk on young people. Don't be afraid to let them step out of the boat and walk on the water, because it's only when you're out on the water that they (and you!) really learn to trust God.

Take Peter, for example. In Matthew 14:29–31, the Lord (effectively Peter's boss) said to him, "Come." Peter got out of the boat and walked on the water, but when he took his eyes off the Lord and looked around, he became afraid and started to sink. He cried out, "Lord, save me!" Immediately Jesus stretched out His hand and caught Peter, saying, "O you of little faith, why do you doubt?" The Lord did not sideline Peter after that. On the contrary, He appointed Peter to be the leader of the apostles after His resurrection.

Wisdom often comes through learning from life's hard knocks. Yet the saying, "There's no fool like an old fool" is also true. White hair isn't necessarily a sign of wisdom—some people just don't learn—and I've met youngsters who are wise beyond their years.

There's much to be gained from the enthusiasm of youth—and the wisdom of the elder. Let's follow God's example and accept both.

PRAYER: Lord, help me to learn from my mistakes, and to allow
others to make mistakes as we all walk toward You. Amen.

February 7

THE GOOD SHEPHERD

"I AM THE GOOD SHEPHERD; AND I KNOW MY SHEEP, AND AM
KNOWN BY MY OWN. AS THE FATHER KNOWS ME, EVEN SO I
KNOW THE FATHER; AND I LAY DOWN MY LIFE FOR THE SHEEP.
AND OTHER SHEEP I HAVE WHICH ARE NOT OF THIS FOLD;
THEM ALSO I MUST BRING, AND THEY WILL HEAR MY VOICE;
AND THERE WILL BE ONE FLOCK AND ONE SHEPHERD."
JOHN 10:14—16

THE GOOD shepherd *leads* his sheep, while the ordinary shepherd *drives* his sheep. Jesus loves us so much that He left His home in heaven to lead by example, showing us how to live and love and providing a way for us to be with Him in heaven one day.

In Luke 15:4–5 we read, "What man of you, having a hundred sheep, if he loses one of them, does not leave the ninety-nine in the wilderness, and go after the one which is lost until he finds it? And when he has found it, he lays it on his shoulders, rejoicing."

Notice what the shepherd in the story did. He did not chase or punish the lost sheep because it ran away. He picked it up, put it on his shoulders, and carried it home. Jesus Christ tells us to come home if we are lost. He will not push us away when we are tired. He will pick us up and carry us home and give us new life.

Don't delay. The Lord is calling to you; He has been looking for you in the wilderness. The Good Shepherd is waiting to carry you in His arms.

PRAYER: Dear Lord, when I am lost and wandering, please help
me to hear Your voice and be carried home again. Amen.

February 8

LIVING BEFORE DYING

"MOST ASSUREDLY, I SAY TO YOU, UNLESS A GRAIN OF
WHEAT FALLS INTO THE GROUND AND DIES, IT REMAINS
ALONE; BUT IF IT DIES, IT PRODUCES MUCH GRAIN."
JOHN 12:24

WE'RE PARTICULARLY conscious of life and death in today's world. The matters of life and death we hear about on the news tend to be frightening or anxiety producing. But in today's verse, we learn that in death there is life. Farmers surely know this principle better than anyone; if we store our seed in a dry room, it will keep for years, but it will also fail to produce anything. However, once it is in the soil, the kernel dies—and through this death there is new birth.

This is a basic principle of the Christian faith. Jesus came to die for our sins, and His death brings new life. Similarly, when we accept Him and "die to sin" in our spirit, we shed the kernel of the old person and bloom anew.

Physical death is not final; it's simply a transition into eternal life. It's like opening a door and walking into another room for those who know and love God.

This knowledge frees us to change our attitude from "What can I get out of life before I die?" to "What can I put into life?" What can we do to make our community a better place to live? How can we be better fathers, husbands, mothers, wives, brothers, sisters, friends—and how can we take care of those less fortunate than ourselves? As we start to live for others, we'll be blessed in life as well as in eternity with Jesus.

PRAYER: God, thank You for this time on earth. Allow me to
die and be reborn spiritually before meeting You in heaven,
so I can make this world better for others. Amen.

February 9
AN IMPERFECT WORLD

WHO IS A GOD LIKE YOU, PARDONING INIQUITY AND PASSING OVER THE TRANSGRESSION OF THE REMNANT OF HIS HERITAGE? HE DOES NOT RETAIN HIS ANGER FOREVER, BECAUSE HE DELIGHTS IN MERCY.
MICAH 7:18

SOME OF you might be angry with God at the moment over a great injustice or painful situation. The Lord is asking you a question today: "What wrong have I done you?"

Though the pain may be deep, in reality we don't have a case against God. Micah 6 reminds us: "'For I brought you up from the land of Egypt, I redeemed you from the house of bondage . . . that you may know the righteousness of the LORD.' . . . He has shown you, O man, what is good; and what does the LORD require of you but to do justly, to love mercy, and to walk humbly with your God?" (vv. 4–5, 8).

God has done nothing wrong to you or to me. We live in a broken world infected by sin and grief, but it was never His will for us to suffer so. In fact, because He hurts for us, He has taken us out of a pit. We were on our way to hell, and He saved us. So when things don't go so well and you raise your eyes with anger to God, speak freely to the One who loves you, but remember all that the Lord has done for you. He asks for only three things: to treat your fellow man with respect, to love mercy, and to walk humbly with your God.

We live in an imperfect world and things will not always go our way, but God loves us and will redeem us in the end.

PRAYER: Lord, when my heart swells with anger over the
unfairness of life, remind me of what You've done for me.
Thank You for Your mercy and deliverance. Amen.

February 10
PLUCKED FROM THE FIRE

THEN HE SHOWED ME JOSHUA THE HIGH PRIEST STANDING BEFORE
THE ANGEL OF THE LORD, AND SATAN STANDING AT HIS RIGHT HAND
TO OPPOSE HIM. AND THE LORD SAID TO SATAN, "THE LORD REBUKE
YOU, SATAN! THE LORD WHO HAS CHOSEN JERUSALEM REBUKE
YOU! IS THIS [MAN] NOT A BRAND PLUCKED FROM THE FIRE?"
ZECHARIAH 3:1–2

THE VISION of the high priest in Zechariah 3:1–10 is a wonderful story. Joshua had been standing ashamed in filthy robes, but God restored the high priest, saying, "See, I have removed your iniquity from you, and I will clothe you with rich robes" (v. 4). The Lord has restored me too, and I trust that He is busy restoring you.

Some of you literally might have been snatched out of a fire like John Wesley. When he was about five years old, a fire broke out in the middle of the night in his childhood home. His mother, pregnant at the time, and his father, the local minister, rushed through the flames to get the children to safety. Once outside, his father realized that John wasn't there. He tried to go back, but by this time the flames had engulfed most of the house. He fell to his knees and started to pray for his son. Two bystanders saw John standing by the open loft window and, one climbing on the other man's shoulders, grabbed him just before the roof of the house collapsed.

From then on, John's mother referred to him as "a brand plucked from the burning." She knew that God had a special plan for him, and she was right—he grew up to be a man who changed the world through Spirit-inspired preaching.

We have all been plucked out of the fire in some way or another; we were all once on our way to a fiery trial. Thank the Lord for the forgiveness of our sins—our rescue.

PRAYER: God, where would I be without You? I praise You
for saving me and continually restoring me. Amen.

February 11

CHARITY BEGINS AT HOME

"IF I THEN, YOUR LORD AND TEACHER, HAVE WASHED YOUR
FEET, YOU ALSO OUGHT TO WASH ONE ANOTHER'S FEET."
JOHN 13:14

SOMETIMES OUR vision for life can be so big that we don't know where to start. Thankfully, God asks us to start with small and manageable steps. Be faithful in the little things; that is how God grows you. You might want to help the whole world, but what does it say if, back at the ranch, you cannot even look after your own family or personal sphere? Start in your own home and with those closest to you. That is what Jesus did: He ministered to His friends and family. He taught the disciples by washing their feet.

God first gives you your vision, then you slowly build on that, layer by layer. Start praying and serving where you are; take what you've got and use it on the nearest person. Jesus saw that there was no one to wash feet, so He took what was in front of Him—a towel and a basin—to serve in a humble way. Of course, this story now echoes through the ages as an example of humility and the inner greatness of Christ.

The Lord is not interested in your ability; He wants your availability. Don't worry about standing up and performing great acts or speeches. Rather, let us be doers of the Word in small ways, so people can come to us for a cup of tea or a warm meal as well as for spiritual nourishment and encouragement.

Today I encourage you to take steps toward getting your personal world in order so that you can be ready when God calls you to greater things.

PRAYER: Lord, show me what small blessings You've given me, and
help me multiply them for You. Turn my eyes to things that need
attention and give me fortitude for those humble first steps. Amen.

February 12

A WARM REFUGE

"YES, MANY PEOPLES AND STRONG NATIONS SHALL
COME TO SEEK THE LORD OF HOSTS IN JERUSALEM,
AND TO PRAY BEFORE THE LORD."
ZECHARIAH 8:22

IN THE context of today's verse, you are Jerusalem. I am Jerusalem. Because we love the Lord, people will come to us to seek counsel, protection, and hope.

Once a farmer who was an unbeliever stopped next to my car at a red traffic light. He told me that it was getting a bit dry and that I had better pray to "the Man upstairs." Then the light turned green, and he drove off. I very much felt like asking him why he didn't ask God himself, but then I realized that he didn't know how to. He didn't have a relationship with God like you and I do.

I often hear little jokes that people make about how it is always raining on Shalom farm where I live. This is, of course, not true. But maybe they see peace in our hearts as believers, and they want that peace. They see our relationship with God and it makes them long for what we have. That is why a person who is cold comes closer to the fire—to be warm.

Be a warm refuge and a shining light for the people of the world.

PRAYER: Lord, I pray for the privilege of being warmth and
light for someone today. Allow me to welcome my neighbors to
Your family and to display the peace You bring. Amen.

February 13

CHILDLIKE FAITH

JESUS TOOK THE LOAVES, AND WHEN HE HAD GIVEN
THANKS HE DISTRIBUTED THEM TO THE DISCIPLES, AND
THE DISCIPLES TO THOSE SITTING DOWN; AND LIKEWISE
OF THE FISH, AS MUCH AS THEY WANTED. SO WHEN THEY
WERE FILLED, HE SAID TO HIS DISCIPLES, "GATHER UP THE
FRAGMENTS THAT REMAIN, SO THAT NOTHING IS LOST."
JOHN 6:11–12

WE ALL know the story above of Jesus feeding five thousand people with only five loaves and two fish. A little boy gave Jesus all he had so that Jesus could feed everyone who had come to hear Him preach. Believe it or not, you too have loaves and fishes the Lord wants to transform.

We can believe God for the impossible just as that boy did. Jesus said, "Assuredly, I say to you, whoever does not receive the kingdom of God as a little child will by no means enter it" (Luke 18:17). If you were to ask a grown man or woman whether it would be possible to feed five thousand men, plus women and children, with only two small fish and five barley loaves, they would tell you it is impossible. And they would be right. It is impossible, and that is precisely why we call it a miracle.

As the boy gave to Jesus, give Jesus your life, your family, and your vision for the future with no strings attached, and He will give it back to you "pressed down, shaken together, and running over" (Luke 6:38).

PRAYER: Lord, thank You for the "loaves" I have in my
possession. I wholeheartedly give them back to You, and I
can't wait to see what You'll do with them. Amen.

February 14
CONVERSATIONS WITH GOD

"WHEN YOU PRAY, GO INTO YOUR ROOM, AND WHEN YOU HAVE SHUT
YOUR DOOR, PRAY TO YOUR FATHER WHO IS IN THE SECRET PLACE;
AND YOUR FATHER WHO SEES IN SECRET WILL REWARD YOU OPENLY."
MATTHEW 6:6

THE *OXFORD* Dictionary says that a conversation is "a talk, especially an informal one, between two or more people, in which news and ideas are exchanged." That's what prayer is—having a conversation with God. I can't start my day without having a good talk with our Lord. In fact, every morning my wife and I pray for our family with desire and faith to believe that God hears our prayers and will answer. The good news is that He does!

An important ingredient for prayer is desire. The great intercessor E. M. Bounds said, "Without desire, prayer is a meaningless mumble of words. . . . Its exercise is a waste of precious time, and from it, no real blessing accrues." It's not how long or how often you pray, but faith and desire that makes for effective prayer.

You can speak to God anytime and anywhere, in the quietness of your heart. The Lord loves to commune with you and to answer your prayers. That's why He created you and me—not for what we can do for Him, but so He can have fellowship with us.

How do we begin? Try starting with a short prayer, and slowly but surely, build from that. Pray from your heart, not your head, and you'll find a whole new dimension opening up in your life.

PRAYER: Dear God, thank You for the gift of prayer. Give me faith
and desire to come to You quietly throughout this day. Amen.

February 15
SHOWING BEFORE SAYING

THEN PILATE SAID TO [JESUS], "DO YOU NOT HEAR HOW MANY
THINGS THEY TESTIFY AGAINST YOU?" BUT HE ANSWERED HIM
NOT ONE WORD, SO THAT THE GOVERNOR MARVELED GREATLY.
MATTHEW 27:13–14

THERE IS a saying that goes like this: "Make sure that your words are sweet, because one day you might have to eat them." Our words carry a lot more impact and weight than we realize. A man who talks much and does little is a man who is not regarded at all.

Doing is louder than speaking. For example, as a farmer I have learned that farming is not only a business, but also a way of life and a culture. It's the same the world over. If you are running your farm in an honorable way, you don't have to speak much to gain respect. Driving onto a man's farm, you will see first the condition of his livestock. When you get to his workshop, you see the condition of his tractors, his tools. Then when you chat with his staff, they will tell you exactly what the farmer is really like. Like the farmer, when Christians model who they are, it speaks more than words ever could.

You see, Jesus did not have to defend Himself because He had absolutely nothing to hide. His lifestyle spoke volumes. He took care of the widows and orphans. He performed miracles, signs, and wonders. He spoke prophetic words. Let us follow His example as we speak less and act more.

PRAYER: God, turn my words and my ideals into actions that glorify You. Amen.

February 16
THE SPIRIT OF TRUTH

"WHEN HE, THE SPIRIT OF TRUTH, HAS COME, HE WILL
GUIDE YOU INTO ALL TRUTH; FOR HE WILL NOT SPEAK ON
HIS OWN AUTHORITY, BUT WHATEVER HE HEARS HE WILL
SPEAK; AND HE WILL TELL YOU THINGS TO COME."
JOHN 16:13

IN THIS Internet age, we're constantly being bombarded with ideas, advice, and opinions. How do we know which are the right ones to take to heart? In today's verse Jesus referred to the Holy Spirit as "the Spirit of truth." It's more important than ever to start listening to the voice of the Holy Spirit, because He is the One who speaks truth.

How do we gain wisdom from the Holy Spirit? First, by revering God and keeping Him in a right place in our lives. The Bible tells us that the fear of the Lord is wisdom and to depart from evil is understanding (Job 28:28). *Fear* in this context doesn't mean "to be afraid"; it means to revere God. Those with a holy fear of God spend time with Him and follow His commandments.

The other side of the coin of holy fear is trust. "Trust in the LORD with all your heart, and lean not on your own understanding; in all your ways acknowledge Him, and He shall direct your paths" (Prov. 3:5–6). God gives us wisdom to guide us. When we try to direct our own paths using pop psychology or the wisdom of the world, we wrest control from Him and show arrogance and confidence in the wrong source. We need to rely on the Spirit of truth to guide our ways.

PRAYER: Lord, teach me how to listen to the Spirit of
truth instead of the spirit of the world. Amen.

February 17
CONSECRATE YOUR FAMILY

"I AM THE LORD YOUR GOD. YOU SHALL THEREFORE CONSECRATE
YOURSELVES, AND YOU SHALL BE HOLY; FOR I AM HOLY."
LEVITICUS 11:44

SOME YEARS ago during our "Healing the Land" crusade, I saw an example of just how important families are to God. After a wonderful meeting, I made the altar call as I usually do, and many people came forward. While ministering to them, I became aware that the Lord wanted to do something special for a certain family.

"There is a family here that God wants to touch," I announced. "A complete family—grandfather, grandmother, father, mother, and children. Please come forward. I believe the Lord wants to meet with you." No one moved. The hall fell silent. I called for those who needed prayer for healing to come forward, and an old gentleman with back trouble stood before me. I was about to pray for him when I sensed the prompting of the Holy Spirit. "Sir," I said, "do you know the Lord Jesus Christ as your personal Savior?"

"No," the man replied.

"Would you like to make your life right with God tonight?"

"Yes," he said emphatically.

I was about to pray when I sensed that the Lord was busy with something more. "Where is your wife?" She came out immediately. Soon their children joined them, followed by their whole family: three generations. We prayed the Sinner's Prayer and the fire of God fell on that meeting.

Never be ashamed of the gospel of Christ or apologize for the truth of God's Word. Truth sets people—and families—free indeed.

PRAYER: God, thank You for the power of Your Spirit and Your love
for the lost. Prompt me today to speak Your will to them. Amen.

February 18
A PRAYER OF FAITH

IS ANYONE AMONG YOU SICK? LET HIM CALL FOR THE ELDERS
OF THE CHURCH, AND LET THEM PRAY OVER HIM, ANOINTING
HIM WITH OIL IN THE NAME OF THE LORD. AND THE PRAYER OF
FAITH WILL SAVE THE SICK, AND THE LORD WILL RAISE HIM UP.
JAMES 5:14–15

ONE DAY a terrible tragedy befell our local doctor and his family when the balcony of their beach flat collapsed. The doctor's beautiful young daughter, Jana (eighteen years old at the time), broke her back. Two specialists told her she would never walk again.

We hold a healing meeting once a quarter on our farm. At the end of one such meeting, Jana came forward in her wheelchair. I asked her if she believed that one day she would walk down the aisle to meet her groom on her wedding day. Jana replied that she believed it would happen.

We anointed her with oil and prayed the prayer of faith—when I felt prompted by the Holy Spirit to ask the men to stand her up. When they raised her from the wheelchair, the pain left her back, her legs locked into position, and she was able to stand on her own.

A few years later, Jana—dressed in a magnificent white wedding gown—walked down the aisle on her father's arm to meet her very handsome groom. When her father lifted the veil from Jana's radiant face and kissed her before handing her gently to her husband-to-be, I don't think there was a dry eye in the whole church, my own included.

I believe our God is a good God, and that He's for us and not against us. And His Word tells us, "If you ask anything in My name, I will do it" (John 14:14).

PRAYER: Lord, Your ways are mysterious. Thank You for always answering prayer and having the best interests of Your children at heart. Amen.

February 19
THE TRUTH WILL COME OUT

"SANCTIFY THEM BY YOUR TRUTH. YOUR WORD IS TRUTH."
JOHN 17:17

HONESTY IS a precious commodity. Where it is absent, things break down. Many of the world's problems stem from blatant lies spoken by people in positions of authority. At home, husbands and wives don't always tell the truth either. Once lies are exposed, a marriage breaks down.

Our sins soon find us out. All lies are equally dangerous. The truth, however, will bring liberty and light to a situation; it will bring harmony to your workplace and to your personal life.

The problem with dishonesty is that once we start telling lies, we have to tell one lie after another to cover up the first one, until we get ourselves in such a deep hole we can't get out of it.

Pride can keep us from telling the truth. Often we don't want people to think badly of us, so we pretend and put up a façade. The problem is that we're living a lie and it's difficult to maintain a false image. But if we come clean—tell the truth and confess our sins—then the Lord Jesus Christ will set us free (1 John 1:9).

Telling the truth is liberating. By contrast, when you continually duck and dive, there is no peace in your heart. Your joy in life evaporates and, slowly but surely, things disintegrate. Let's make a decision today to put the truth first. When we start speaking the truth at home, and then at work, it will filter right up to government. Then we'll have a country that the world can look to as an example of truth.

PRAYER: Lord, please point out areas where truth is needed
in my life. Help me to speak it today. Amen.

February 20
THE "UNKNOWN GOD"

"GO THEREFORE AND MAKE DISCIPLES OF ALL NATIONS,
BAPTIZING THEM IN THE NAME OF THE FATHER AND OF
THE SON AND OF THE HOLY SPIRIT, TEACHING THEM TO
OBSERVE ALL THINGS THAT I HAVE COMMANDED YOU."
MATTHEW 28:19–20

IN ATHENS, Paul preached to the Jews and the Gentiles about Jesus. A few philosophers who had heard Paul preach took him to the Areopagus to find out more about his God. Here Paul came across an altar that read, "TO THE UNKNOWN GOD." Paul told them that he knew the name of this unknown God. This immediately piqued their interest, and he was able to tell them more about the Lord.

He said, "The One whom you worship without knowing, Him I proclaim to you: God, who made the world and everything in it, since He is Lord of heaven and earth, does not dwell in temples made with hands. Nor is He worshiped with men's hands, as though He needed anything, since He gives to all life, breath, and all things. . . . He is not far from each one of us; for in Him we live and move and have our being" (Acts 17:23–25, 27–28).

This unknown God was Jesus Christ Himself, who does not live in tombs, or in shrines, or even in statues. Paul went and spoke to unbelievers in their own backyard, showed them who this unknown God was, and told them all about Him. We are called to go and do the same.

PRAYER: Dear Jesus, when I talk to others about You, lead me
to address the ways You have already been speaking to them.
Show me how to make their "unknown God" known. Amen.

February 21

GONE FISHING

JESUS SHOWED HIMSELF AGAIN TO THE DISCIPLES AT THE
SEA OF TIBERIAS . . . SIMON PETER SAID TO [THE DISCIPLES],
"I AM GOING FISHING." THEY SAID TO HIM, "WE ARE GOING
WITH YOU ALSO." THEY WENT OUT AND IMMEDIATELY GOT
INTO THE BOAT, AND THAT NIGHT THEY CAUGHT NOTHING.
JOHN 21:1, 3

WHENEVER YOU see the sign "Gone fishing," you know that the occupants aren't there. They might have literally gone fishing . . . or they might have had enough for the day. When Peter and the disciples saw the death of Jesus, who was their hope, their vision, and their future, their entire world crumbled. They decided to go back to fishing because it was all they knew.

The good news, though, is that the Lord Jesus rose from the dead. He came to the disciples at the Sea of Galilee and challenged them to continue the work and to take care of His sheep (John 21:17). In other words, He wanted them to continue with the work He had called them to.

We must never, ever give up. After all, we never know just how close we might be to victory. In the Gospels, Peter may have gone fishing because he believed he was a failure. But Jesus showed up, and in the end, instead of "nothing," they had a miraculous catch of fish (John 21:6).

I encourage you to lift up your eyes and look to the future. God has placed you where you are because He has something He wants you to do there. Do it with all your heart, and the Lord may take you forward into something greater.

PRAYER: God, thank You for Your miraculous provision. When I feel like checking out, please help me to keep dropping my nets in faith. Amen.

February 22
EARNEST PRAYER

ELIJAH WAS A MAN WITH A NATURE LIKE OURS, AND HE
PRAYED EARNESTLY THAT IT WOULD NOT RAIN; AND IT DID NOT
RAIN ON THE LAND FOR THREE YEARS AND SIX MONTHS.
JAMES 5:17

IN TODAY'S verse we read about Elijah, who prayed earnestly that it would not rain. Elijah wasn't supernatural; he was an ordinary man who prayed that it would not rain, and it didn't. He just prayed in faith.

You might be praying for a baby. Well, that's exactly what Sarah and Abraham did: they believed God, and God gave them a child. Hannah prayed for a baby, and she gave birth to Samuel.

Our whole ministry operates on faith. If the Lord tells us to go and do something, He will supply. God will pull you though every situation and fulfill His promises.

I want to encourage you to start praying with a different attitude. You don't have because you don't ask in faith (James 4:2–3). And faith comes by hearing, and hearing comes by the Word of God. Start spending time in the Word of God and get direction from Him, not from the people around you. That is effective prayer.

God answers fervent prayer offered in faith. Make sure your life is in order with God, seek His will, and thank Him in anticipation.

PRAYER: Lord, please strengthen my faith as I pray. I thank
You ahead of time for answering this prayer! Amen.

February 23

STAND STRONG

WHY ARE YOU CAST DOWN, O MY SOUL? AND WHY ARE YOU
DISQUIETED WITHIN ME? HOPE IN GOD; FOR I SHALL YET
PRAISE HIM, THE HELP OF MY COUNTENANCE AND MY GOD.
PSALM 42:11

ARE YOU going through difficult circumstances in your life at the moment? Maybe you have been serving the Lord for many years, and though the Lord said you would receive abundantly, you are still struggling. You are not necessarily doing anything wrong; don't let some "super-Christian" come and tell you that there must be some unconfessed sin in your life. You are planted exactly where God wants you to be. However, we are not subject to special treatment because we live on earth and we love Jesus—we go through the same storms as everybody else. The question is, how will we handle it?

In today's scripture, the Lord is telling us to stand strong until the storm passes. On my farm we've got some very strong oak trees that are 150 years old. They are tilted because they grow into the prevailing wind. It's almost as if they are putting their shoulder to the wind. Such trees have character because they've been subject to the storms of life. When you do cut them down or they fall over, they weigh a ton because they have been through times of testing and have developed a strong core.

Be like an oak tree: stand in the storm and rejoice in your tribulation. If you want to become a strong believer, then you've got to be tested by the storms of life. But remember: God will never leave you.

PRAYER: God, thank You that strength comes from my struggles. I pray that You will give me faith and strength to put my shoulder to the wind. Amen.

February 24
A TWO-WAY RELATIONSHIP

[JESUS] SAID TO HIM THE THIRD TIME, "SIMON, SON OF
JONAH, DO YOU LOVE ME?" PETER WAS GRIEVED BECAUSE
HE SAID TO HIM THE THIRD TIME, "DO YOU LOVE ME?" AND
HE SAID TO HIM, "LORD, YOU KNOW ALL THINGS; YOU KNOW
THAT I LOVE YOU." JESUS SAID TO HIM, "FEED MY SHEEP."
JOHN 21:17

WHAT DOES "Feed My sheep" mean? It is literal—meaning taking care of others—but it also means we must look after that which God has given to us.

I have found from experience that if a business looks after its employees, the business will almost run itself. But so many employers try to do it the other way around in their earnestness to put bread on their own tables. They forget to "feed the sheep" who have been placed in their trust: the staff, their families, and the community as a whole. I don't just mean financial responsibility; I'm talking about taking care of the whole person.

Your colleagues, family, and subordinates need to know that they can confide in you when they have a problem. It takes a long time to earn people's trust, but when someone starts asking you for help with a personal issue—a marital problem, trouble with a child, a personal problem—then you know you are feeding the Lord's sheep in a spiritual way.

Many years ago, I had a personal tragedy. Apart from my wife and children, the staff on my farm comforted me more than anyone else. Let's learn to laugh together, go through tough times together, feed each other, and walk this road together with humility, trust, and love.

PRAYER: Lord, thank You for those in my care and my circle of influence. Show me how to feed them more effectively. Amen.

February 25

A CLEAR CONSCIENCE

I MYSELF ALWAYS STRIVE TO HAVE A CONSCIENCE
WITHOUT OFFENSE TOWARD GOD AND MEN.
ACTS 24:16

YOUR CONSCIENCE is your sense of right and wrong. I believe that the Holy Spirit is a Christian's conscience. If we obey and listen to the gentle motivation of the Spirit of God in us, then we'll make the right decisions and have peace in our hearts.

The Christian author Oswald Chambers once wrote, "Conscience . . . is the eye of the soul which looks out either toward God or toward what it regards as the highest authority." If you keep your conscience sensitive to the needs of others, you will walk without offending others because you'll be walking according to the will of the Lord.

The world in which we live is desperately seeking peace, and the only peace we shall ever have comes from a conscience free from guilt. Charles H. Spurgeon, the great British preacher, once said, "I would bear any affliction rather than be burdened with a guilty conscience." A guilty conscience will prevent us from sleeping well, from making sound decisions, from being good spouses, and from enjoying work. So as you continue to allow the Holy Spirit to direct you at home, school, or work, be assured that if you have a clear conscience, you can face the world with confidence.

PRAYER: Lord, make Your Sprit bother me about things I need to change and clean up so I can have a victorious life in You. Amen.

February 26
SAVED BY JESUS ALONE

THE RIGHTEOUSNESS OF GOD IS REVEALED FROM FAITH TO
FAITH; AS IT IS WRITTEN, "THE JUST SHALL LIVE BY FAITH."
ROMANS 1:17

ONE MAN, Adam, brought sin into the world, and one Man, Jesus, dealt with it.

Romans 5:20–21 reads, "But where sin abounded, grace abounded much more, so that as sin reigned in death, even so grace might reign through righteousness to eternal life through Jesus Christ our Lord."

Before Christ came into the world, people had to live by the law, which exposed sin in their lives. However, we can't be saved simply by obeying the law. It took the Son of God, Jesus Christ, to come into this world and to die for our sins so we could believe in Him and have eternal life. That is how it works. The law cannot save us, but it shows us the sin in our lives. It is grace that saves us—undeserved lovingkindness.

Since we are all saved by grace, we have no right to be judgmental of other people. Rather, we are called to be compassionate and full of mercy, because if it were not for the grace of God, we would all be in exactly the same place.

There is no hope for us outside the grace of Christ, so let us believe and be grateful.

PRAYER: Dear Jesus, thank You for Your saving grace. Give me a right
understanding of Your law and compassion for all of Your creation. Amen.

February 27
TIMES OF ADVERSITY

FOR YOU HAVE NEED OF ENDURANCE, SO THAT AFTER YOU HAVE
DONE THE WILL OF GOD, YOU MAY RECEIVE THE PROMISE.
HEBREWS 10:36

ADVERSITY IS something we all experience sooner or later. Even after you have given your life to the Lord, you will have setbacks. Why? The Son of God faced adversity, and all the disciples faced adversity too; that's because we do not live in a perfect world.

Mark 5:21–43 tells the story of Jairus's dying daughter: "One of the rulers of the synagogue came, Jairus by name. And when he saw Him, he fell at His feet and begged Him earnestly, saying, 'My little daughter lies at the point of death. Come and lay Your hands on her, that she may be healed, and she will live'" (vv. 22–23).

Jesus went to the house, but before He got there He was told He was too late and that the girl was already dead. Jesus, however, said that she was not dead, but only sleeping, and He brought her back to life. Even though the story has a happy ending, this must have been a very trying time for Jairus.

There can be no doubt that adversity brings us closer to God. Almost every testimony you will hear from Christian men and women describes how they came closer to Jesus in a time of hardship. In the midst of troublesome times, may we run to Jesus as Jairus did. He probably would not have turned to Jesus if his little daughter hadn't fallen terribly ill, but he ended up getting a miracle. We too can turn to Jesus in our tribulations; in return, He will produce in us perseverance, character, and hope.

PRAYER: God, it's so easy to panic when everything seems to go dramatically wrong. Help me to run to You, the only source of healing. Amen.

February 28
SIMPLY BELIEVE

THEN [JESUS] AROSE AND REBUKED THE WIND AND THE RAGING OF
THE WATER. AND THEY CEASED, AND THERE WAS A CALM. BUT HE
SAID TO THEM, "WHERE IS YOUR FAITH?" AND THEY WERE AFRAID,
AND MARVELED, SAYING TO ONE ANOTHER, "WHO CAN THIS BE? FOR
HE COMMANDS EVEN THE WINDS AND WATER, AND THEY OBEY HIM!"
LUKE 8:24–25

THE ORIGIN of the word *miracle* comes from the Latin word *miraculum*, meaning "object of wonder." I can confirm that miracles are not obsolete, because I've experienced many.

The greatest miracle I've experienced so far was at Ein Gedi in 2012. The wind rarely blows there, and it rarely rains. I had been invited to speak to people from all over the world as part of the Feast of Tabernacles, a celebration that takes places in Israel each year.

Before the meeting, we asked the Lord to show us His tangible power. When I closed my Bible and walked to the front of the pulpit, a gentle wind started to blow. Before long, it became mighty. It was so strong that it blew my four-pound Bible right off the pulpit! As if that were not enough, it began to rain. The fire of God fell on us that night at Ein Gedi.

The Lord has promised us very clearly that He will never leave or forsake us. When we are in great need, we must ask Him to undertake for us in a miraculous way, and then believe He will. Believe God once again for that miracle in your marriage, in your home, with your children, with your exam, with your business. As we start to believe Him for the small things, our faith will grow to believe Him for bigger miracles.

PRAYER: God, thank You for being a God of miracles.
Increase my faith today. Amen.

February 29
GUILTY NO MORE

WHO IS HE WHO CONDEMNS? IT IS CHRIST WHO DIED, AND
FURTHERMORE IS ALSO RISEN, WHO IS EVEN AT THE RIGHT
HAND OF GOD, WHO ALSO MAKES INTERCESSION FOR US.
ROMANS 8:34

DO YOU feel guilty when you have let someone down? Guilt can nag at us as we consider our conduct or the way we spoke to someone. The disciples probably felt that way in the Garden of Gethsemane. The Lord begged His friends to watch with Him for just an hour, but they couldn't stay awake. When Jesus woke them up a third time, He said to them, "Are you still sleeping and resting? It is enough! The hour has come; behold, the Son of Man is being betrayed into the hands of sinners" (Mark 14:41).

The disciples had let Him down. Maybe you have been in that position as well. You are absolutely exhausted, and your brother or sister wants to come over and see you. You say you are too busy, then you find out later that something terrible has happened.

Once we've asked for forgiveness, we cannot continue to live with guilt. The best way to move on is to look forward, which is why it's such a privilege for us to know the Lord Jesus Christ.

Dr. David Livingstone once said, "I'll go anywhere with God, as long as it is forward." We need to learn from our mistakes. What is past is past. It's water under the bridge. Now is the time to receive God's forgiveness and move forward in faith, rather refusing to do the next thing God is calling us to because we are wallowing in our guilt.

PRAYER: Lord God, thank You for patience and forgiveness. Show
me how to move forward out of my guilt today. Amen.

MARCH

March 1

THE REALITY OF OUR FAITH

JESUS ANSWERED AND SAID TO THEM, "THIS IS THE WORK
OF GOD, THAT YOU BELIEVE IN HIM WHOM HE SENT."
JOHN 6:29

SOMETIMES WE wonder, did Jesus really rise from the dead? Is the Lord Jesus really
the Son of God? Was the Lord Jesus really conceived by the Holy Spirit and born of
the Virgin Mary?

With all the evidence God has given us, it takes more faith to believe in false
religions than it does to believe that Jesus Christ is the Son of God, that He came
down from heaven in the form of a baby, that He lived among us to show us how to
live, and that He was crucified, buried, and raised from the dead after three days.
The reality of faith is that Jesus Christ *is* the Son of the living God and He *is* coming
back soon.

I am a child of God, not because I am a good man, but because the Word of God
says so in 1 John 1:9: "If we confess our sins, He is faithful and just to forgive us our
sins and to cleanse us from all unrighteousness." That's why I am alive. That's why
I don't feel guilty about my life before I met Jesus. The Lord Jesus Christ is alive
and well. The bedrock of my faith and my life is that Jesus Christ is the Son of God.
What is the bedrock of your faith?

PRAYER: Lord God, help me to examine the source of my faith
and to strengthen it daily by spending time with You. Amen.

March 2

FAVOR WITH MAN OR GOD?

DO NOT BE CONFORMED TO THIS WORLD, BUT BE TRANSFORMED
BY THE RENEWING OF YOUR MIND, THAT YOU MAY PROVE WHAT
IS THAT GOOD AND ACCEPTABLE AND PERFECT WILL OF GOD.
ROMANS 12:2

KING HEROD threw John the Baptist in jail because John had said it was unlawful for Herod to be involved with Herodias, his brother's wife (Matt. 14:1–12). Although Herod wanted to kill John, he knew that the people greatly respected John and that he would fall into disfavor if he hurt the prophet.

However, on his birthday, Herod promised the daughter of Herodias that he would give her anything she wanted because she had danced before him and pleased him. She promptly asked for John's head, and because the king had made a promise in front of many people, he had no choice but to have John the Baptist beheaded.

Herod killed John in order to stay in one woman's good graces and save face before his guests. And like it or not, we tend to do the same thing: we do whatever we know will make others happy and keep us in good standing with them. But it is better to keep the favor of the Lord than the favor of people.

John the Baptist did what God told him to do until the end; and as a result, he now rests in God's arms. King Herod, on the other hand, sought favor with man instead. He is now infamous in the eyes of history. Let's start doing things God's way and put peer pressure behind us. God's favor is all we need.

PRAYER: Dear God, please help me to keep the wider perspective today.
Cause my heart to long for Your approval above all others'. Amen.

March 3

WE ALL STAND TOGETHER

MAY THE GOD OF PATIENCE AND COMFORT GRANT YOU TO BE
LIKE-MINDED TOWARD ONE ANOTHER, ACCORDING TO CHRIST
JESUS, THAT YOU MAY WITH ONE MIND AND ONE MOUTH
GLORIFY THE GOD AND FATHER OF OUR LORD JESUS CHRIST.
ROMANS 15:5–6

RECENTLY, MY son asked me to help him bring in a herd of cattle on our farm. It was a Sunday afternoon, and he didn't have staff to help him. While saddling my horse, I could see my grandson and his dad saddling up their horses. The sight touched my heart deeply. Three generations out riding together!

All families have their good times and their tough times. Whether it's financial woes, the weather, problems with the market, or our relationships with each other and those outside the family circle, families need to talk things through.

When my children were young, I would share our difficulties openly with them. The only way for the family to stand together is by talking to each other and sharing experiences and feelings. Another key to a happy family is not to let the sun go down on a disagreement (Eph. 4:26). When you have a conflict with your spouse, children, or extended family, sit down, talk it through, settle the matter, and move on together.

As we went to round up the cattle, my little grandson looked small on top of his big horse, but he was confident because he had his father on one side and his grandfather on the other. We went out as a team, and I could see how proud my son was of his little boy. God is proud of us when we work together and rely on Him.

PRAYER: Lord, thank You for my family, and for those who have been like family to me. Show me how to preserve and protect those relationships today. Amen.

March 4
OUR GUIDE

"NOW I GO AWAY TO HIM WHO SENT ME, AND NONE OF YOU
ASKS ME, 'WHERE ARE YOU GOING?' BUT BECAUSE I HAVE
SAID THESE THINGS TO YOU, SORROW HAS FILLED YOUR
HEART. . . . I WILL SEND [THE HOLY SPIRIT] TO YOU."
JOHN 16:5–7

TIMES ARE hard, and the bad news is that they are going to get tougher. Without the Holy Spirit you are not going to make it. The good news is that when you invite Him into your home and your life, He answers. When you were born again, the Holy Spirit came into your heart; but when you are baptized in the Holy Spirit, that is when you are enveloped in the power of God.

After Jesus' resurrection and ascension, He sent the Holy Spirit to His disciples (Acts 2:1–4). The disciples were already born again, but when Jesus left, the Holy Spirit came into their hearts.

We too need that power. It is the power that gives us strength. When we get up in the morning and everything seems to be going wrong, we can rejoice and know that the Lord promised to never leave us (Heb. 13:5), that we can do all things with Him by our side, and that He will give us everything we need (Phil. 4:19).

The moment you understand and accept this is the moment you will start to walk in the power of the Holy Spirit. Once you invite the Holy Spirit into your heart, you will become different from the world. You will shine when everybody else is afraid; you will be strengthened just like the early saints.

PRAYER: Dear God, please send Your Holy Spirit into my
life. I offer up my heart today and every day. Amen.

March 5

VICTORY OVER DEATH

"O DEATH, WHERE IS YOUR STING? O HADES, WHERE IS YOUR
VICTORY?" THE STING OF DEATH IS SIN, AND THE STRENGTH
OF SIN IS THE LAW. BUT THANKS BE TO GOD, WHO GIVES
US THE VICTORY THROUGH OUR LORD JESUS CHRIST.
1 CORINTHIANS 15:55–57

WHAT HAPPENS when a person dies? Maybe you have recently lost a loved one and you just cannot come to terms with their passing. You don't know where your loved one has gone and you are frightened. You needn't be afraid because God through Jesus Christ has dealt with the sting of death forever.

You may have heard the verse, "to live is Christ, and to die is gain" (Phil. 1:21). For a believer, if we live, we live for the Lord; and if we die, we go home to heaven. There is nothing to fear; if your loved one knew Jesus Christ, they are waiting for you in heaven. They are free from all pain and suffering, and experiencing wholeness and joy.

Look forward to the day when you will join them, by the grace of God. Our hope is in eternal life, not in the here and now.

Jesus said that He is going ahead to prepare a place for us (John 14:2). And we will be there together with our loved ones forever. Death has lost its sting. God bless you and help you to keep looking up; your redemption draws near.

PRAYER: God, thank You for Your victory over death. When I grieve
a loved one, remind me of this all-important fact. Amen.

March 6

OBEY HIS COMMANDS

"IF YOU LOVE ME, KEEP MY COMMANDMENTS."
JOHN 14:15

ONE OF the older boys at the children's home we run came to see me to talk about his future. He had just completed his final school year and, thankfully, was able to get a job as an apprentice electrician, which he was very excited about. I told him that in the big world, there are certain rules and statutes that he would need to adhere to if he wanted to succeed.

He would have to follow the rules, arrive on time, dress well, and show humility. It would be hard for him in the beginning; he would probably have to take a lot of flak from the electrician teaching him, but he could take a deep breath and persevere. If he did all this, I told him, he would become a successful man.

Then we turned to Ezekiel 20:18–20, which reads, "But I said to their children in the wilderness, 'Do not walk in the statutes of your fathers, nor observe their judgments, nor defile yourselves with their idols. I am the LORD your God: Walk in My statutes, keep My judgments, and do them; hallow My Sabbaths, and they will be a sign between Me and you, that you may know that I am the LORD your God.'"

Many people are put off by Christianity because of the hypocrisy in the church—Christians are "holier than thou" on Sundays, but show no compassion, integrity, or love toward others for the other six days of the week. Our entire lifestyle must measure up to the Word of God. Obedience to Him is the only way to success.

PRAYER: Dear God, thank You for giving us Your wise laws. Help me to learn them and follow them, and to coach others in Your ways. Amen.

March 7

MINISTERING BY ACTION

WHO IS WISE AND UNDERSTANDING AMONG YOU?
LET HIM SHOW BY GOOD CONDUCT THAT HIS WORKS
ARE DONE IN THE MEEKNESS OF WISDOM.
JAMES 3:13

IT IS very easy to say, "God bless you; keep warm," and leave that poor, homeless person in his plight. But in the book of James, the Lord says our faith is made perfect by our actions.

Many years ago I was preaching the gospel in the Great Lakes area of Central Africa in a big yellow truck that we called the Seed Sower. I remember being extremely homesick. I had been away from home for five weeks and was feeling the strain. We were battling all kinds of things: that area is renowned for malaria, food was quite short, and accommodation was almost nonexistent. We slept in the truck and preached from the back of it, day in and day out. I was feeling rough, to put it mildly.

Then one day I came to a little fishing village on Lake Mweru, which is on the border between Congo and Zambia. As I walked into the village, I saw a Zambian lady sitting and listening to Christian music. It brought a tear to my eye; I thought, *Lord, You are everywhere.* I explained to her who we were and what we were doing, and immediately she called one of her clerks and gave him the keys to her house. She instructed us to go to her home and take hot baths. While we were bathing, her house servant made us the most delicious papaya salad I think I have ever eaten in my life. I have never forgotten that extravagant gesture, though it happened well over twenty years ago. She wanted nothing back in exchange. Actions always speak louder than words, and this woman's actions spoke of Christ.

PRAYER: Lord, thank You for the generosity shown through Your children.
Cause my actions to bring relief to others and to glorify You. Amen.

March 8

BIND YOUR THOUGHTS

FAITH COMES BY HEARING, AND HEARING BY THE WORD OF GOD.
ROMANS 10:17

AS CHRISTIANS, we are called to keep our imaginations in check. What we read, what we watch on TV, and the conversations we have with others all influence the way we think. The best way to start taking control of our thoughts and our dreams is to concentrate on what the Lord says and thinks about us. The devil is not called "the father of all lies" for nothing. Deceit is the only power that he has, and he will use it to try to warp your knowledge of God's love for you. Let us remember that he can only influence people who are afraid. The opposite of fear is faith, and the way to become faithful is by reading the Bible—spending time in the Word and learning God's will.

In 2 Corinthians 10:4, Paul describes the battle of the mind: "For the weapons of our warfare are not carnal but mighty in God for pulling down strongholds." To harness that power properly, and to keep your heart and mind open to Him instead of the world, try spending quiet time with the Lord every day before you begin work. You'll find that your day will go much better as a result. Spend time with people who are positive about life and about the future, and who are prepared to live according to God's principles. Read wholesome books, especially the Bible. Be careful what you watch on TV and read on the Internet. And, finally, form friendships with men and women who have a heart for the Lord Jesus.

PRAYER: Dear God, please help me to control my thought life today.
Keep me from ingesting anything that does not bring You joy. Amen.

March 9

AMBASSADORS FOR CHRIST

WE ARE AMBASSADORS FOR CHRIST, AS THOUGH GOD
WERE PLEADING THROUGH US: WE IMPLORE YOU ON
CHRIST'S BEHALF, BE RECONCILED TO GOD.
2 CORINTHIANS 5:20

THE GREATEST ambassador in the Word of God was Paul the apostle. He was a clever man who used everything at his disposal to be effective. May we to do the same and use everything at our disposal in order to win souls for Christ.

Acts 23:1–3 tells of one incident: "Then Paul, looking earnestly at the council, said, 'Men and brethren, I have lived in all good conscience before God until this day.' And the high priest Ananias commanded those who stood by him to strike him on the mouth. Then Paul said to him, 'God will strike you, you whitewashed wall!'"

As ambassadors for Christ, we don't have to be weak. Humble, yes; submitted to God, yes; but when the crunch comes, like Paul, we must stand up for what we believe in.

Paul was smart. He looked around him and saw that there were Pharisees and Sadducees in the court. He got them arguing with one another over the issue of life after death. This gave him a bit of breathing room in the situation.

Use the wits God has given you as you defend the gospel. Analyze your situation and use arguments that will reach your audience. But remember your ultimate goal: to bring glory to God and turn people's hearts to Him.

Avoid thinking that you are better than others, and don't forget where you come from. You are also just a sinner saved by grace. Most of all, love them and show compassion.

PRAYER: God, help me to develop my ambassadorial approach. Grant
me wisdom, tact, and passion for spreading Your Word. Amen.

March 10
PRAYER CHANGES THINGS

CONTINUE EARNESTLY IN PRAYER, BEING
VIGILANT IN IT WITH THANKSGIVING.
COLOSSIANS 4:2

SOMETHING WORTH having is always worth praying for. When we seek to spread God's Word, it's not medical help, education, or impressive speeches that will turn the tide, but undiluted prayer and nothing less. We are working toward Jesus Christ's harvest, so why wouldn't we communicate with Him above all else?

What is truly special is that Christ Himself prays for us. He is our ultimate Intercessor in this dying world. It is always touching to know that one of our friends or family members is praying for us, but how much more wonderful to know that the very Son of God is praying for you and me! He also sets a towering example of the way we should pray (Matt. 6:5–13).

Do not neglect the "prayer closet," the place where you pray alone to God. It is like the roots of a tree: without the roots the tree cannot grow strong and survive when the rough wind blows. Daily communion with our heavenly Father is absolutely critical to the Christian life. Give the firstfruits of every morning, and indeed the rest of the day, to Jesus by spending time in prayer with Him.

When you pray, go to a quiet place and keep it personal. Ask the Lord to visit you in a special and fresh way so that you can feel His powerful presence in your quiet time.

PRAYER: God, please make prayer my fuel for life. Thank
You, Jesus, for interceding for me always. Amen.

March 11

THE FEAR OF MAN

I HAVE BEEN CRUCIFIED WITH CHRIST; IT IS NO LONGER I
WHO LIVE, BUT CHRIST LIVES IN ME; AND THE LIFE WHICH
I NOW LIVE IN THE FLESH I LIVE BY FAITH IN THE SON OF
GOD, WHO LOVED ME AND GAVE HIMSELF FOR ME.
GALATIANS 2:20

FEARING MAN can really get in the way of action. We wonder, *What will people think?* But what does it matter? The important thing is what Jesus thinks.

The greatest evangelist that we know of was Paul the apostle. He learned that the fear of man is what holds a person back. He wrote in Galatians 6:12, "As many as desire to make a good showing in the flesh, these would compel you to be circumcised, only that they may not suffer persecution for the cross of Christ."

In other words, some in Galatia spoke about circumcision rather than being born again, because they did not want to upset the public. Paul concluded by saying, "But God forbid that I should boast except in the cross of our Lord Jesus Christ, by whom the world has been crucified to me, and I to the world. For in Christ Jesus neither circumcision nor uncircumcision avails anything, but a new creation" (vv. 14–15).

Paul did not preach about circumcision; he did not try to find favor with man. Instead, he was obedient to God, and that is where his liberty came from. Wherever Paul went, there was either riot or a revival because he preached from his heart. He had no concern for what people thought about him. He loved people, which is why he told them the truth.

PRAYER: Dear God, please help me to tell Your truth in love
instead of saying what people want to hear today. Amen.

March 12

SPEAKING OUT

IF INDEED YOU HAVE HEARD HIM AND HAVE BEEN
TAUGHT BY HIM, AS THE TRUTH IS IN JESUS . . . PUT OFF,
CONCERNING YOUR FORMER CONDUCT, THE OLD MAN
WHICH GROWS CORRUPT ACCORDING TO THE DECEITFUL
LUSTS, AND BE RENEWED IN THE SPIRIT OF YOUR MIND.
EPHESIANS 4:21–23

ONE MORNING in 1979, I made a conscious commitment to Jesus Christ. I went to the front of the church and accepted Jesus Christ into my life as my Lord and Savior.

After we got home, a man from the church whom I had never met before came to me and asked whether I had meant it when I prayed the Sinner's Prayer. I got defensive and quickly declared that I had of course meant every word. He then challenged me to tell the first three people I met the next morning what I had done.

The next morning, as I sat in a pickup with my next-door neighbor, I had a tremendous internal wrestling match. On the one hand, the devil was telling me that if I said anything, this man would laugh at me. On the other hand, the Lord was telling me that if I didn't speak up, He would not speak up for me. Finally, I told him about my accepting Christ. His face went gray, but he told me that even though it was not for him at that stage, he was happy for me.

Not long after that he called me up and asked me about my faith. Later that day he and his entire family accepted Jesus Christ into their lives.

Who knows what will happen when we speak up? Telling people about our faith cements our stand for Christ.

PRAYER: God, give me the bravery to speak for You today. Amen.

March 13
THE MEASURE OF COMMITMENT

BE STEADFAST, IMMOVABLE, ALWAYS ABOUNDING IN THE WORK OF
THE LORD, KNOWING THAT YOUR LABOR IS NOT IN VAIN IN THE LORD.
1 CORINTHIANS 15:58

WHETHER YOU are starting a business, bringing up a family, completing a degree, or fulfilling a dream, there's always a price. Anything that costs nothing isn't worth having. It requires commitment and sacrifice to see our vision completed. One of the biggest dangers is starting off with great gusto and then, when the going gets tough, throwing in the towel. That's not the way to a successful life. Instead, we need zeal!

William Carey, who took the gospel to India, committed himself to bringing the good news to those who had never heard it. He was known as the "father of modern missions." Even though his wife and one of his sons died in India, Carey never turned back. God used him to establish a printing press, which printed the full Bible or parts of it in dozens of languages and dialects during Carey's lifetime. He was committed to fulfilling what God had called him to do.

God never promised us a bed of roses. In fact, He never promised that He would take us out of the fire; instead, He told us He would walk through the fire with us (Isa. 43:1–2). Hardships build character. They mold us and make us more humble, more understanding, more teachable, and more loving. The measure of our commitment through trials and obstacles will determine the success of any enterprise.

PRAYER: Dear Lord, please renew my zeal for seeing Your mission in
my life completed. Thank You for using my trials to grow me. Amen.

March 14

THE UNDILUTED GOSPEL MESSAGE

NOW MAY THE GOD OF HOPE FILL YOU WITH ALL JOY
AND PEACE IN BELIEVING, THAT YOU MAY ABOUND
IN HOPE BY THE POWER OF THE HOLY SPIRIT.
ROMANS 15:13

WHEN YOU talk to unbelievers about God, it is not your personality or your eloquence that will sway them; it's the power of the Holy Spirit. It is not about how well you can memorize the message; it is what is in a person's heart that will convert him or her to Jesus.

Let's consider 1 Corinthians 2, which reads, "And I, brethren, when I came to you, did not come with excellence of speech or of wisdom declaring to you the testimony of God. . . . [M]y speech and my preaching were not with persuasive words of human wisdom, but in demonstration of the Spirit and of power, that your faith should not be in the wisdom of men but in the power of God" (vv. 1, 4–5).

Paul was a highly intelligent and articulate man who did not go to people and witness using his intellectual gifts. Rather, he went to preach a simple gospel message, knowing that the power of God is what would change them—not his wisdom, qualifications, or experience.

Unbelievers need help from God, and it is our duty to lead them to Him. At the end of the day, it is the simple message, the undiluted Word of God, that convicts people to follow the Lord. It is the gospel that draws people to Him—not us. Keep it simple, keep it passionate, keep it personal, and keep it relevant, and God will use you powerfully.

PRAYER: Dear God, thank You that You are the One who
brings people to You—not me! I pray for Your voice to
speak through me as I tell others about You. Amen.

March 15
EFFECTIVE COMMUNICATION

LET NO CORRUPT WORD PROCEED OUT OF YOUR MOUTH,
BUT WHAT IS GOOD FOR NECESSARY EDIFICATION,
THAT IT MAY IMPART GRACE TO THE HEARERS.
EPHESIANS 4:29

I'M A firm believer in stating the obvious. The first thing I do when I wake up every morning is tell my wife that I love her. Sure, she already knows, but there's so much negativity and stress in the world that we build each other up and reassure each other by saying what's on our hearts. Poor communication can cause mistrust and lead to a breakdown in a relationship. By not communicating clearly, people develop misconceptions and unnecessary problems arise.

There's a lack of effective communication in many communities at the moment. Speak to those around you, ask for advice, share ideas. The solutions to your challenges may be as close as your neighbor next door.

This goes for work life as well. As part of a team, it's important to build each other up and be clear about what we expect from people and what we are doing. Communication builds security and confidence within the workplace environment.

It's true that in this day and age we are challenged by the elements, by the economic situation, by the political climate. We need each other more than ever. So let us stand together and encourage one another daily. When we watch out for and encourage our colleagues, employees, clients, and friends, and when we speak freely and truthfully, then real growth can occur.

PRAYER: God, please bless my communication with those around me today.
Help me to build others up with encouragement and truthfulness. Amen.

March 16

UNEQUALLY YOKED

DO NOT BE UNEQUALLY YOKED TOGETHER WITH UNBELIEVERS. FOR WHAT
FELLOWSHIP HAS RIGHTEOUSNESS WITH LAWLESSNESS? AND WHAT
COMMUNION HAS LIGHT WITH DARKNESS? AND WHAT ACCORD HAS CHRIST
WITH BELIAL? OR WHAT PART HAS A BELIEVER WITH AN UNBELIEVER?
2 CORINTHIANS 6:14–15

BE CAREFUL of the company you keep, because you don't want to be unequally yoked. Just as oil and water cannot mix, and light and darkness cannot blend, so believers and unbelievers cannot be bound together. Therefore, the Lord says to come out from among them and be separate (2 Cor. 6:17). We are new creations in Christ (5:17), so we should surround ourselves with people who will help us live a life of godliness.

It is our duty as Christians to reach out to people, but we are not to become entangled with unbelievers. When people see that you stand for righteousness, they will come to you. And when they come to you and want to know why you have peace and joy and freedom, then you can tell them about Jesus.

It is easy to make bad choices when you are tied to people who are not followers of Jesus. King Ahab, for example, was a good and wise king according to the Word of God, until he got mixed up with bad company. They influence you, whether you like it or not.

Some people believe they will be able to change their unbelieving spouse once they are married. You won't change them; they will change you. Let us make sure our closest friends and spouses are those of the faith so we can live godly lives, unhindered.

PRAYER: Dear God, I ask Your blessing in guiding me
to the right friends and relationships. Amen.

March 17

CAUGHT UP IN SELF

OUR OLD MAN WAS CRUCIFIED WITH HIM, THAT
THE BODY OF SIN MIGHT BE DONE AWAY WITH, THAT
WE SHOULD NO LONGER BE SLAVES OF SIN.
ROMANS 6:6

JESUS SAID that He came to set the captives free, and the greatest freedom we can ever know is to be set free from ourselves.

We see the symptoms of self-obsession all around us: anxiousness that people should think well of us, that we should be accepted into their circles or groups. Anxiousness over living in the right house, the right neighborhood, what make of car we drive, the clothes we wear, and the friends we spend time with. We are anxious about having enough money, eating at the right places, and taking a vacation where everyone else does. The stress of this sort of lifestyle can affect most of us physically and mentally. Our reputations, looks, and fitness levels keep us totally absorbed. Sadly, many resort to drinking, medication, and drugs to cope with life.

In John 8:36 we read these words: "Therefore if the Son makes you free, you shall be free indeed." Only a sovereign work of God can set us free from self. With that freedom comes liberty, and we find that reverence for God replaces the fear of man in our hearts. We acknowledge Him as greater than ourselves.

As we come to know God's love, we can reach beyond ourselves to love others. So let's make a decision to die to self so that we can live free of anxiety—to the glory of Jesus and for others.

PRAYER: Jesus, please reveal to me where I am focused on myself today, and turn that gaze outward to You and the work You have for me to do. Amen.

March 18

DON'T QUIT

FIGHT THE GOOD FIGHT OF FAITH, LAY HOLD ON ETERNAL LIFE,
TO WHICH YOU WERE ALSO CALLED AND HAVE CONFESSED THE
GOOD CONFESSION IN THE PRESENCE OF MANY WITNESSES.
1 TIMOTHY 6:12

THE BIBLE tells us very clearly not to quit or give up. Instead, we are called to press on and carry our load, just as our Lord did. All too often when we've nearly had enough, when our burden seems heavier than ever, we are close to winning. To give up at this stage would truly be a shame. If we persevere, the next few steps might take us to the crest of the mountain at last, with success right there for the taking.

Even Paul, the mighty man of God who wrote so much of the New Testament, became disappointed in himself and his own behavior. In Romans 7:19 he wrote, "For the good that I will to do, I do not do; but the evil that I will not to do, that I practice." He continued in verse 24: "O wretched man that I am! Who will deliver me from this body of death?"

If Paul can become disheartened and still persevere, there is hope for you and me! The secret is to walk and operate by faith and not by sight. We will reap a bountiful crop if we do not falter. Let us put energy and passion into whatever we do, using our God-given gifts for His glory.

PRAYER: Dear God, please give me the faith to carry on when things look darkest. I look to You today to make my burdens bearable. Amen.

March 19

CUT YOUR LOSSES AND PRESS ON

FORGETTING THOSE THINGS WHICH ARE BEHIND AND REACHING
FORWARD TO THOSE THINGS WHICH ARE AHEAD . . .
PHILIPPIANS 3:13

WE ALL make mistakes, often falling into despair when we realize we can't make things right on our own. Instead, I want to encourage you to remember the old saying, "Don't cry over spilled milk." Or, as Oswald Chambers wrote, "Never let the sense of failure corrupt your new action."

Despair is a very normal human experience. If we have lost an opportunity to do something good, we feel despondent over it.

I once planted a maize crop and made a mess of the planter calibration. This resulted in far fewer plants than normal. I remember despairing month after month because of the mistake I'd made. I thought it might cost me my farm. Then, one morning, I felt the Holy Spirit say to me, "Stop despairing, stop looking at the gaps in the maize crop, and start looking at the cobs." As it turned out, the extra spacing between the plants allowed the cobs to develop well—which was profitable, since we were paid by weight rather than volume.

The devil wants us to lose hope, whereas the Lord wants us to move on. If we've made a mistake or haven't taken advantage of an opportunity, the only solution is to put it behind us. The Lord will make more opportunities available to us in the future.

Cut your losses and press on, because many more wonderful opportunities will be waiting up ahead. You can move on with Jesus guiding you.

PRAYER: Dear God, it's so easy to fall into despair. Please help me to keep my eye on the bigger picture and take confident steps forward instead. Amen.

March 20

DIFFERENT POINTS OF VIEW

"BE ANGRY, AND DO NOT SIN": DO NOT LET THE SUN GO
DOWN ON YOUR WRATH, NOR GIVE PLACE TO THE DEVIL.
EPHESIANS 4:26–27

FROM TIME to time believers lose their tempers. Though there may be no good reason for it, even Christians can be hotheaded. When we lose our tempers, we tend to think we will not be able to recover our relationship and our reputation. God, however, works all things together for the good of those who love Him and are called according to His purpose (Rom. 8:28).

If you have a serious disagreement with someone, the first step to healing is to repent and seek reconciliation; but don't feel condemned if you lost your temper. It happens to the best of us. It even happened to Paul and Barnabas.

In Acts 15:39–40 we read, "Then the contention became so sharp that they parted from one another. And so Barnabas took Mark and sailed to Cyprus; but Paul chose Silas and departed, being commended by the brethren to the grace of God." These are two men of God, giants of the faith, who had a serious disagreement over whether to take John (called Mark) with them (Acts 15:36–41).

Of course, public disagreements between believers do not set a good example to the world, but when it happens, we are not condemned. It's what happens next that matters; in the end, Paul and Barnabas reconciled. God uses all kinds of people in His ministry. He will fulfill His purposes even in the midst of—and sometimes because of—our disputes.

PRAYER: God, thank You for showing grace to Your children,
and for using me despite my failings. Amen.

March 21

BACK TO BASICS

A BISHOP THEN MUST BE BLAMELESS, THE HUSBAND OF ONE
WIFE, TEMPERATE, SOBER-MINDED, OF GOOD BEHAVIOR,
HOSPITABLE, ABLE TO TEACH; NOT GIVEN TO WINE, NOT VIOLENT,
NOT GREEDY FOR MONEY, BUT GENTLE, NOT QUARRELSOME, NOT
COVETOUS; ONE WHO RULES HIS OWN HOUSE WELL, HAVING
HIS CHILDREN IN SUBMISSION WITH ALL REVERENCE.
1 TIMOTHY 3:2–4

THIS SECTION of 1 Timothy describes the qualities required of church leaders, and many of them relate to leading in home life. Strong families ensure a strong church and nation. Revival and change won't come through government, but rather through the strength and peace found in the home. The devil is hell-bent on destroying the family. He knows that when we're so busy worrying about issues outside the front door, he can walk right through the kitchen door. So let's get back to basics. Put God first, then your family, and then your work and ministry. If we get our priorities back in order, our homes will be vibrant, happy places in which to live and grow.

Children imitate what they see. If you're unfaithful to your spouse, there's a good chance your child will grow up to be unfaithful too. If you don't respect your spouse, don't expect your child to respect others.

Jesus Christ is our role model: He never abused a woman or a child, He never took advantage of the poor or the needy. In fact, He was their champion. He was never married, nor did He have children, but He knew the basics started with honoring His Father and loving His neighbors.

PRAYER: Dear God, thank You for my family and those You've put
in my life. Help me to refocus on the basics today. Amen.

March 22

GOD'S FAITHFULNESS

HE WHO CALLS YOU IS FAITHFUL, WHO ALSO WILL DO IT.
1 THESSALONIANS 5:24

THIS MORNING I was sitting quietly in my study, listening to some beautiful country-western music (my favorite). There are a few mainstay themes in country music, including dogs, trucks, and cheating spouses. When a song came up about a wronged woman, I suddenly felt deeply saddened, and was reminded of the value of faithfulness.

When someone becomes unfaithful to their spouse, to their partner in business, or to their childhood friend, it can tear out the heart of a person. Yet today's scripture reminds us that our God is a faithful God. The apostle Paul wrote to the Romans, "Let God be true but every man a liar" (3:4).

Faithfulness is one of the most beautiful fruits of the Spirit of God. When we are unfaithful, He still remains faithful. He promises us that He will never leave us nor forsake us (Heb. 13:5). Some will hurt us and some will disappoint us, but I can promise you one thing: our God will never ever leave us, never disappoint us, and most of all, never be unfaithful to us. You might not be able to trust your bank, you might not be able to trust the weather, and you might not even be able to trust the government; but you can trust the man from Galilee, Jesus Christ, who is faithful indeed.

PRAYER: Dear God, the true strength of Your faithfulness is
beyond my imagining. Thank You for always staying with me,
and help me to be faithful to You in return. Amen.

March 23

DON'T COMPROMISE

IF THAT IS THE CASE, OUR GOD WHOM WE SERVE IS ABLE TO DELIVER US FROM THE BURNING FIERY FURNACE, AND HE WILL DELIVER US FROM YOUR HAND, O KING. BUT IF NOT, LET IT BE KNOWN TO YOU, O KING, THAT WE DO NOT SERVE YOUR GODS, NOR WILL WE WORSHIP THE GOLD IMAGE WHICH YOU HAVE SET UP.
DANIEL 3:17–18

A COMPROMISER is a person who moves goalposts and plays to the crowd. Compromisers tell people what they want to hear because they want to be popular. They do not stand for truth. But being a Christian calls for firm resolve against compromise.

We must be prepared; following Jesus without compromise invites continual criticism. We cannot be controlled by what others say about us. That is why it is so important for men and women of God to spend time alone in prayer and to listen to what the Spirit of God tells them to do.

God is looking for people like Shadrach, Meshach, and Abed-Nego—who, according to today's verse, refused to compromise in the face of danger. They faced a fiery furnace after refusing to worship a golden idol, but God protected them. If you are grounded in the Word, sure of your calling, and sure of your walk with Jesus, not even fire can destroy your foundation. Stand your ground. Never compromise because of criticism. D. L. Moody, one of my American heroes, once said, "The man that is popular with the world is not a friend to Jesus Christ. . . . You may be sure that something is wrong with you when everybody is your friend."

If Jesus is the most important Person in your life, then you will be able to withstand any kind of buffeting.

PRAYER: God, my heart is resolved against compromise. Lead me to stay pure, strong, and faithful to Your will no matter what others say. Amen

March 24
ETERNITY IN YOUR HEART

HE HAS PUT ETERNITY IN THEIR HEARTS.
ECCLESIASTES 3:11

EVERY PERSON knows there is a God, because He put eternity in every human heart.

There was a program recently on the History Channel about a man who lives with remote groups of people. One week he'll be with the Eskimos, and the next he'll be with a group of people in the Amazon jungle. One thing that fascinated me is that all of these remote groups acknowledge that there is a God, even though many of them have never been evangelized by a preacher of the Word. It is God who put eternity in their hearts.

An eternal perspective causes us not to live for ourselves but for others. With eternity in mind, we sow into our children's lives, into the lives of the community, and into the nation—knowing that whatever we sow, we will reap.

The last chapter in the book of Ecclesiastes says, "Fear God and keep His commandments, for this is man's all" (12:13). If this advice was good enough for Solomon, the wisest man in history, then it's good enough for the rest of us.

Fear (or respect) God, so that you may keep His commandments. If you treat others as eternal beings loved by God, you'll find that life never loses its meaning. You'll begin to celebrate on earth what will come to pass in heaven.

PRAYER: Dear Lord, thank You for placing eternity in all our hearts. Let it influence everything I do. Amen.

March 25

A DISCIPLINED LIFE IS A HAPPY LIFE

NO CHASTENING SEEMS TO BE JOYFUL FOR THE
PRESENT, BUT PAINFUL; NEVERTHELESS, AFTERWARD
IT YIELDS THE PEACEABLE FRUIT OF RIGHTEOUSNESS
TO THOSE WHO HAVE BEEN TRAINED BY IT.
HEBREWS 12:11

ELI WAS the high priest in the house of the Lord (1 Sam. 1–4). He was a diligent man and a hard worker, someone who had been anointed and chosen by God. Eli was not just a leader—everybody sought counsel from him whenever they needed guidance. The Bible says that he was a good man and a man of God. But despite all this, he did not take his responsibility at home seriously.

He had two sons who were priests in the house of God, even though they did not know Him. They were corrupt men who abused their positions, taking portions of the sacrifices the people brought to honor God (1 Sam. 2:12–17). Their behavior was brought to Eli's attention, but when he addressed the matter with his sons, they ignored his words.

If Eli had put his foot down and "cleaned house," he might have saved his family from heartache. His sons died because they sinned against God, and Eli himself died after the ark of God was captured by the enemy (1 Sam. 4:10–18).

You might be the best leader in the world, the CEO of a big company, or a success at everything else you do, but if your home life is not in order, you will pay the price. If you have a spouse and children, take time out to spend with them. If not, focus on your closest relationships and the state of your personal affairs. God has called you to minister to your household first, whoever that may be.

PRAYER: Lord, open my eyes to those elements of
my home life that need attention. Amen.

March 26

A GRATEFUL HEART

OH, GIVE THANKS TO THE LORD! CALL UPON HIS NAME;
MAKE KNOWN HIS DEEDS AMONG THE PEOPLES!
1 CHRONICLES 16:8

OFTEN MY wife comes with me when I go for a jog early in the morning, just as the sun is coming up. We run past the plowed fields, we hear the birds singing as they build nests, and we occasionally see small antelope darting across the fields. There's a bird sanctuary near our farm in South Africa, and we often observe flocks of geese flying over in formation. We always agree that we are so grateful to live in such a beautiful place.

If I allow myself to be consumed with work or my worldly problems, I'll miss it all, jogging right past it without really seeing. In the same way, without an attitude of gratitude in life, we might fail to see the blessings that God gives us daily. Why focus on the negative and cloud our vision, missing the beauty right in front of us?

There's always something to be grateful for. Even when life is tough, the things in life that are really worth having are the things that money can't buy: true friendship, the love of family, and good health. Some of the most unhappy people I have met in my life are those who have so much money that they could never spend it in two lifetimes, let alone one. Gratefulness is priceless!

Let's decide to have a godly mind-set and to thank the Lord for the good things we have. Go out today with new eyes—the eyes of faith—and have a wonderful day.

PRAYER: Dear God, thank You for the gifts You've set around me!
Allow my eyes to see them for all that they are. Amen.

March 27

LIVING FOR TODAY

LET YOUR CONDUCT BE WITHOUT COVETOUSNESS; BE CONTENT
WITH SUCH THINGS AS YOU HAVE. FOR HE HIMSELF HAS
SAID, "I WILL NEVER LEAVE YOU NOR FORSAKE YOU."
HEBREWS 13:5

THE JOY of living is found in each moment, and the future is in God's hands. Remember the popular saying, "Yesterday is history, tomorrow is a mystery, today is a gift."

When we start to live this life day by day, we can handle the challenges that come our way. Jesus said that we should not be concerned about tomorrow, because today has enough concerns of its own (Matt. 6:34). It's the *process* of living, and not the end, that glorifies the Lord. When we enjoy the little things in life—the sunrise, the blessings of family and friends, the new opportunities given to us every day—we will give thanks to God, the Giver of every good gift. The Lord gives us the strength to live one day at a time. How do you enjoy each day? Perhaps it starts with disciplining ourselves not to always worry about the future. Let's take care of little things, and leave the big things in God's hands.

When we trustingly take care of the work God has given us for this day, we will become good citizens and, most of all, better disciples of the living God. After all, Jesus spent thirty years in a carpenter's shop in preparation for a mere three years of service, and that changed the world!

PRAYER: Dear God, thank You for these twenty-four hours. Allow me to enjoy them, and to trust that if I do what I can, You'll do the rest. Amen.

March 28

THE GIFT OF FAITH

"HAVE FAITH IN GOD."
MARK 11:22

TODAY'S SCRIPTURE is one of the easiest scriptures in the Bible to remember, and one of the most important. The Lord holds faith as the number one priority on His list. He tells us to walk by faith and not by sight (2 Cor. 5:7). If we walk by sight, we can easily become discouraged when things don't go our way; but in the faith realm, God has everything under control.

An anonymous writer wrote, "Faith follows God implicitly, albeit with trembling on occasion; while sight calculates, considers, cautions, and cringes." When we walk by sight, our understanding of our situation may be very bleak indeed; but when we look through God's eyes, the mountain before us becomes a molehill.

Martin Luther said, "Faith is not an achievement. It is a gift. Yet it comes only through the hearing and study of the Word." The gift of faith is something you can lay hold of. The more time you spend reading the newspapers, the more fear will enter into your heart; but the more time you spend reading God's Word, the more you will be able to walk by faith, and the stronger your faith will become. God has promised you that, through faith in Jesus Christ, you too become His child and heir (Gal. 3:26–29). What a gift!

PRAYER: God, please grow my faith in You. Amen.

March 29

FIGHT THE GOOD FIGHT

LET US LAY ASIDE EVERY WEIGHT, AND THE SIN WHICH SO
EASILY ENSNARES US, AND LET US RUN WITH ENDURANCE
THE RACE THAT IS SET BEFORE US, LOOKING UNTO
JESUS, THE AUTHOR AND FINISHER OF OUR FAITH.
HEBREWS 12:1–2

I RECENTLY had the privilege of speaking to a group of young sportsmen. The meeting opened with a passionate prayer, then the boys read from 1 Corinthians 9:24–27, where the Word of God speaks of running the true race and fighting the good fight. It was well-chosen and appropriate for these young men.

I then addressed the audience and spoke about vision, not only in sport, but in life in general. And as I spoke, I could see that these disciplined young men were ready and waiting to go forward: physically, spiritually, and mentally, they were prepared for the good fight. At the end, we prayed a prayer of commitment to the Lord Jesus Christ and to our families. I felt as if I were speaking to wild horses about to break free—all they needed was some direction!

To every employer, every leader, and every responsible, caring adult, I say this: There is a desperate need for mentors and godly leaders in the world today. If we don't step into the breach and help these young people, someone else will. They're more than ready to run. Let's make sure they have someone godly to emulate.

The answers we all need are in the Word of God. It is the blueprint, the game plan. All we need to do as their seniors is to guide the youth in following biblical precepts. And before long, they will become fine role models for others in turn.

PRAYER: Dear God, thank You for youthful energy. Open my heart to
young people and help me to be the example they so need. Amen.

March 30
MY BROTHER'S KEEPER

THEN THE LORD SAID TO CAIN, "WHERE IS ABEL YOUR BROTHER?"
HE SAID, "I DO NOT KNOW. AM I MY BROTHER'S KEEPER?"
GENESIS 4:9

ONCE YOU become a child of God, you are responsible for your brother. Who is this "brother" exactly? It's your neighbor, your friend, your colleague, a stranger, anyone you come into contact with. Deuteronomy 22:1–2 tells us:

> You shall not see your brother's ox or his sheep going astray, and hide yourself from them; you shall certainly bring them back to your brother. And if your brother is not near you, or if you do not know him, then you shall bring it to your own house, and it shall remain with you until your brother seeks it; then you shall restore it to him.

When I was a young man learning about farming, I was taught that if you see an animal walking down the road, you don't just look the other way. You stop and take the animal back to its owner. If you don't know who the owner is, then you look after the animal until its owner can be found.

In the same way, when you see somebody in trouble, as a Christian you must stop and help. When you see a parking attendant trying her best, or a waiter doing his job well, make sure that you reward each one generously. Why? Because you are your brother's keeper. We need to take care of each other, knowing that God will take care of us. You can never invest too much into somebody else's life. God will always honor you for that.

PRAYER: God, please show me who my neighbors are,
and how You want me to help them. Amen.

March 31

A QUIET SPIRIT

DO NOT LET YOUR ADORNMENT BE MERELY OUTWARD—
ARRANGING THE HAIR, WEARING GOLD, OR PUTTING ON FINE
APPAREL—RATHER LET IT BE THE HIDDEN PERSON OF THE
HEART, WITH THE INCORRUPTIBLE BEAUTY OF A GENTLE AND
QUIET SPIRIT, WHICH IS VERY PRECIOUS IN THE SIGHT OF GOD.
1 PETER 3:3–4

WHEN THINGS go wrong, the world looks to people of faith to see how we will handle it. And sometimes, I am sorry to say, we look even more anxious than the people in the world. But if we develop a peaceful spirit and learn to sit still and listen to God, we will watch Him pull through for us.

Today's verse speaks of tranquility within and the "incorruptible beauty" of a quiet spirit. The Bible tells us that God treasures it. I can tell you that mankind finds this beauty extremely attractive, because true peace is one of the most elusive things in the world for those who do not yet know God. That peace is a side effect of knowing and enjoying a relationship with your Creator.

Quiet time is so much more than just reading the Bible, or doing a devotional, or praying (as important as those things are). Quiet time is also being still before God and enjoying His presence. A spirit of restlessness or anxiety can hinder God's work in your life, but a quiet spirit is a great asset to any man or woman of God. Philippians 4:6 reads, "Be anxious for nothing, but in everything by prayer and supplication, with thanksgiving, let your requests be made known to God."

I pray that you will know the joys of quietness in God's presence today.

PRAYER: Lord, please promote a quiet spirit within me,
and allow me to experience Your peace. Amen.

APRIL

April 1

TREASURE EVERY MOMENT

BELOVED, LET US LOVE ONE ANOTHER, FOR LOVE IS OF GOD; AND
EVERYONE WHO LOVES IS BORN OF GOD AND KNOWS GOD.
1 JOHN 4:7

WHEN I was a young farmer in Zambia many years ago, an elderly gentleman taught me how to grow maize. I remember asking him one day, "How often should I check my maize crop?"

"Every day," he said. "You should check your maize crop every single day."

Farmers know that something new takes place each day. The color of a plant may change, indicating a need for extra nitrogen. There may be a sudden fungus attack on a young emerging crop, or there might be an infestation of insects. Taking stock doesn't mean viewing things from a distance; it means getting in close and examining the situation carefully.

Take stock every day—that applies to every aspect of your life. Spend quality time (and quantity time) with your loved ones. Go for long walks and talk to your family. You'll find out a great deal about what's actually going on in their lives. Things you thought were okay might not be; and once you know about it, you can support them. Take stock and adjust accordingly.

Take time to make sure that the wheels aren't coming off, as the saying goes. It's easy to become too busy trying to please others at the expense of those whom God has placed in your closest circle. You have them with you for such a short time. Be wise and treasure every moment.

PRAYER: Dear Lord, please open my eyes to what's really going on with my
loved ones, and help me to keep loving eyes on them every day. Amen.

April 2
THE POWER OF LOVE

NO ONE HAS SEEN GOD AT ANY TIME. IF WE LOVE ONE ANOTHER,
GOD ABIDES IN US, AND HIS LOVE HAS BEEN PERFECTED IN US.
1 JOHN 4:12

HENRY MOREHOUSE was a preacher who worked at about the same time as Dwight L. Moody. An Englishman, Morehouse attended some of the meetings that Moody held in Great Britain. This young man came up and asked Moody if he could come to Moody's hometown, Chicago, to preach. Moody reluctantly agreed, thinking Morehouse would not make good on his pledge to visit.

The young preacher traveled to Chicago, and Moody had to make good on his word, thinking that Morehouse could not do much harm in just one evening. Morehouse absolutely transformed the crowd, preaching the message of John 3:16 with such passion that Moody insisted he stay and continue. This young lad got onto the platform and preached about the love of Jesus for several nights in a row.

The most powerful weapon we have as believers is love. When the love of Christ dominates you, overwhelms you, and saturates you, people get saved. Love turns people's hearts—not hatred, fear, or intimidation.

Morehouse was converted by the love of God. And the same love of God sent him all the way to another country on the other side of the world. The love of God got Morehouse up on that platform and inspired his message.

I want to encourage you to start loving others intentionally—even if you don't feel like it—and see how they respond.

PRAYER: Dear Lord, thank You for Your message of love.
Show me how to live it in a new way each day. Amen.

April 3
THE ULTIMATE PRICE

AND THEY OVERCAME HIM BY THE BLOOD OF THE LAMB
AND BY THE WORD OF THEIR TESTIMONY, AND THEY
DID NOT LOVE THEIR LIVES TO THE DEATH.
REVELATION 12:11

ARE YOU prepared to pay the ultimate price for your faith? In these last days God might require many of us to go the whole distance. Perhaps you feel as though you don't have the strength to do that. Don't worry—God will give it to you.

Stephen was one of the first Christians to be martyred for his faith. He told people the truth about the Lord, but some of the people did not agree. They made up stories, claiming that Stephen had blasphemed the Lord by saying that Jesus would destroy the temple and that He wanted to change the customs of Moses.

To defend himself, Stephen referred to Scripture to prove that the laws of Moses were not being undermined, but rather fulfilled. He went so far as to accuse the council of being like their ancestors, who resisted the Holy Spirit and murdered the Lord Jesus Christ. Furious, they chased Stephen out of the city and stoned him to death. With his dying breaths, Stephen asked the Lord to receive his spirit and to "not charge them with this sin" (Acts 7:60).

Stephen stayed strong until the end. I believe that the Lord also gives us the strength to live, and the strength to die. You don't have to be concerned about what will happen when your day comes. Focus on living one day at a time for the Lord and strengthening yourself as a Christian, and in the day of your testing He will be with you.

PRAYER: Lord, please keep me strong as I tell the
truth about You to the very end. Amen.

April 4
HAND OVER THE REINS

"BE STRONG AND OF GOOD COURAGE; DO NOT BE
AFRAID, NOR BE DISMAYED, FOR THE LORD YOUR
GOD IS WITH YOU WHEREVER YOU GO."
JOSHUA 1:9

A YOUNG man wrote to me recently and included a story:

"When I was young, my dad had a carriage with horses. One day he asked me if I would like to take the reins, and I was overjoyed. I was in control, steering the horses, and it was wonderful—except the pace was too slow for me. I wanted excitement, so I tugged on the reins to make them trot. Then the horses decided they could get me home in half the time if they went full speed! So they started galloping faster.

"I realized we were in a very dangerous situation, and I tried my best to gain control, but nothing worked. I glanced at my father, who was calmly watching the world speeding past. By now I was quite anxious, my hands bruised and bleeding, and tears were streaming down my cheeks. Eventually I turned to my father and said, 'Here, Dad. Please take the reins. I don't want them anymore.'"

The young man concluded, "It doesn't matter how old we are or how skilled we think we are—there will always be a time when our only choice will be to turn to our heavenly Father and say, 'Here, Father. Take the reins. I don't want to be in control anymore.'"

So often we think we can handle things ourselves. We say, "Stand back, Lord, I'll do it," only to realize we can't handle the situation anymore. But He is right next to us at all times, ready to take the reins—and all we have to do is ask.

PRAYER: God, thank You for sitting calmly beside me and taking
control when I need You. I relinquish the reins to You today. Amen.

April 5
A DAY OF REST

ON THE SEVENTH DAY GOD ENDED HIS WORK WHICH HE HAD
DONE, AND HE RESTED ON THE SEVENTH DAY FROM ALL HIS
WORK WHICH HE HAD DONE. THEN GOD BLESSED THE SEVENTH
DAY AND SANCTIFIED IT, BECAUSE IN IT HE RESTED FROM
ALL HIS WORK WHICH GOD HAD CREATED AND MADE.
GENESIS 2:2–3

GOD NEVER designed us to work seven days of the week. Even God Himself rested on the seventh day. My dear friend, if God rested after six days, do we think we can work harder? It's foolishness, and yet we do it.

What does rest mean? It means to sit down and be quiet. It means to take your Bible and to meditate on the things of God. It means to go for a walk and appreciate God's creation, have a good meal, and spend time with your loved ones.

So many problems can arise if we don't respect the day that God has set aside for us to rest. If you are going to use that day to fix your truck or to do your shopping, on Monday morning you will be exhausted before you even start the week.

My busiest day is the day of the Sabbath, the day I preach the gospel. So I make sure to take off another day in the week to rest and read God's Word. This is when I am rejuvenated: mentally, physically, emotionally, and spiritually.

God purposefully gave you the gift of a day of rest. If you refuse it, you will break down. Let's thank Him for His foresight, and appreciate His wisdom in giving us a day to recharge.

PRAYER: Dear God, show me how to rest as You did on the seventh day, enjoying Your creation and seeing that it is good. Amen.

April 6

THE GLORY DUE HIS NAME

GIVE TO THE LORD THE GLORY DUE HIS NAME; BRING
AN OFFERING, AND COME BEFORE HIM. OH, WORSHIP
THE LORD IN THE BEAUTY OF HOLINESS!
1 CHRONICLES 16:29

GOD LOVES His people to worship Him. He created us for worship and for fellowship with Him. David said, "One thing I have desired of the LORD . . . that I may dwell in the house of the LORD all the days of my life, to behold the beauty of the LORD" (Ps. 27:4). David wasn't interested in any crown; he just wanted to be a doorkeeper in the house of the Lord where he could worship Him day and night.

David wasn't an angel. He made many mistakes: he committed adultery, he had someone murdered, he lied, and did many other terrible things. But he knew to repent and say sorry, and to come back and worship God. Worshiping God is not about how well you can sing or how saintly you are; it's about spending time in His presence.

I like to jog early in the morning, and that is when I worship God. As the sun starts breaking over the tops of the trees, I smell the fresh air and I hear the birds calling. I thank Him for His creation, for His goodness. I adore Him, and then I confess my sins and ask for forgiveness. Then I thank God for all He has blessed me with . . . and then I start to run with renewed energy! It's a wonderful way to begin the day.

Do you want to grow in the Lord? Worship God more and you will find your whole outlook becoming more positive and filled with joy.

PRAYER: God, please make my heart worshipful, and meet
me when I open my mouth to praise You. Amen.

April 7
DIRECTION FROM GOD

THEN [GOD] SAW WISDOM AND DECLARED IT; HE PREPARED
IT, INDEED, HE SEARCHED IT OUT. AND TO MAN HE SAID,
"BEHOLD, THE FEAR OF THE LORD, THAT IS WISDOM."
JOB 28:27–28

YOU'LL RECEIVE lots of advice in life, but true wisdom comes only from the Lord. It helps to obtain advice from godly counselors or mentors, but at the end of the day, we must seek the face of God. With His counsel, we can't put a foot wrong.

Civil rights activist and minister Jesse Jackson wrote, "Nothing about our faith makes us pain-proof. It does hurt. It does make us cry. And we must dry our eyes and continue our work until our time is finished."

Being a believer doesn't exempt you from troubles. Often it's the other way around—troubles seem to increase. But the good news is that you aren't alone: God walks with you. Don't run from the only Person in the world who can help you. When the going gets tough, draw closer to God and regain the purpose He has planned for you.

When I look back on my farming life, there have been many times when I was directed by God to do things that, as a farmer, I thought were outrageous. Yet they saved the day for me financially, and I learned to trust God before my instincts.

Listen for that small voice giving you direction, saying to you, "Your ears shall hear a word behind you, saying, 'This is the way, walk in it,' whenever you turn to the right hand or whenever you turn to the left" (Isa. 30:21).

PRAYER: Dear Lord, thank You for guiding and speaking to me.
Help me to hear Your direction and walk in it. Amen.

April 8

FIRST PLACE

LEAD ME, O LORD, IN YOUR RIGHTEOUSNESS BECAUSE OF MY
ENEMIES; MAKE YOUR WAY STRAIGHT BEFORE MY FACE.
PSALM 5:8

IT IS so wonderful to get confirmation from the Lord of heaven and earth about the way forward. Many years ago, on November 17, 1989, the Lord told me that if I had the same faith that other great men and women of God had, I should go and book stadiums and city halls in order to share the good news with people, and He would fill each and every venue to the brim—a promise He has always kept. The 2013 Mighty Men Conference in America took place on November 17, exactly twenty-four years after God had given me this promise. From that time to this, we have had more men in the Mighty Men conference than the combined forces of the South African army, air force, and navy put together. What an amazing blessing.

The most important blessing that the Lord ever gave to Jacob was when He promised that He would be with Jacob wherever he went: "Behold, I am with you and will keep you wherever you go, and will bring you back to this land; for I will not leave you until I have done what I have spoken to you" (Gen. 28:15).

The Lord keeps His promises. He promised that He would always be with me throughout every conference and meeting, and that the conferences would be well attended. And He has kept His promises every step of the way. God will be there for you too. Be willing to give Him first place in every aspect of your life. He will stay with you until His promises are fulfilled.

PRAYER: God, thank You that I can count on You to go with
me. Please help me to keep You first in my life. Amen.

April 9
ASK IN FAITH

IF ANY OF YOU LACKS WISDOM, LET HIM ASK OF GOD, WHO
GIVES TO ALL LIBERALLY AND WITHOUT REPROACH, AND IT
WILL BE GIVEN TO HIM. BUT LET HIM ASK IN FAITH, WITH NO
DOUBTING, FOR HE WHO DOUBTS IS LIKE A WAVE OF THE SEA
DRIVEN AND TOSSED BY THE WIND. FOR LET NOT THAT MAN
SUPPOSE THAT HE WILL RECEIVE ANYTHING FROM THE LORD.
JAMES 1:5–7

ARE YOU like the waves of the sea? Are you being tossed to and fro because of your circumstances? I've got a good message for you today from the Lord Himself: believe that He is in control.

You may say, "But God doesn't answer prayer. I've prayed and prayed, but nothing has happened." But look at today's verse: if you use prayer as a last resort and you don't really believe it, God does not answer. But He does answer the prayer of faith.

One of my favorite scriptures is Mark 11:24: "Therefore I say to you, whatever things you ask when you pray, believe that you receive them, and you will have them." When I pray for rain, I believe that the rain will come; and when I pray for sick people, I believe that they will be healed. I don't hope so; I believe so.

When you pray, spend time in the Word to find out God's will for you in your situation. Is it right to pray for God to help you find employment because you need to care for your family? Yes, that is an honorable prayer. Do you believe that God will provide a way? If you do, then pray the prayer of faith and believe for God's provision.

PRAYER: Lord, please build my faith so I can come
to You confidently in prayer. Amen.

April 10
FOLLOW MY LEADER

TEACH ME TO DO YOUR WILL, FOR YOU ARE MY GOD; YOUR
SPIRIT IS GOOD. LEAD ME IN THE LAND OF UPRIGHTNESS.
PSALM 143:10

WHOM DO you follow when things are darkest?

Mark 8:22–25 reads, "Then [Jesus] came to Bethsaida; and they brought a blind man to Him, and begged Him to touch him. So He took the blind man by the hand and led him out of the town. And when He had spit on his eyes and put His hands on him, He asked him if he saw anything.

"And he looked up and said, 'I see men like trees, walking.' Then He put His hands on his eyes again and made him look up. And he was restored and saw everyone clearly." The blind man trusted Jesus completely. The Lord led him out of the town, blind and vulnerable though he was, and then healed him.

Who is leading you today? I hope you are putting your hand in the hand of the Lord Jesus Christ. And if you are being led by Him but don't know where you are going, you can rest assured that you are still in the safest place you could possibly be.

If you are making your own plans, following your own path, who knows where you'll end up? But when you put your faith in Jesus, you declare that you will walk one day at a time, one step at a time, and will keep going forward toward healing. Don't be afraid to let the world know who it is that you follow. He will lead you every step of the way.

PRAYER: Lord, thank You for guiding me when I cannot see. Keep
my hand firmly in Yours as we walk forward together. Amen.

April 11
TRUST GOD TO SEE YOU THROUGH

WHEN THE WHIRLWIND PASSES BY, THE WICKED IS NO MORE,
BUT THE RIGHTEOUS HAS AN EVERLASTING FOUNDATION.
PROVERBS 10:25

AT ANY given moment, each of us faces a whirlwind in life. It might be financial difficulties, sickness, depression, marital problems, or conflict with our children. During times of testing, people are often not sure what they should do. Should they go or stay, say something or keep quiet? At these times, remember your calling as it corresponds with God's will; God will protect you and keep His promises.

In Acts 27:13–17, a big storm hit as Paul was being taken by ship to Rome to appear before Caesar. It looked like smooth sailing at first, "But not long after, a tempestuous head wind arose" (v. 14). Soon they were caught in big trouble. They were sailing close to an island when a strong wind took the ship right out to sea. The boat could not be controlled. Paul tried to tell the sailors that all would be well, but they panicked (vv. 21–38). They started throwing the cargo overboard in order to keep the ship afloat. But Paul, a man of God, wasn't worried because he knew he had a destination: he had to stand trial in Rome.

Paul knew that because it was God's will for him to appear before Caesar, all he had to do was trust God to get him safely there. Maybe you are in serious trouble today. You are stuck, not knowing what to do next. As long as you trust God, you have nothing to fear. Cling to Him in your time of difficulty, and He will see you through.

PRAYER: Dear Lord, please build my faith in Your
promises as I face my storms today. Amen.

April 12
OUTSIDE INTERESTS

WHETHER YOU EAT OR DRINK, OR WHATEVER
YOU DO, DO ALL TO THE GLORY OF GOD.
1 CORINTHIANS 10:31

IN RELATIONSHIPS, the importance of giving each other space cannot be overstated.

It is fatal for a marriage if the wife cannot release her husband—with her blessing—to spend time with his friends now and again. If a wife wants her man to remain the person she fell in love with when they first met, then she needs to allow him to explore the mountains or enjoy a sport with his friends from time to time. The same thing applies to the husband: he needs to give his spouse space to express herself, enjoy her own hobbies, and spend time with friends who have her same interests. After this healthy time apart, each significant other will come back and love the other all the more.

For all close relationships in life—including children, friends, family, and romantic relationships—be careful not to destroy the character and qualities you so love in the other person. If you close your hand and make a fist, you squash all the life out of what was in your hand. So it is with your loved one; that person will start to wither away under your tight grip. However, if you open your hand and let them fly, they will come back twice as strong and full of energy and joy.

Each party in a relationship needs the opportunity to mature separately as well as together. They will become individuals with so much more to offer each other and the community in which they live.

PRAYER: Dear Lord, please help me to trust You with the most important relationships in my life, and let my loved ones fly on their own. Amen.

April 13

THE TRUTH SHALL SET YOU FREE

THE TIME WILL COME WHEN THEY WILL NOT ENDURE SOUND DOCTRINE, BUT
ACCORDING TO THEIR OWN DESIRES, BECAUSE THEY HAVE ITCHING EARS,
THEY WILL HEAP UP FOR THEMSELVES TEACHERS; AND THEY WILL TURN
THEIR EARS AWAY FROM THE TRUTH, AND BE TURNED ASIDE TO FABLES.
2 TIMOTHY 4:3–4

WHICH VOICE speaks the truth? When there is no moral standard, when the church seems irrelevant or weak, or when we do not call sin by its name, we become just another voice in the wind, giving generic life advice or "fables" to "itching ears."

Let us feel free to be outspoken as believers, to broadcast the truth to a jaded generation. We can learn much from the good old faithful revivalists—men like Martin Luther, Charles Finney, and Evan Roberts. When these men came to town, the town exploded. Wherever they went, men and women were compelled to shrug off indifference and make a true commitment to God. They called out the truth and did not sugarcoat sin.

One might think that the best way to impact others is to be concerned with whether they like us or not. But that's not true. What is more important is that the world *respects* Christians as men and women of righteousness. In years gone by, the world used to set its moral standards on what the church stood for. But as we have become more lukewarm and equivocating, the church's pull has weakened.

We are to be a light on the hill—steadfast, bright, and shining. As things become more uncertain in this world, this is actually the finest hour for the Christian. We can be sure of where we're going, where we've come from, and in whom we believe.

PRAYER: Lord Jesus, please give me the strength to stand
up for righteousness in thought, word, and deed, no matter
what's popular or politically correct. Amen.

April 14
SETTLE YOUR ACCOUNTS

WEALTH GAINED BY DISHONESTY WILL BE DIMINISHED,
BUT HE WHO GATHERS BY LABOR WILL INCREASE.
PROVERBS 13:11

THE BIBLE is very clear that we should be no one's debtor. I'm aware that this statement may go against the grain of modern-day thinking. Many say that you should hold on to your money as long as you can and only pay your debtors when you really have to (just before they hand you over to the debt collector).

I don't believe that's the way the Lord wants us to act. If God has blessed you with a good crop or good sales and you owe people money, pay them immediately, even if the debt has not come due.

In Matthew 19, a rich man approaches Jesus saying he has obeyed every commandment in the Bible. He wants to know what else he needs to do to ensure eternal life The Lord replies that he needs to sell all his treasures and give the money to the poor. Upon hearing this, the rich man bows his head and walks away. But Jesus does not run after him. He leaves the poor "rich" man to walk away from God and eternal life.

A man whose god is money will not part with it easily—whether it's his or someone else's. Often he skates on the edge, only paying his debts after the last warning. I believe that there is freedom in not owing anything to anyone, and in not holding on to money too tightly. When a hand is clasped in a fist, you cannot put anything in it, but when it is held open, it's very easy to put more into that hand.

PRAYER: Lord, thank You for trusting me with my resources.
Help me to use them in godly ways. Amen.

April 15
GROWING OLD WITH GRACE

THE GLORY OF YOUNG MEN IS THEIR STRENGTH, AND
THE SPLENDOR OF OLD MEN IS THEIR GRAY HEAD.
PROVERBS 20:29

IT'S UNBELIEVABLE how much money some people spend in order to try and stay young. It's a good thing to keep fit, but getting cosmetic surgery and trying to dress like a youngster is going a bit far, I feel. What do they say about such people? "Mutton dressed up as lamb."

On the other hand, there's nothing nicer than seeing a mature man or woman who presents him- or herself with taste and restraint. Young people can look up to them as an example of what it is to be mature, wise, and dignified. And older people can be proud of the "glory" of the youthful energy surrounding them.

Be like the eagle, that solitary bird, and come apart for a while to work on your "inner man." Apart from the madding crowd, God can speak to you and work on your life and character. Be gentle, loving, encouraging, and positive when stepping into later seasons of life. A gray head does not have to mean being grumpy, insecure, or envious of God's younger children, but rather thankful for experience and hard-earned wisdom.

As a young man I was always trying to prove a point, trying to be successful and the best at everything. Now that I'm older, I've "been there, done that." I've had my time in the limelight, and it is the turn of the next generation. Now I want to leave a legacy. I'm grateful to God that I don't have to prove anything now; I just have to be.

Let's act our age and make every year a year of grace.

PRAYER: God, thank You for every day and year I'm on this planet. Help me to change and grow appropriately to my stage in life. Amen.

April 16
VISION AND PURPOSE FROM GOD

WHERE THERE IS NO REVELATION, THE PEOPLE CAST OFF
RESTRAINT; BUT HAPPY IS HE WHO KEEPS THE LAW.
PROVERBS 29:18

WHAT IS your vision? If you say you don't have one, that's as good as aiming at nothing—and you're sure to hit it!

When men and women seek God for vision and direction, this will make opportunities for everybody, and we can only have a better and brighter future. The most important ingredient for a successful vision is to make sure it's from God, through prayer, counsel, and study. "A good idea is not always a God idea," I often say. But if you're confident your vision is from God, then you have nothing to fear as you pursue it.

My father used to say that if you get up in the morning and you don't feel like going to work, change your job, because that's where you'll spend most of your life.

If your vision is your work, and you have passion for your vision because it's something you love doing, you will go the extra mile and work much harder—and you will surely succeed. Even if it doesn't seem to be working out in the beginning, that doesn't mean it's not from God. Don't be scared of a few trials and tests—they will surely come. If it were easy, everybody would be doing it, wouldn't they?

Nothing is too hard if you have a vision of great things to come.

PRAYER: Lord, renew my vision and give me strength
and confidence to do Your will. Amen.

April 17

LOVE THY NEIGHBOR

TWO ARE BETTER THAN ONE, BECAUSE THEY HAVE A GOOD
REWARD FOR THEIR LABOR. FOR IF THEY FALL, ONE WILL
LIFT UP HIS COMPANION. BUT WOE TO HIM WHO IS ALONE
WHEN HE FALLS, FOR HE HAS NO ONE TO HELP HIM UP.
ECCLESIASTES 4:9–10

RECENTLY WE invited our neighbors of thirty years to our house. It was one of the most pleasurable times we've enjoyed for a long while. We laughed and shed a few tears. We spoke about our grown children and reminisced about the good times and the bad.

It doesn't matter how busy we are—spending time with your neighbors is critical. Without my neighbors, I never would have made it on my farm. When we arrived from Zambia with just a truck and a trailer, there was no electricity or water, and my wife was pregnant with our fourth child. Our neighbors brought over a water cart and helped take our children to school. They taught us the times to plant, what insects to watch out for, and many other things.

When we first arrived, our family was literally camping in the bush and I was busy digging a deep hole for a latrine. Our neighbor John drove up and told me to stop working, come over to his and Dawn's house, and spend the afternoon with them. I didn't want to. The land had to be prepared, and I needed to build a house for my family, repair some old tractors, and do a hundred other things. But we went over and shared a meal together, and my family enjoyed their first real bath in weeks! It helped keep us going.

If you want a friend, be a friend. If you can lend a hand in any way, don't hesitate, because before long you will need a helping hand yourself.

PRAYER: Lord, please show me new ways to love my neighbors today. Amen.

April 18

PRINCE OF PEACE

FOR UNTO US A CHILD IS BORN, UNTO US A SON IS GIVEN;
AND THE GOVERNMENT WILL BE UPON HIS SHOULDER.
AND HIS NAME WILL BE CALLED WONDERFUL, COUNSELOR,
MIGHTY GOD, EVERLASTING FATHER, PRINCE OF PEACE.
ISAIAH 9:6

PEACE . . . IT'S what the whole world is looking for, and it can only be found in one place, and that is in the Prince of Peace—the Lord Jesus Christ. To everyone who believes in Him He freely offers this wonderful peace.

In John 14:27 the Lord said, "Peace I leave with you, My peace I give to you; not as the world gives do I give to you. Let not your heart be troubled, neither let it be afraid." This means that peace cannot be found in the secular world. Rather, it comes in Jesus, who bears our burdens and conquers the world. We can rest easy and hand our problems over to Him.

When Jesus saved us and brought us out of the darkness, He brought us into a peace that is meant to be shared. This peace is not exclusive; it is available to anyone who believes and accepts the Lord Jesus Christ as their Savior. And so we are brought into a wonderful cycle of thankfulness, praise, and peace—one leads to another, and then another.

Hear Him calling you into His peace today: "Come to Me, all you who labor and are heavy laden, and I will give you rest" (Matt. 11:28).

PRAYER: Lord, I pray for a thankful, peaceful heart. Help me to
share this peace with others at every opportunity. Amen.

April 19
THE GIFT OF PAIN

HE IS DESPISED AND REJECTED BY MEN, A MAN OF
SORROWS AND ACQUAINTED WITH GRIEF.
ISAIAH 53:3

THE WORD *pain* comes from a Latin word that also means "penalty." Our Lord Jesus Christ paid the penalty for our sins by dying on the cross. He understood what pain meant.

Although He was God, Christ was also very much a man. He was despised and rejected by men, and he became acquainted with grief. In the Garden of Gethsemane, His sweat became like great drops of blood falling to the ground (Luke 22:44). Medical experts will tell you that this can occur when someone is under extreme stress or shock. When we cry out to God, He really does know exactly what we're going through.

The worst thing to do for someone who's just lost a loved one is to tell them to pull themselves together, to read the Bible, and to pray. They won't hear you because their heart is so full of grief. Just tell them you care for them and you're there for them. When you yourself have been through suffering, you can truly pass on the gift of love and compassion to others.

Pain also slows us down. It teaches us to listen and to speak less. That's why you'll often find that older people aren't as spontaneous and impulsive as young people. Because they've been through much pain, they count the cost before acting. Remember, however, that tribulation produces perseverance; and perseverance, character; and character, hope (Rom. 5:3–4).

PRAYER: Lord, give me the grace to see pain as a gift and the
mercy to help others through it with compassion. Amen.

April 20
IDOL WORSHIP

AMONG ALL THE WISE MEN OF THE NATIONS, AND IN
ALL THEIR KINGDOMS, THERE IS NONE LIKE YOU. BUT
THEY ARE ALTOGETHER DULL-HEARTED AND FOOLISH;
A WOODEN IDOL IS A WORTHLESS DOCTRINE.
JEREMIAH 10:7–8

IDOL WORSHIP is a very serious thing in God's eyes. God says, "What could be more futile?" How can we be so foolish to worship a statue or an idol that has been made by man? Rather, worship the living God who can help you, who can communicate with you, who can listen, whom you can talk to about your problems, and who can undertake anything for you.

You may not have wooden statues in your house, but really an idol is anything in your life that is more important than God. Maybe you love running or going to the gym. There's nothing wrong with that, but if it becomes more important to you than the Lord Jesus Christ, then it must be put in its place. Perhaps money is an idol in your life. Be careful: the Lord is your security, not money. Maybe you want to own your own business or buy that big car one day and you are working toward that with everything you've got. My dear friend, be careful, because that idol cannot fulfill you one bit.

The Lord says very clearly how futile, foolish, and ridiculous it is to make an idol with your own hands and then worship it (Jer. 10:1–8). It can't speak, it can't talk, it can't hear, and it can't help you. Instead, spend time with God in the presence of the Holy Spirit and He will change your life forever.

PRAYER: Heavenly Father, if there is an idol in my life, please point it out
to me through Your Spirit. Help me to put You above all else. Amen.

April 21
COME WHAT MAY

THE LORD IS GOOD, A STRONGHOLD IN THE DAY OF
TROUBLE; AND HE KNOWS THOSE WHO TRUST IN HIM.
NAHUM 1:7

LAZARUS WAS probably one of Jesus' best friends. So when he fell ill, his two sisters, Mary and Martha, sent someone to tell Jesus, believing He would come at once and heal their brother (John 11:1–44).

But Jesus only arrived after Lazarus had passed away and had been in the tomb for four days. Mary and Martha were devastated that Jesus had not come immediately to heal him, before it was too late.

Mary and Martha gave up hope. When Jesus did come, Mary said to Him, "Lord, if You had been here, my brother would not have died" (John 11:32). If only they had not lost hope in Jesus, they could have spared themselves a lot of grief.

Jesus said to Martha, "I am the resurrection and the life. He who believes in Me, though he may die, he shall live. And whoever lives and believes in Me shall never die" (John 11:25–26). After this He brought Lazarus back to life.

In times of despair, Jesus is the only one who can help us. Never stop hoping in the Lord, even when it looks as though there's no way out; He is the only one who is completely reliable in the end, and the only one who sees the big picture, though our pain may be great. When my little nephew passed away after falling off a tractor I was driving, my family and I were overcome with grief, but the hope of Jesus did not abandon us even in our deepest moments of pain. Heaven is to be with Jesus and hell is to be without Him. Hold on to your relationship with the Lord at all costs.

PRAYER: God, thank You for Your faithfulness, even when I can't understand what's happening around me. Build my faith in You. Amen.

April 22
RUNNING IN THE LIGHT

FOR I CONSIDER THAT THE SUFFERINGS OF THIS PRESENT
TIME ARE NOT WORTHY TO BE COMPARED WITH THE
GLORY WHICH SHALL BE REVEALED IN US.
ROMANS 8:18

I'VE HAD the privilege of running in several long-distance marathons. The experienced runners understand that they are not going to finish the race if they run too fast at the beginning. It is not a hundred-yard sprint, but a long-distance race.

The race of life is even longer than that. The Lord instructs us to run with patience, no matter how hard it gets, no matter how hard the pain is to bear, no matter how difficult the course becomes. Jesus gives us the strength to keep going.

In a marathon, seasoned men and women often carry a small flag. On that flag is printed "sub 3," "sub 4," indicating the speed at which the group will be running. If you stick with these pacers, they will help to get you home. When you can hardly breathe, they keep talking and encouraging. They are feeling the same pain, sweating just as much, yet they motivate the runners to keep them going. They do it for no personal reward but the satisfaction of helping others.

I see Jesus as one of those pacers. When we are going through steep mountain passes, He keeps saying, "Come on, everyone. It's not much farther. Keep going." When He sees that we can't take much more, He tells us to slow down and have a drink. We'll walk briskly till we catch our breath and then start jogging again.

We are called to finish the race we are running. We cannot slink off to a dark place and sit there quietly by ourselves. We must continue by confessing our sins, putting them behind us, and running forward in the light.

PRAYER: Jesus, please help me to hear Your encouraging
voice as I run forward today. Amen.

April 23

THE BIBLE IS OUR COMPASS

"SEEK FIRST THE KINGDOM OF GOD AND HIS RIGHTEOUSNESS,
AND ALL THESE THINGS SHALL BE ADDED TO YOU."
MATTHEW 6:33

I WAS recently asked to take part in a panel discussion on ethics in the business world, and the thing that weighed most heavily on my heart was to speak about moral principles starting at home and then flowing out into the business sector.

In the Bible, God gives us specifics on how to live our daily lives. If you sow bad seed, you will reap a bad crop. If you sow no seed, you will reap no crop. However, if you sow good seed, you will reap an abundant crop.

Remember, though, that before we can go out into the world and tell people how to live, we should start in our own homes. As never before, we need to speak the truth in love to our children. In John 17:17, the Lord said to His Father, "Sanctify them by Your truth. Your word is truth." We need to model and teach our children the basic morals of life according to the Ten Commandments, and show them in our everyday interactions.

If I had my life to live over again, I'd spend more time with my family and less time trying to have the smartest farm in the area, or the fattest cattle, or the straightest fences. At the end of the day, our loved ones are the most important thing. Focus on order in the home and order in our hearts, and it will set us in the right direction for the rest of life and business.

Let's use the Bible as our compass and our standard for moral principles and all we set out to do.

PRAYER: Dear Lord, please let the Bible and its
principles guide my every move. Amen.

April 24

FAITH LIKE A MUSTARD SEED

"IF YOU HAVE FAITH AS A MUSTARD SEED, YOU WILL SAY TO
THIS MOUNTAIN, 'MOVE FROM HERE TO THERE,' AND IT WILL
MOVE; AND NOTHING WILL BE IMPOSSIBLE FOR YOU."
MATTHEW 17:20

I GREW seed maize for one of the leading seed companies for many years, and it gave me an understanding of the importance of pure seed—the genetic requirements, the vigor that's needed for germination, the size of the seed, and the color.

God always honors faith if He sees that your heart is sincere, your motives are pure, and that you have a real desire to succeed for His kingdom—for the community, your fellow man, your family, and your workers. If your heart is pure, God will honor that step of faith every time.

An amazing thing I discovered as a young farmer was that the more time I spent with God, the better things seemed to go in my business. Conversely, the less time I spent with Him, the less effective my farming was. Time with God purifies us.

When you've spent time with the Lord and you truly feel that He has told you to go a certain route in your life or in business, set your face toward that goal and go for it with all you have. Sow that seed. It's a wonderful thing to have the Lord Jesus Christ as your business partner; to be able to talk to Him about your dreams and what you need; to be able to pray to Him in times when the market is down or there's a seemingly insurmountable problem.

When you take a step of faith, you can trust God to honor it. Remember that you don't have to be lonely during your times of decision making because He is just one prayer away.

PRAYER: God, please guide me today as I make
decisions. Grow my faith in You. Amen.

April 25
BEING PREPARED

"WHAT WILL IT PROFIT A MAN IF HE GAINS THE
WHOLE WORLD, AND LOSES HIS OWN SOUL?"
MARK 8:36

RECENTLY MY next-door neighbor died of a massive heart attack. He said good-bye to his dear wife in the morning and left for work. Later, his car was found parked on the side of the road, my friend dead at the wheel. How can we ever be prepared for something like this?

We can make provision for our families and work hard to keep ahead, but not at the cost of thinking we'll live forever. The question is, where will we go when we die? We don't want to "win" the world but lose our souls.

When I think of my departed friend, I realize how much we need to put things in place and be in a position to leave. If God were to call you today, would you have to say, "Lord, I can't leave yet because I'll leave behind too many debts," or "Lord, I haven't reconciled with a certain person yet, and there is unforgiveness in my heart." What a relief it would be to say, "Lord, I am ready."

Keep short accounts with God and short accounts with men. Martin Luther, when asked what he would do if he knew God was coming to fetch him the next day, said, "I would still plant my apple tree." We are to carry on living, certainly, but we need to be ready when He calls us.

PRAYER: God, please cause me to live with eternity in mind. Show me what
I need to do, even now, to prepare to leave the world behind. Amen.

April 26
FOCUS ON THE FUTURE

"NO ONE, HAVING PUT HIS HAND TO THE PLOW, AND
LOOKING BACK, IS FIT FOR THE KINGDOM OF GOD."
LUKE 9:62

HOW CAN a man continue to plow in a straight line if he keeps looking backward? Answer: he can't. Today's verse tells us to let bygones be bygones. Only when we forgive those who have disappointed and hurt us in the past can we start again with a clean slate.

In Matthew 8:22, Jesus said the same thing when He told His disciples, "Follow Me, and let the dead bury their own dead." What He meant was that we need to move on with what is at hand and stop living in the past.

People who refuse to move on, who prefer to live in the past, tend to be very negative. Seek out those who are looking ahead and who believe the best is yet to come. Invest in the future instead. Be prepared for change—because if there's one certainty in this life, it is that things will change.

In Isaiah 43:18 and 19 we are told, "Do not remember the former things, nor consider the things of old. Behold, I will do a new thing, now it shall spring forth; shall you not know it?" What an amazing breath of encouragement. When we're tempted to look back in anguish, embarrassment, or disappointment on things of the past, God tells us that He's bringing us something much better. So let us seize the day, enjoy it, and live it to the full, because we don't know what tomorrow will bring.

PRAYER: Dear God, thank You for doing new things in my life.
Keep my eyes straight ahead and not looking back. Amen.

April 27

THE FRIEND OF SINNERS

DRAW NEAR TO GOD AND HE WILL DRAW NEAR TO YOU.
JAMES 4:8

ARE YOU feeling downhearted today? Maybe you feel that you are not good enough for the Lord. Well, the bottom line is, no one is, but He is more than good enough for you.

If you take one step toward Jesus, He takes three steps toward you. Isn't that amazing? Maybe you've made a big mistake in your life and you think that the Lord will never take you back, but I can promise you that He will. He came for sinners, not the righteous. He is known as the Friend of sinners, and He wants to be your friend today.

Follow the example of the prodigal son—come to Jesus as you are, even though you have sinned and the world has messed you up. Sometimes we think that when we get our lives together, or stop doing this or that, then we'll come to God, but then we'll never get there. You have to come right now, with all your problems, your bad habits—the whole package. Just take that one step in His direction.

In the story of the prodigal son, the father ran toward his son, hugged him with all his dirt and filth and brokenness, and kissed him. He took him home, cleaned him up and dressed him, and prepared a feast in celebration (Luke 15:11–32). That is exactly how Jesus feels about you. Second Corinthians 5:17 says, "Therefore, if anyone is in Christ, he is a new creation; old things have passed away; behold, all things have become new."

PRAYER: Lord, thank You for welcoming me. I come to You today with
all of my brokenness, and ask that You make me whole. Amen.

April 28
LOST AND FOUND

"FOR THE SON OF MAN HAS COME TO SEEK AND
TO SAVE THAT WHICH WAS LOST."
LUKE 19:10

EARLY ONE morning as I set off for my run, I saw a goose flying back and forth across the sky all by himself. As you may know, geese do not fly alone; they fly in flocks. This goose was calling for his friends. He was well and truly lost, and my heart went out to him.

How about you? Are you flying on your own? There's no doubt we need each other. There is no such thing as a solitary Christian or a lone ranger in God's kingdom. In John 14:6, Jesus said, "I am the way, the truth, and the life. No one comes to the Father except through Me." If you are lost today, know that the Lord is calling you to join Him and His family.

Jesus is the Good Shepherd. Luke 15:1–7 says that the shepherd will leave all his sheep to look for the one sheep that is lost, and when he finds it, all heaven will rejoice. Jesus came for the sick, the lost, and the downhearted; He came for people like you and me.

Are you like the lost goose, flying across the sky and crying out for help, or the one wandering sheep—each looking for its flock? Know that the Lord hears you. You might be lonely, going through a difficult time and feeling lost, but the Lord says, "Call to Me, and I will answer you, and show you great and mighty things, which you do not know" (Jer. 33:3). Take heart, for the Lord will come to your aid.

PRAYER: Dear Lord, thank You that You come after me and bring me back to You and Your family. Hear me when I call out in fear, and bring me home. Amen.

April 29

NOT BY WORKS

THEN THEY SAID TO HIM, "WHAT SHALL WE DO,
THAT WE MAY WORK THE WORKS OF GOD?"
JOHN 6:28

FAITH IN the Spirit gets us much further in our walk with Christ than flesh and the law. We will not always be able to obey the law. That is why Jesus came and introduced us to the concept of grace, which is undeserved lovingkindness.

In Philippians 3, the Jews tried to ensure the "letter of the law" was obeyed by saying that a believer must be circumcised. Paul disagreed. He said that it is by faith in Jesus Christ that we are saved, and not by works (Eph. 2:8). Paul himself was a Jew and had done everything by the book, but without faith in Jesus he could not be saved. Don't let people persuade you that you will only go to heaven if you conform to certain rules and regulations. It is only faith in Jesus that brings you to Him.

We will not obtain eternal life based only on the good works we do—this is one of the most fundamental differences between Christianity and other religions. It doesn't matter how hard we try or what good deeds we do, because it just doesn't work that way—no matter how much charity work you do.

So be encouraged. Don't beat yourself up because you aren't righteous enough. Just be grateful for the amazing free gift of eternal life through Jesus.

PRAYER: Lord, I just keep falling short. Thank You for bringing me to You through Your Spirit and faith, rather than based on my perfection. That's the only way I could ever know You! Amen.

April 30

THE PEACE JESUS GIVES

"PEACE I LEAVE WITH YOU, MY PEACE I GIVE TO YOU; NOT
AS THE WORLD GIVES DO I GIVE TO YOU. LET NOT YOUR
HEART BE TROUBLED, NEITHER LET IT BE AFRAID."
JOHN 14:27

A FEW years ago I attended a Mighty Men Conference held in the Yorkshire Dales in the UK. I had an amazing time, and the weather was magnificent (bearing in mind that they'd had floods up until a few days before the event). Early each morning, I went for a jog through the most beautiful setting you could wish to see. Everything was green, the flowers were in full bloom, and the villages had been standing for hundreds of years. The scene reminded me of 1 Timothy 6:6: "Godliness with contentment is great gain."

What is contentment? What is peace? The *Oxford Dictionary* says peace is "freedom from disturbance; quiet and tranquility." But I've come to realize that peace doesn't come from the outside—it comes from within. It has commonly been defined as the "conscious possession of adequate resources." In other words, peace comes when we realize that we have enough.

Some of the wealthiest men I've met have the least peace in their lives. They're continually trying to hold on to their possessions. I've also had the privilege of meeting people who aren't wealthy, but who are totally at peace. Peace isn't found by making lots of money; it is found by walking with God. Where there is God, there is peace—there is gratefulness for what we have, rather than yearning for what we don't. Let's concentrate on the things in life that money can't buy.

PRAYER: Dear Lord, please make my heart grateful for the
blessings You give, which money can't buy. Amen.

MAY

May 1

LONELY NO MORE

"BE STRONG AND OF GOOD COURAGE; FOR YOU SHALL
BRING THE CHILDREN OF ISRAEL INTO THE LAND OF
WHICH I SWORE TO THEM, AND I WILL BE WITH YOU."
DEUTERONOMY 31:23

ARE YOU feeling lonely today? Do you feel as though you are all by yourself? That is exactly how Elisha must have felt when he stood by the great Jordan River after his mentor Elijah—his spiritual father—had been taken up to heaven by God in a whirlwind (2 Kings 2:1–18).

The scene had been dramatic. After he saw the whirlwind, Elisha cried out, "'My father, my father, the chariot of Israel and its horsemen!' So he saw him no more. And he took hold of his own clothes and tore them into two pieces" (2 Kings 2:12). But though he may have been alone physically, he was not truly alone. The Lord was always with him, and you do not have to stand alone either.

Like Elisha, you might be overcome with grief and loneliness, missing companionship you have always relied upon. But look at what Elisha did next: he took up the mantle that Elijah left behind and, believing, he rolled it up and struck the Jordan River just as his mentor had done moments before.

Just as before, the river parted in a miraculous way and he walked across on dry land. God will give you what you need to carry on with your life. You don't have to remain in despair. Thank God for past mentors and press on, putting into practice the things they taught you. You will always have a spiritual mentor—Jesus Christ. Look to Him, and He will teach you all you need to know.

PRAYER: Lord, thank You for those who have shaped my life; cause
me to take what they've taught me and carry on. Amen.

May 2
THE HELPER

"NEVERTHELESS I TELL YOU THE TRUTH. IT IS TO YOUR ADVANTAGE
THAT I GO AWAY; FOR IF I DO NOT GO AWAY, THE HELPER WILL
NOT COME TO YOU; BUT IF I DEPART, I WILL SEND HIM TO YOU."
JOHN 16:7

SOME OF you might feel friendless today, but I want to tell you about a Friend who sticks closer than any brother. You might be going through a court case, and I want to tell you about the greatest Advocate who has ever lived—someone who doesn't even charge you. Some readers might be looking for counseling: Should you marry that young man? Should you marry that young woman? Should you go into business? I want to tell you about a Counselor who never gives bad advice.

Who are we talking about? Of course, it's the Holy Spirit. Many of us are not using the gift of the Holy Spirit to our advantage. The Lord said that He was sending us a Helper, someone who is there to help us (John 16:7).

The baptism of the Holy Spirit is the power that you have, the power that God gives you—the peace, the *shalom*, the joy, and the wisdom that come with walking in the fullness of God. You and I believe in the holy Trinity: the Father, the Son, and the Holy Spirit—let us not forget about the last one. My dear friend, open your heart, seek Him while He may be found. Start asking the Counselor to give you advice, and you will become wiser than your years. Allow the Helper to help until Jesus comes.

PRAYER: Holy Spirit, thank You for the gift of Your counsel and comfort, and for praying for me continually. Help me to come to You in everything. Amen.

May 3
CAST YOUR BURDEN ON GOD

CAST YOUR BURDEN ON THE LORD, AND HE SHALL SUSTAIN YOU;
HE SHALL NEVER PERMIT THE RIGHTEOUS TO BE MOVED.
PSALM 55:22

ARE YOU a person who frets a lot? Do you tend to panic easily? Most people walk around worrying about one thing or another, and many seek advice and help from those around them. But there is a limit to what people can do to help; only God can really provide the solution you are looking for.

If there is anything in your life that is giving you sleepless nights, take it to the Lord in prayer. Psalm 37:1 says, "Do not fret because of evildoers." Don't be afraid: the Lord says that He will never leave you or forsake you (Deut. 31:6). So why worry?

Constantly worrying tends to make us tired, because we cannot sleep. And when we're tired, we begin to worry even more. It's a vicious cycle. Plus, people tend to stay away from negative worrywarts. They want to be around people who are positive and know the source of their help. Worry can affect every aspect of who we are—including our health. And the only cure is prayer and petition, and accepting God's sovereignty.

"Every evening I turn my worries over to God. He's going to be up all night anyway," said businesswoman Mary Crowley. You have a heavenly Father who watches over you; God has everything under control.

PRAYER: Lord, I turn my worries over to You. Please direct
my steps to make things better, but at the same time grow my
faith so that worry does not suck my life away. Amen.

May 4
TRUSTING IN GOD

TRUST IN HIM AT ALL TIMES, YOU PEOPLE; POUR OUT
YOUR HEART BEFORE HIM; GOD IS A REFUGE FOR US.
PSALM 62:8

AT THE beginning of a recent planting season in the district where I live, the rain was delayed and many farmers were wondering whether they should plant. Some men went ahead and planted by faith. It didn't look like much of a season at the start, but it ended up being a magnificent one in the end. Second Corinthians 5:7 tells us to walk by faith and not by sight; that is why I have called my Bible my "agricultural handbook" for many years now.

Our walk with God is the same. We don't walk according to our feelings or what we see with our eyes, but according to the promises of God and His faithfulness to us in the past.

We look to the future by faith and remind ourselves there are so many things for believers to be thankful for—and hopeful for. Remember, one of the most offensive things to God is lack of belief (Heb. 11:6). When we don't believe God will pull us through, that's when we're in trouble—fear and anxiety move in and faith moves out. As we continue in our work, let's take hold of new opportunities and move ahead in faith, remembering that "faith comes by hearing, and hearing by the word of God" (Rom. 10:17). We live by faith when we seek the face of the Lord every day. And God is faithful indeed.

PRAYER: Dear God, I believe that You work all things for my good. Show
me how to act in faith, so I can see You do mighty things. Amen.

May 5

THE POWER OF THE HOLY SPIRIT

"YOU SHALL RECEIVE POWER WHEN THE HOLY SPIRIT HAS COME
UPON YOU; AND YOU SHALL BE WITNESSES TO ME IN JERUSALEM,
AND IN ALL JUDEA AND SAMARIA, AND TO THE END OF THE EARTH."
ACTS 1:8

THE POWER of the Holy Spirit is what gets us through this life. I am not talking about getting up onstage and preaching, but rather getting from one day to another—getting up in the morning, getting the children ready for school, getting prepared for work, going to school or university. We need sustained power—perseverance and persistence—to get through life, and we obtain this by waiting on God.

Remember Peter? He was absolutely downcast after he denied the Lord three times. He had said to the Lord, "I'll fight for You. Don't worry, I'll never leave You." But then he was the first one to run away. He just didn't have it in him. However, after he was reinstated by Christ and baptized by the Spirit in the Upper Room, Peter went out and preached. And after the first sermon he gave, three thousand people came to know Jesus as Lord and Savior. What happened? He was filled with power from on high.

God baptizes us in His Holy Spirit so that we will be bold and so full of love, grace, mercy, and compassion that we will tell the whole world what the Lord has done for us. I cannot wait to go to distant countries and tell people about Jesus, encouraging them and reminding them how much God loves them. Of course, I need power to do that, and it comes from the Holy Spirit.

You are not alone; go out in the power of the Holy Spirit today.

PRAYER: Lord, sustain me with Your power this and every day. Amen.

May 6
THE HARD YARDS

THE LORD YOUR GOD WILL BLESS YOU IN ALL YOUR PRODUCE AND
IN ALL THE WORK OF YOUR HANDS, SO THAT YOU SURELY REJOICE.
DEUTERONOMY 16:15

NOTHING COMES without effort. Ask any professional sports player or successful businessperson, any artist or filmmaker. It's the "blood, sweat, and tears" that bring the blessing. There is no shortcut to success.

If you want to be a good horse rider, you've got to spend time on your horse; if you want to be a good rugby player, you have to spend time in the gym and on the field.

A famous tennis player told me that he used to spend time on a family farm with all his cousins when he was a boy. The others would go off into the bush and have fun, while he practiced on the tennis court. He is one of history's most accomplished tennis players, and a big part of the reason is that he put in the hard work. Another example is Usain Bolt, who is an absolute phenomenon—the fastest human on the planet. He says he struggles to get to the gym every morning because he has to train so hard. You don't become the best just by coincidence—it takes much work.

Likewise, if we refuse to do the hard work in our spiritual lives, we will miss out on God's blessings. I get up early in the morning and spend time with the Lord every single day because I want to learn from Him. So roll up your sleeves and work hard, because God created us for work and He wants to bless us through it.

PRAYER: Lord, build my resolve and strength for the work You've
given me to do. Help me to be persistent and tenacious. Amen.

May 7

A LAMP UNTO MY FEET

THESE ARE WRITTEN THAT YOU MAY BELIEVE THAT
JESUS IS THE CHRIST, THE SON OF GOD, AND THAT
BELIEVING YOU MAY HAVE LIFE IN HIS NAME.
JOHN 20:31

THE BIBLE is the Word of Life, the Sword of the Spirit, the Living Water, the good news, the Bread of Life. Its purpose is to confirm that Jesus Christ is the Son of God.

If your friends ask you to show them this Jesus that you are always talking about, just give them a Bible. I have walked with the Lord now for forty years, and He has never failed me, nor have I found His Word to be untrue.

Sometimes people come to me and say, "Can you pray that God will give me more faith?" And I always tell them that I won't pray for God to give them more faith, but I will pray that God would give a hunger for the Bible, because reading the Scriptures builds up faith.

If you are not reading your Bible systematically, I encourage you to start doing so today. I suggest that you start reading from Psalm 1 every day, along with another portion of the Old Testament and the New Testament. Buy a notebook and write down what God tells you every day.

This practice keeps me alive—it keeps me going and gives me messages every time I need to speak. So let's take advantage of the mighty power of the Word of God, whose purpose is to set the captives free, to heal the brokenhearted, to give us hope and a new start, and, of course, to point us to everlasting life.

PRAYER: Lord, thank You for the Bible. Let me never see it as
just a book, but rather as a powerful tool for life. Amen.

May 8

THE HEART OF THE HOME

WHO CAN FIND A VIRTUOUS WIFE? FOR HER WORTH IS
FAR ABOVE RUBIES. THE HEART OF HER HUSBAND SAFELY
TRUSTS HER . . . HER CHILDREN RISE UP AND CALL HER
BLESSED; HER HUSBAND ALSO, AND HE PRAISES HER.
PROVERBS 31:10–11, 28

MY WIFE is my best friend. I thank God for her every morning when I open my eyes. I agree with Proverbs 18:22, which says, "He who finds a wife finds a good thing, and obtains favor from the LORD." She is the mother of my children and the light of my life.

I want to salute mothers and wives today. Indeed, you hold one of the key positions in society, and you have one of the most honorable professions there is. I also think that Father God agrees.

Why do I say that? Quite simply because God trusted a young peasant girl by the name of Mary to look after His Son, our Savior, Jesus Christ. She was to teach Him, feed Him, love Him, and grow Him into the greatest single influence this world has ever known. The Father chose this young woman to do it, not a group of professors or a seminary or a monastery. No, He selected a regular, everyday family and put His Son in the hands of a wife and mother. Women have been given a stamina that few men have. We men salute you! We do not know what we would do without you.

PRAYER: Lord God, thank You for all the strong women who have touched my life. Help me to find ways to honor them today. Amen.

May 9
WHO IS IN CONTROL?

TO BE CARNALLY MINDED IS DEATH, BUT TO BE
SPIRITUALLY MINDED IS LIFE AND PEACE.
ROMANS 8:6

YOU'VE PROBABLY heard the story about the grandfather telling his grandson a tale about life. He described two wolves within him: one evil and one good. "They are constantly fighting," he told the boy. "Which wolf will win?" the grandson asked. The grandfather replied, "It depends on which wolf I am feeding." Who is in control of your life? Is it the Lord or the devil? Is it the sinful nature or the Spirit of God? Let's be wary of becoming more concerned with what the world thinks is important—what we look like and what we are doing to impress others—than the spiritual condition of our lives.

If we want to talk about the things of the Spirit, we need to be spiritual people; and to be spiritual people, we have to feed the spirit.

Let me ask you a question: Which wolf are *you* feeding? If you are spending time in prayer, in reading your Bible, and in serving the Lord, you are feeding the Holy Spirit. If you are spending your time absorbed with worldly things, the carnal spirit will take over, developing depression, fear, dissatisfaction, and anxiety. Be cognizant of what you are feeding today.

PRAYER: Dear God, show me how I am feeding the wrong things in life.
Help me to devote all my resources to becoming closer to You. Amen.

May 10

DYING TO SELF

IF CHRIST IS IN YOU, THE BODY IS DEAD BECAUSE OF SIN,
BUT THE SPIRIT IS LIFE BECAUSE OF RIGHTEOUSNESS.
ROMANS 8:10

OF ALL the dangers in the world, our biggest enemy is ourselves. Even the great evangelist Paul struggled with his human nature. He said, "For what I am doing, I do not understand. For what I will to do, that I do not practice; but what I hate, that I do" (Rom. 7:15). Paul personally met Jesus Christ, and yet he still struggled with sinful desires! Dying to self is something we'll have to do over and over again in our lives, and the easiest way to do it is to concentrate on the Lord. If we can get out of the way and let Jesus Christ live in us, then we will have eternal victorious life.

How do you start? Every time you find yourself concerned with what other people think of you, refocus on what God thinks of you. Set yourself apart. When people start to see Jesus in you, then you know you are making a difference.

The world needs men and women who are different—who have died to self. If you haven't already, now is the time for you to do so, so that Jesus Christ can live in you. You will become a new person in Christ, and God will give you a new reason to live.

PRAYER: Lord, help me to walk in the newness of Christ.
Show me new ways to die to myself each day. Amen.

May 11
DEALING WITH DISILLUSIONMENT

TRULY MY SOUL SILENTLY WAITS FOR GOD;
FROM HIM COMES MY SALVATION.
PSALM 62:1

SOMETIMES WE find ourselves expecting things from our fellow human beings that are impossible for them to deliver. A young bride is a good example. Newly married, she has such high expectations of her husband that she forgets that ordinary blood flows through his veins. He's not a supernatural being. Likewise, a young man may expect his young bride to take care of him exactly the way his mother did. This situation will naturally lead to disappointment.

We have great expectations of our government, our neighbors, our employers, and our colleagues. When they don't meet the standards we expect of them, we become disillusioned. This can lead us to judge others harshly, while we ourselves become cynical, distrustful, and isolated.

Our trust is misplaced—only one person can satisfy that aching hole in the human heart: our Lord Jesus. When we realize that people are exactly like us, limited in what we (and they) can do, we find freedom. The pressure is taken off our fellow humans.

Let's start to put our trust, our hope, and our future in the Lord. In this way, we won't be so disappointed in the behavior, or lack of behavior, in others or even ourselves. In being patient and gracious with one another, we'll find that our relationships with our spouses, friends, and children will grow stronger.

PRAYER: God, I'm so easily disillusioned with myself and with others.
Whenever this happens, help me to check where I place my hope. Amen.

May 12

ONE FLESH

THEREFORE A MAN SHALL LEAVE HIS FATHER AND MOTHER AND
BE JOINED TO HIS WIFE, AND THEY SHALL BECOME ONE FLESH.
GENESIS 2:24

MANY OF us have embarked on, or at least contemplated, a marriage relationship. As friends, family, and part of a larger community, it is our duty as well to support healthy marriages—both for ourselves and for those around us. Let us not forget that marriage takes a great deal of work. The greatest responsibility of married people, next to God, is to our spouses. There is nothing closer than a husband and a wife. It is a deeper relationship than a man has with his son or a woman has with her daughter.

I have seen many marriages strained because parents are interfering. Parents, respect your married children's boundaries. Married children, guard your relationship from others who want to get involved. Friends, encourage your married friends and give them space to grow. Our loved ones mean so much to us that we want to air our opinions on their relationship, but we must remember that first, they belong to each other.

God says married people are joined to become one flesh. We need to love them and support them in their marriage by giving them godly counsel. But we should never interfere; they have their own family. However, we should pray for them. That is the best thing we can do for those who have undertaken this blessed commitment: pray for them and love them.

PRAYER: Lord, please show me how I can nurture and protect
marriage, whether my own or my loved ones'. Amen.

May 13
FAILURE REDEEMED

IF THE SPIRIT OF HIM WHO RAISED JESUS FROM THE
DEAD DWELLS IN YOU, HE WHO RAISED CHRIST FROM
THE DEAD WILL ALSO GIVE LIFE TO YOUR MORTAL
BODIES THROUGH HIS SPIRIT WHO DWELLS IN YOU.
ROMANS 8:11

SUCCESS IS merely failure turned inside out. If we look at the Easter story, we see that Good Friday was an absolute disaster. The disciples panicked and fled. Then, on Easter Sunday, Christ rose from the dead. He visited His disciples on the shores of Galilee. He called to them, asking if they'd caught anything.

When they replied, "Nothing," He told them to throw the net on the other side; and they caught 153 fish (John 21:11). The first miracle was that the net never broke, and the second was the sheer quantity of fish. The lesson is to step out in faith, even after failure, because God can work with that.

I was recently called down to the coastal area of Zululand, an extensive sugarcane area, where farmers were experiencing a terrible drought. We came before God at a huge school sports field—farmers, townsfolk, young, and old. We repented together, and prayed for Jesus to send rain.

Within a few days, God opened the heavens and the rain bucketed down for days.

There is nothing that is impossible for the Lord—even when it seems all is lost. We can be confident putting our trust in Him, because He has the power to turn everything around.

PRAYER: God, You know my many failures. I trust that You
have the power to change them to successes! Amen.

May 14
LIVING IN FREEDOM

STAND FAST THEREFORE IN THE LIBERTY BY WHICH
CHRIST HAS MADE US FREE, AND DO NOT BE
ENTANGLED AGAIN WITH A YOKE OF BONDAGE.
GALATIANS 5:1

FREEDOM IS a multilayered concept. At this very moment, even if you're in jail, lying in a hospital bed, without a job, or completely oppressed, you can still be free. The Lord says if the Son has set you free, "you shall be free indeed" (John 8:36).

When Paul and Silas were thrown into jail, they were still free (Acts 16:23–40). They sang hymns and praised God because of this. When you are set free by the Holy Spirit, nothing can ever imprison you. You can be waiting in chains, but if you are a child of God, you are free in the way that really matters—in your soul.

Second Corinthians 3:17 says, "Now the Lord is the Spirit; and where the Spirit of the Lord is, there is liberty." Freedom is the ability to serve the Lord regardless of the situation you are in. I have met people who are disabled and confined to a wheelchair, yet they are free in the Lord. On the other hand, I have seen people who are amazing athletes, who can run and jump, but they are prisoners because the Lord Jesus Christ has not come into their hearts and set them free.

Since becoming a Christian I have attempted things that I never would have dreamed of doing before, because I did not have the courage, the strength, or the vision for them. But with freedom through Christ, I do now!

If you have the Holy Spirit, you too have liberty. The world is your oyster when you are free in God. This is the world that the Father has made, and if He sets you free, you are free indeed.

PRAYER: Lord, I celebrate my freedom! Thank You for
freeing me, regardless of my situation. Amen.

May 15

THE POWER OF PRAYER

FOR THIS REASON I BOW MY KNEES TO THE FATHER
OF OUR LORD JESUS CHRIST, FROM WHOM THE WHOLE
FAMILY IN HEAVEN AND EARTH IS NAMED.
EPHESIANS 3:14—15

ARE YOU concerned about your loved ones? Maybe you have some prodigal sons or daughters in the family who are living a wild life, and every time you try and talk to them, they don't listen to you. What can you do?

How much time are you spending on your knees for your children, family, friends? Here comes the challenge: If you are not praying for them, how do you expect things to change? Billy Graham said that if he had to live his life again he would preach less and pray more. Why? Because there is power in prayer.

The Bible tells us that "the effective, fervent prayer of a righteous man avails much" (James 5:16). Talking can turn to nagging, but prayer is the way to true change.

John Wesley's mother prayed for her son every day. I've heard many stories of men and women whose mothers prayed for them. God raised these evangelists up to be giants in the kingdom. This is what can come from encouraging and praying more and criticizing less.

Start believing what God says about your loved ones, and not what other people say. Keep believing and praying, and God will answer your prayers.

PRAYER: Lord, when I'm frustrated about a loved one, remind
me to come where the power is: to You in prayer. Amen.

May 16

WHO CAN BE SAVED?

BELIEVE ON THE LORD JESUS CHRIST, AND YOU WILL BE SAVED.
ACTS 16:31

THERE IS a reason John 3:16 is perhaps the most famous Bible verse in the world: "For God so loved the world that He gave His only begotten Son, that whoever believes in Him should not perish but have everlasting life." It says *whoever believes in Him*, not whoever is a good person, not whoever tries their best. Whoever believes in Him shall be saved and have eternal life.

It is so simple and so amazing. People come to me and say, "No, it can't be that simple. There must be some catch. There must be something I've got to do." But all you have to do is believe.

Jesus says, "Behold, I stand at the door and knock. If anyone hears My voice and opens the door, I will come in to him and dine with him, and he with Me" (Rev. 3:20). The handle is on the inside of the door. Unless you open the door and invite Jesus to come in and dine with you, He cannot have fellowship with you.

Will you let Him in? God has given us the freedom to choose whether or not to open the door. No matter what bad decisions you might have made in the past, you always have a second chance with the Lord. If you repent of your past and ask Jesus to be Lord of your life, He will cancel your sins. He came for those who are lost.

PRAYER: God, thank You for sacrificing Your Son
to make me right with You. Amen.

May 17
GOOD JUDGMENT

THIS I PRAY, THAT YOUR LOVE MAY ABOUND STILL MORE AND
MORE IN KNOWLEDGE AND ALL DISCERNMENT, THAT YOU MAY
APPROVE THE THINGS THAT ARE EXCELLENT, THAT YOU MAY BE
SINCERE AND WITHOUT OFFENSE TILL THE DAY OF CHRIST,
PHILIPPIANS 1:9–10

SO MANY people today say one thing and mean something totally different. This is when discernment is required. We need to ask God for the gift of discernment or good judgment—to show us what's in a person's heart.

Jesus pointed out that an apple tree will not produce oranges, nor a fig tree, grapes: "You will know them by their fruits. Do men gather grapes from thornbushes or figs from thistles?" He said (Matt. 7:16). We need to trust people, but at the same time be wise and discerning. Perception is not necessarily truth. Perception is what we *think* the truth is, and often we find ourselves totally wrong. We should look for the fruit before we make a judgment!

Discernment comes from God, and also from experience. When I was a young man doing my agricultural training in Scotland, I loved to sit with the elderly farmers. In those days there were no computerized weather forecasts, but because of their experience, those farmers could tell what the coming season would be like. Invariably, they would be spot-on.

We need to discern the times in which we live, through observation and hard-earned wisdom, in order to be prepared—spiritually and practically—for life. Keep your eyes open and heart tuned to God for His wisdom.

PRAYER: Lord, increase my discernment and give me wisdom
to see people's fruit before rushing to judgment. Amen.

May 18

BETTER TO PERSEVERE THAN ENDURE

NOT THAT I HAVE ALREADY ATTAINED, OR AM ALREADY
PERFECTED; BUT I PRESS ON, THAT I MAY LAY HOLD OF THAT
FOR WHICH CHRIST JESUS HAS ALSO LAID HOLD OF ME.
PHILIPPIANS 3:12

MY WIFE and I once watched an epic battle between two tennis players. They must have come close to breaking the record for the longest tennis final. I was moved by the perseverance the two young men showed, especially when taking into account the many hours they'd spent in training.

Perseverance is about continuing with a course of action despite difficulties and little sign of immediate success. What is it you seek to "lay hold of" in your life? It might be to become a loving husband or wife, a successful student, a responsible citizen of your country, or a young person whose parents are proud of them. Whatever the case, it will take perseverance to "lay hold of" your goals.

"*Endurance* is the ability to stand up under adversity; *perseverance* is the ability to progress in spite of it," wrote evangelist Jerry Bridges. I really believe that God wants us as Christians to persevere rather than to endure.

In the tennis match, one player continually took the game to his opponent, while the other player simply "endured." He played defensively behind the baseline, but his opponent would move forward with attack. As a result, his opponent won.

In the thirty or so years I've been serving God, I've seen that those who mean business for the Lord are the ones who persevere to the end. Just enduring won't get us far; it's all or nothing.

PRAYER: Lord, show me how to move from endurance
to perseverance in my life today. Amen.

May 19

WITNESSING FOR JESUS

TO THEM GOD WILLED TO MAKE KNOWN WHAT ARE THE
RICHES OF THE GLORY OF THIS MYSTERY AMONG THE
GENTILES: WHICH IS CHRIST IN YOU, THE HOPE OF GLORY.
COLOSSIANS 1:27

THE HARDER things get in the world, the easier it is for us to shine as children of God. The harder things get, the more opportunities we have to be different. When someone sins against us, we have an opportunity to respond with love, grace, and understanding.

Jesus never acted or spoke in haste; He always took time to hear what the Holy Spirit was telling Him. In the same way, let us take time out to listen to what God says before we act. Quiet your spirit and your soul before you go out to face the day and be an ambassador for Jesus Christ, a person who is different from the world.

Allow the Holy Spirit to come into your life. Be like Jesus. In the end it is not so much what you say that will make a difference, but who you are.

I'll never forget a particular day when I was speaking to a packed hall filled with salt-of-the-earth farmers and cattlemen. We had a break to have some refreshments halfway through the meeting, and an old, seasoned farmer came up to me and said, "Son, preach so that we can see *you*." I have never forgotten that remark and its lesson: often people are more moved by who you are rather than what you say.

The peace God gives you will be your witness to the world, because in the world there is no peace. Your peace comes from the Prince of Peace, and if you let that shine through you into a dark world, the Lord will be with you all the way.

PRAYER: Dear God, help me to see the dark times as an opportunity
to shine. Fill my heart with grace and compassion for those who
suffer, so I can be a beacon pointing the way to You. Amen.

May 20
OPEN YOUR HEART

YOUR WORD IS A LAMP TO MY FEET AND A LIGHT TO MY PATH.
PSALM 119:105

THOMAS À Kempis was a German priest, monk, and author who wrote *The Imitation of Christ*, a book that is said to be the most widely read devotional work after the Bible. In it he considered God's Word to be "the light of [his] soul," saying that without it, he "could not properly live." He read and wrote many books himself, but he loved God's Word the most.

There's nothing more important in this life than getting to know God, and the way we get to heaven is by knowing the Author of the Good Book. On the Day of Judgment we will not be judged by what we have read but by faith in Jesus alone.

The Bible will introduce you to the King and direct you in how to live your life. It's a personal revelation that you need from the Lord—a love letter from Him to you. Let your knowledge of and relationship with God move from the head to the heart. It was only after I accepted Jesus Christ as my personal Lord and Savior that I became emotional—I cry more than I preach sometimes—because God breaks my heart for people.

People can say whatever they like, but I know that my Redeemer lives. I don't hope He lives; I don't deduce that He lives; I *know* He lives—with all my heart. Open your heart today and allow the knowledge to travel from your head to your very deepest soul.

PRAYER: Dear God, thank You for the wisdom in Your Word. Allow
it to soak into me and change me to the core. Amen.

May 21
THE VALUE OF WATER

IN EVERYTHING GIVE THANKS; FOR THIS IS THE
WILL OF GOD IN CHRIST JESUS FOR YOU.
1 THESSALONIANS 5:18

SOME YEARS ago we had a long dry spell on the farm and surrounding area. When at last it started to rain properly, the relief in the community was palpable. There was a turnaround in the crops on all the farms.

I firmly believe we can only truly appreciate something when we've suffered. My children will tell you that if there's one thing that really upsets me, even at my age, it is wasting water. This is because I've experienced several severe droughts. In fact, in my area, many farmers lost their farms because of the continuous drought we experienced in the 1980s. That drought gave me an acute awareness of the value of water.

Suffering and hardship develop character and new appreciation. The apostle Paul was shipwrecked, stoned, whipped, imprisoned, deprived of food, and eventually beheaded in Rome. Yet he pressed on in hope to the end.

When you've been through a near-death experience, you start to appreciate every moment of living. You value your family and friends, your employer and employees, the smell of rain on dry ground, a newborn baby, or a sunrise. I encourage you to appreciate God, your loved ones, and your community. We have everything we need. So let us thank God in our trials, and treasure the strength gained through them.

PRAYER: God, thank You for turning hardship into perseverance, compassion, and strength. Help me to remember this day by day. Amen.

May 22

WORDS REMAIN FOREVER

THERE IS ONE WHO SPEAKS LIKE THE PIERCINGS OF A SWORD,
BUT THE TONGUE OF THE WISE PROMOTES HEALTH.
PROVERBS 12:18

THE OLD saying, "Sticks and stones may break my bones, but words will never harm me" is probably the most untrue statement I have ever heard. In fact, it works in reverse: bones can mend, but words stay in your heart forever.

Teachers, leaders, parents, and siblings can have a serious, positive impact on a child's life by what they say. Instead of being negative, decide to empower and encourage those around you. Our words can reflect our faith too; the Lord Jesus said if you have faith the size of a mustard seed, you can move mountains, and that's the kind of faith and encouragement we need (Matt. 17:20).

When can you take the opportunity to say something positive about your colleague or classmate? How can you compliment the person who prepared your dinner? When can you tell your parents that you love them? We can never be told enough times that we are loved and appreciated.

We can change the tide of negativity around us by returning a biting, sarcastic comment with a positive reply; and a gentle reply will turn away wrath (Prov. 15:1). Let us be known as peacemakers who soothe and comfort in a world that tears others down.

PRAYER: Dear Lord, You gave great power to words for a reason. Help me to use them to bring joy and build up the people around me today. Amen.

May 23

SINNERS LIKE YOU AND ME

THIS IS A FAITHFUL SAYING AND WORTHY OF ALL
ACCEPTANCE, THAT CHRIST JESUS CAME INTO THE
WORLD TO SAVE SINNERS, OF WHOM I AM CHIEF.
1 TIMOTHY 1:15

WHY DID Jesus come into the world? It's true that He came to heal the sick, to set the captives free, and even to give us direction for our lives. But the main reason Jesus came into the world was to save sinners.

This gives hope to people who are struggling, people who are still walking in darkness. Jesus came to save those who are not walking in the light.

Even the disciples had to be saved from sin. They weren't always believers—they started out as fishermen and tax collectors who didn't know the Lord. Then Jesus called them and they followed Him, taking the gospel of Jesus to the whole world. What hope this brings.

Jesus is known by many names—the Lily of the Valley, the Good Shepherd, the Lamb of God—but the name I love the most is the Friend of sinners. As His followers, that is our name too. We are called to be patient with one another, with people who don't have the beliefs we do, because Jesus was patient with us.

PRAYER: Dear God, I am in awe of Your unrelenting love of us, though we
sin. Help me to reflect this love to others who don't know You. Amen.

May 24

LAY YOUR BURDENS DOWN

I HAVE TRUSTED IN YOUR MERCY; MY HEART SHALL
REJOICE IN YOUR SALVATION. I WILL SING TO THE LORD,
BECAUSE HE HAS DEALT BOUNTIFULLY WITH ME.
PSALM 13:5—6

YOU WILL find in the Bible that the men who disappointed the Lord the most were also the ones who learned to cling to grace. Consider David, who used to play those beautiful psalms to the Lord up in the hills when he was looking after his father's sheep. He fell when he saw a beautiful woman bathing, succumbing to temptation. As we know, he committed adultery and later had the woman's husband killed (2 Sam. 12, 13). But David admitted his guilt, and God forgave him. That's one special thing about David: he knew how to repent. And his psalms give us some of the most beautiful portraits of grace in the Bible.

We will never stop doing things we regret. The good news is, the Lord forgives us. Don't keep beating yourself up; lay your burdens down at the foot of the cross and walk away. There might be areas in your life where you don't have the strength to put them right. But do you know something? God knows that. Just ask for His forgiveness and He'll forgive you. Remember, Jesus said that He came for those who were lost.

Of course, we want to learn a lesson and not repeat the mistake. Then we can be set free, leaving our baggage behind and walking in holiness.

PRAYER: Lord, I accept Your grace, which I so desperately need.
Forgive me and show me how to move ahead. Amen.

May 25

FAITH AND A GOOD CONSCIENCE

THIS CHARGE I COMMIT TO YOU . . . ACCORDING TO THE PROPHECIES
PREVIOUSLY MADE CONCERNING YOU, THAT BY THEM YOU MAY WAGE
THE GOOD WARFARE, HAVING FAITH AND A GOOD CONSCIENCE.
1 TIMOTHY 1:18–19

WE ARE in a war. Yes, we ultimately have the victory because of the Lord Jesus Christ, but we are still in a full-scale war. That is why, before we start our day, we need to put on the armor of God during time with Him each morning (Eph. 6:11–17). Remember, the devil is going around like a roaring lion seeking whom he may devour (1 Peter 5:8).

One powerful way the devil acts is to lull us into complacency. He'll tell believers that they've done everything right in the beginning, so now they can just sit back and coast. But even as the Lord is challenging us to fight the good fight and to run the race, we must remind ourselves that He is not interested in good starters, but good finishers. We must finish strong and keep the faith. In this war, if we sit back and neglect to put on our armor for just one day, we become vulnerable to the enemy's hands.

The words "This is just the way I am. Get used to it" are like music to his ears. We must nip complacency in the bud and fight the good fight every day, not just when we feel like it.

PRAYER: Lord, the fight we fight is so important! Keep me strong and
vigilant, dressed in the indestructible armor You have given me. Amen.

May 26

A SEASON FOR SLOWING DOWN

"BE STILL, AND KNOW THAT I AM GOD."
PSALM 46:10

RECENTLY ON a predawn jog I saw two beautiful owls. One was sitting in a tree, her eyes shining brightly in the light of my headlamp. A little farther on, another owl flew just past my head. It was extremely cold, yet there was a calmness in the air. As I ran along the road, the frost on the grass shone like millions of little diamonds.

It was absolutely quiet, and the scene impressed upon me how important it is for us to sometimes slow down. We move too fast, and if we don't take the time to regenerate our bodies, and more importantly our spirits, we shall not be able to complete the task and run the race that God has set before us.

So many people these days end up seeking help from psychologists and doctors because they're mentally fatigued, which leads to physical exhaustion. This is a natural law: if the Lord gives us time to work, He also gives us time to rest.

This life is not a hundred-yard sprint, but a long-distance race. I once attempted the Comrades Marathon and fell short eight miles from the finish, simply because I drove myself too hard and didn't drink enough liquid. We can accomplish much more for God and our loved ones if we discipline ourselves to rest. So let's take time to slow down. Most of all, let's spend more time with our families and with the Lord. I believe you'll be surprised at the results.

PRAYER: God, thank You for the precious gift of rest. Show
me new ways to make it a part of my life. Amen.

May 27

MORE THAN A STORY

ALL SCRIPTURE IS GIVEN BY INSPIRATION OF GOD, AND IS
PROFITABLE FOR DOCTRINE, FOR REPROOF, FOR CORRECTION, FOR
INSTRUCTION IN RIGHTEOUSNESS, THAT THE MAN OF GOD MAY BE
COMPLETE, THOROUGHLY EQUIPPED FOR EVERY GOOD WORK.
2 TIMOTHY 3:16–17

THE BIBLE is the most important book in the world. Some call it "the greatest story ever told," but it's so much more than some old wives' tale or fable. When I was little, I was told that one should never cross two knives at the table or walk underneath a ladder as it was considered bad luck. This is nonsense; mere superstition. There is no truth in it whatsoever. But the statutes given in the Bible are something completely different.

Paul told us how to approach telling the story of God: "If you instruct the brethren in these things, you will be a good minister of Jesus Christ, nourished in the words of faith and of the good doctrine which you have carefully followed. But reject profane and old wives' fables, and exercise yourself toward godliness" (1 Tim. 4:6–7). Paul was telling young Timothy to keep his focus on the value of the Word: it's not a magic trick or superstition, but a life-changing power.

When you go out and tell people the good news, be wary of cheapening the message or reducing it to a mere trick or tip that people can use in their lives. If you don't know what to say, just tell them the stories of the Bible and what Jesus means to you. When we have a real relationship with God, we don't need anything else to help witness to the world. The Bible is complete. It is Jesus in print, and He is enough.

PRAYER: Lord, I gain a new respect for Your Word each day. Show me its true depth, and help me to communicate it to others with life-changing love. Amen.

May 28
CLAIM THE VICTORY

BY FAITH THE WALLS OF JERICHO FELL DOWN.
HEBREWS 11:30

THE WALLS of Jericho fell with one shout of faith (Josh. 6). The Lord directed the Israelites: "Make a long blast with the ram's horn, and when you hear the sound of the trumpet, that all the people shall shout with a great shout; then the wall of the city will fall down flat. And the people shall go up every man straight before him" (v. 5). Like the Israelites, we can shout out and lay claim to those things that God has promised us.

A great shout of faith is much more effective than a whimper of doubt. We need faith in order for the walls in our lives to come tumbling down. Jesus is not going to give us the victory; He already *has* the victory. We just need to take that step of faith and claim it.

God answers the prayer of faith. He does not answer presumption or hoping; He answers faith. So when you pray, give a shout of faith as Joshua's men did. As you stand up and shout, feel the hesitation slip away. Are you held back by sickness, fear, or brokenness? Start shouting the Word of faith with confidence. Claim your rightful place in the name of Jesus Christ, and God will answer your prayers in His wisdom.

PRAYER: Dear God, Your victory is complete and our blessing secure. Thank You that we can lay hold of it with confidence! Amen.

May 29

THE POWER OF THE WIND

FOR HE COMMANDS AND RAISES THE STORMY WIND, WHICH
LIFTS UP THE WAVES OF THE SEA. . . . THEY REEL TO AND FRO,
AND STAGGER LIKE A DRUNKEN MAN, AND ARE AT THEIR WITS'
END. THEN THEY CRY OUT TO THE LORD IN THEIR TROUBLE,
AND HE BRINGS THEM OUT OF THEIR DISTRESSES.
PSALM 107:25, 27–28

THE BOOK of Genesis tells us about the end of the great flood: "Then God remembered Noah, and every living thing, and all the animals that were with him in the ark. And God made a wind to pass over the earth, and the waters subsided. The fountains of the deep and the windows of heaven were also stopped, and the rain from heaven was restrained. And the waters receded continually from the earth" (8:1–3).

Noah was a man of great faith, so when God instructed him to build an ark, he built it, even though the people ridiculed him. But the story wasn't finished yet. The flood did come, but finally a wind blew the water back and the water receded.

The Lord can stop the flood in your life too. It doesn't matter what the flood might be. It could be sickness or unemployment, disappointment or failure; but know that the Lord will stop that flood by the power of the Holy Spirit. Trust God to send that wind. God will send it—the wind will blow and the flood will recede, and there will be new life and a new opportunity. The wind of God will change your situation.

PRAYER: God, thank You that floods subside. I look forward to seeing the
new life and new birth that will come of the flood in my life. Amen.

May 30
RIVERS OF LIVING WATER

THIS WATER FLOWS TOWARD THE EASTERN REGION, GOES DOWN
INTO THE VALLEY, AND ENTERS THE SEA. WHEN IT REACHES
THE SEA, ITS WATERS ARE HEALED. AND IT SHALL BE THAT
EVERY LIVING THING THAT MOVES, WHEREVER THE RIVERS GO,
WILL LIVE. THERE WILL BE A VERY GREAT MULTITUDE OF FISH,
BECAUSE THESE WATERS GO THERE; FOR THEY WILL BE HEALED,
AND EVERYTHING WILL LIVE WHEREVER THE RIVER GOES."
EZEKIEL 47:8—9

THE DEAD Sea is the lowest point on earth, and it is a truly lifeless place. There's a strong smell of sulfur, and the hills are barren. What's more, the water is so salty that it's impossible to drown in it—you just float on the top.

Yet Ezekiel tells us that rivers will sweeten the water there. There will be lots of fish, while fruit-bearing trees will grow on the banks of the lake and the leaves will be used for medicinal purposes (Ezek. 47:8–12).

Our conversations can be like rivers of life and positivity to others. After all, we have so much for which to be thankful. We are called to step forward and speak life and not death—if we don't, who will?

I'm reminded of what Jesus said in John 4:14: "Whoever drinks of the water that I shall give him will never thirst. But the water that I shall give him will become in him a fountain of water springing up into everlasting life."

Let us be living water to those who are thirsty, who have lost hope and purpose and have given up.

PRAYER: Dear God, You refresh us and bring new life to every corner
of this dry world. May I be a river for others to drink from. Amen.

May 31

CHANGE YOUR OUTLOOK

FOR GOD HAS NOT GIVEN US A SPIRIT OF FEAR, BUT OF
POWER AND OF LOVE AND OF A SOUND MIND.
2 TIMOTHY 1:7

HAVE YOU ever lived in a state of fear? The devil wants to put fear into our hearts, to paralyze us so that we cannot think straight. Perhaps we don't allow our children to play outside because something might happen. Or we don't travel to new places in case we are mugged or get into an accident. We often stand panicked in the face of change or challenges.

This is why the Lord has given us the armor of God to put on when we get up in the morning (Eph. 6:13–17). Fears large and small can be fought by dressing your family every morning in the Spirit: the helmet of salvation, the breastplate of righteousness, the belt of truth, the shoes of the gospel of peace, the shield of faith, and the sword of the Spirit—the Word of God. God longs to answer our prayers for protection and courage.

When city dwellers see black clouds approaching, they tend to get worried, or afraid about the bad weather that is on its way. Farmers, on the other hand, rejoice because rain is coming, and rain brings life. It's true that bad things might (and will) happen, but God is with us, and we can be assured that He is guiding our lives when we ask Him to. Let's stand up to fear and trust in Him.

PRAYER: God, in the face of fear, I accept the gift of Your armor, which
protects me. Thank You for Your ceaseless care for me. Amen.

JUNE

∾

June 1

THE BLESSINGS OF DISCIPLINE

IF YOU ARE WITHOUT CHASTENING, OF WHICH ALL HAVE
BECOME PARTAKERS, THEN YOU ARE ILLEGITIMATE AND
NOT SONS. FURTHERMORE, WE HAVE HAD HUMAN FATHERS
WHO CORRECTED US, AND WE PAID THEM RESPECT.
HEBREWS 12:8−9

YOU'VE HEARD the proverb, "Spare the rod, spoil the child." But the concept of discipline is not very popular today. There are even governments that regulate the discipline of children in the home. My dear friend, the government is not responsible for your child; you are. If you really love your children, you will discipline them because of that love. You want them to be the best they can be.

God loves you and me, and that is why He disciplines us. If we resist that discipline, we are refusing the Holy Spirit. When the Holy Spirit comes and convicts you in your heart or prompts you to do something, do it—because He is disciplining you for your own good—not because He dislikes you, but because He loves you.

I want to encourage you to start obeying the Word of God; that is what makes good soldiers of the cross. Then the world will sit up and say, "We want to be like them." Let us start to honor our fathers and mothers, to love our spouses, to respect our elders, and to discipline our children. Let us listen, most of all, to God. He did not put the instructions in the Bible in place for His benefit but for ours. If we want to be good soldiers of the cross, let's allow the Holy Spirit to sanctify us and set us apart so that we can be different for His glory.

PRAYER: Lord, I accept Your discipline however it comes. Teach me
its value and help me enact Your principles in my life. Amen.

June 2

PERSIST AND PURSUE

THE EFFECTIVE, FERVENT PRAYER OF A
RIGHTEOUS MAN AVAILS MUCH.
JAMES 5:16

HERE ARE two key ideas that are essential to getting anywhere worth going: *persist* and *pursue*. If we give up or keep changing direction, we never really get anywhere. Instead, let us persist in seeking God's will and then pursue it with our whole heart.

Think of the two blind men who wanted Jesus to heal them. They pursued Him, and when they caught up with Him, Jesus asked them, "Do you believe that I can?" Jesus prayed for them, and their eyes were opened. They went away rejoicing once their faith had made them well (Matt. 9:27–30).

You can either believe that the Lord answers prayer, or you can say it is a coincidence. But as a Christian, you cannot continue to think it is coincidence for the rest of your life. We serve a mighty God who expects us to pursue and to persist in prayer. If you keep knocking on that door, it's going to open.

God honors the fervent prayer of the righteous. For me it's become a lifestyle to first seek God's will and then persist in prayer until it comes to pass. It's very exciting and so very rewarding. As Christians we have been sorely tested in numerous ways, and we will continue to be tested. Many have become disillusioned, but I encourage you to once more pursue the dream that God gave you by persistently praying until it comes to pass.

PRAYER: Dear Lord, when I become tired or complacent,
help me to pursue You and persist in prayer. Amen.

June 3

THE FAMILY OF GOD

YOU ARE A CHOSEN GENERATION, A ROYAL PRIESTHOOD,
A HOLY NATION, HIS OWN SPECIAL PEOPLE, THAT YOU
MAY PROCLAIM THE PRAISES OF HIM WHO CALLED YOU
OUT OF DARKNESS INTO HIS MARVELOUS LIGHT.
1 PETER 2:9

HOW AMAZING it is that before the foundation of the world, God chose us to be His children, to be a part of His heavenly family.

He has called us to be holy, saying, "I the LORD am holy, and have separated you from the peoples, that you should be Mine" (Lev. 20:26). God has given us His very own Holy Spirit to help us to walk in His ways.

Our heavenly Father took His love for us a step further by giving His only begotten Son, Jesus Christ, because He loves us and wants us to live an abundant life. Jesus came, He said, "that they may have life, and that they may have it more abundantly" (John 10:10).

We are God's chosen people, His royal priesthood, His special people—given an indescribable gift so that we might one day be united with our heavenly family. And what does God ask in return? That we obey the directions and commandments that He has put in place for us, His people. This is not for His sake, but rather for our own—not to control us, but to prevent us from getting hurt.

The Lord wants fellowship with us, His children, so very much. This is something we should not take for granted. Let's wait patiently for Him to meet with us so that we might live according to His purpose for our lives.

PRAYER: God, I am so grateful to be part of Your family. Thank You for
the gift You gave me when You brought me in as Your own. Amen.

June 4

SEPARATED NO MORE

"IF YOU HAD KNOWN ME, YOU WOULD HAVE KNOW MY FATHER
ALSO; AND FROM NOW ON YOU KNOW HIM AND HAVE SEEN HIM."
JOHN 14:7

YOU CAN sometimes spend a lot of time with someone and still not truly know that person. In the same way, one can know all about Jesus without truly knowing Him as Lord and Savior. It is in meeting Him and spending time with Him that we get to know God's true character. And we begin to understand the mind-blowing sacrifice Jesus made for us.

We have the privilege of getting to know God because of what Jesus accomplished on the cross. He gave His life so that we might be reconciled to our heavenly Father. Isn't that truly amazing? The separation between God and man was bridged the moment Jesus said, "It is finished." The temple veil that was torn when He died signifies that Jesus opened the way for us (Matt. 27:51). The division between us and Him is now gone. We are now free to know Him personally and to develop an intimate relationship with Him.

John Gerstner put it beautifully when he said, "To the artist he is the one altogether lovely. To the educator he is the master teacher. To the philosopher he is the wisdom of God. To the lonely he is a brother; to the sorrowful, a comforter; to the bereaved, the resurrection and the life. And to the sinner he is the Lamb of God who takes away the sin of the world."

PRAYER: Jesus, thank You for performing the unimaginable
feat of reuniting us with You. I worship You! Amen.

June 5

BEARING THE COST

TO HIM WHO LOVED US AND WASHED US FROM OUR SINS IN HIS OWN
BLOOD, AND HAS MADE US KINGS AND PRIESTS TO HIS GOD AND
FATHER, TO HIM BE GLORY AND DOMINION FOREVER AND EVER.
REVELATION 1:5–6

MANY MEN and women have died for the sake of the gospel. Jim Elliot was one of them. He, together with four other missionaries, sought to bring the gospel to the Auca tribe in Ecuador.

The Auca were considered by outsiders to be a violent and murderous people. The group first approached them from an airplane, dropping down gifts from above. After several weeks, they built a base near their village and had some interaction with them. Encouraged by this, they made plans to witness to them. Before they could do so, however, ten warriors appeared and confronted the men, killing all five. Their bodies were later discovered downstream, pierced with spears.

Although Elliott died that day, his wife and other missionaries were able to continue his work by forgiving the Auca tribe and going back to share God's love and forgiveness with them. Jim's wife, Elisabeth, later published two books on his life and the Auca ministry.

The gospel comes at a cost, not only to you, but also to your family. I myself have to leave my family on a regular basis to spread the gospel. However, it is a small price to pay when I think of what others have given and what Jesus gave for me.

We have a saying here at Shalom farm where I live: "If your faith is costing you nothing, it is worth nothing. If your faith is costing you everything, then it is worth everything."

PRAYER: God, thank You for paying the price to reunite us with You. Help
me to do what it takes, without fear, to spread Your Word. Amen.

June 6

A SIGN FROM ABOVE

SO GIDEON SAID TO GOD, "IF YOU WILL SAVE ISRAEL BY MY HAND
AS YOU HAVE SAID—LOOK, I SHALL PUT A FLEECE OF WOOL ON
THE THRESHING FLOOR; IF THERE IS DEW ON THE FLEECE ONLY,
AND IT IS DRY ON ALL THE GROUND, THEN I SHALL KNOW THAT
YOU WILL SAVE ISRAEL BY MY HAND, AS YOU HAVE SAID."
JUDGES 6:36–37

GIDEON RECEIVED a vision from God. But because of everything that had happened to the Israelites, Gideon was reluctant to believe that God would be with him. Why would God use him, of all people, to save the Israelites? So he asked God for the sign of the fleece so he would know for sure.

After making his request to the Lord, Gideon got up early the following morning and found the wet fleece. He wrung out the dew, releasing a bowlful water (Judges 6:38). How's that for a sign from God? Yet Gideon still doubted. He wanted a second confirmation, which God gave him (vv. 6:39–40). Finally, Gideon was convinced that God was with him and he was no longer afraid.

At the end of all the Mighty Men Conferences we've held on our farm, it has started raining. The rain seems to be a sign from God, as when God gave Noah a beautiful rainbow. It is almost as if the Lord is saying, "Well done, good and faithful servants."

Do you need a sign from God today? Something to remind you that He is with you? Do you want Him to replace fear with assurance and courage? Ask the Lord to strengthen your faith through a sign or a word, and He will give it to you—even if that answer is "Be still and wait."

PRAYER: Lord, please open my eyes to the signs You are giving me today. Amen.

June 7

THE FAITHFULNESS OF THE LORD

SO BOAZ TOOK RUTH AND SHE BECAME HIS WIFE; AND WHEN HE
WENT IN TO HER, THE LORD GAVE HER CONCEPTION, AND SHE BORE
A SON. THEN THE WOMEN SAID TO NAOMI, "BLESSED BE THE LORD,
WHO HAS NOT LEFT YOU THIS DAY WITHOUT A CLOSE RELATIVE;
AND MAY HIS NAME BE FAMOUS IN ISRAEL! AND MAY HE BE TO
YOU A RESTORER OF LIFE AND A NOURISHER OF YOUR OLD AGE."
RUTH 4:13—15

NAOMI AND Ruth had obeyed God when He told Naomi it was time for her to return to Bethlehem, her hometown. And God was faithful to Ruth when He brought Boaz across her path and honored her loyalty. When Ruth married Boaz, the Lord blessed Ruth with a son named Obed, who was King David's grandfather. And, as we know, Jesus was a descendant of King David. Be faithful to God and He will bless you.

God will tell us when we need to go, or make a big change in our lives, as He did for Ruth and Naomi. It takes a lot of faith, but God always honors faithfulness. We will experience wonderful, prosperous times, and less pleasant times. In difficult times it would be easy to question God, but instead let us follow in Ruth's footsteps and trust God for His care and faithfulness.

From our youth to our old age, God is always with us. When life's storms threaten to overwhelm us, He is there. There is nowhere that God has not been and nothing that He has not seen. God is real, and He will never fail us.

PRAYER: God, thank You for walking with me when I step out and take
a risk for You. I trust You with my future and my legacy. Amen.

June 8

AFFIRMING WORDS

FOR WHO IS GOD, EXCEPT THE LORD? . . . GOD IS MY STRENGTH
AND POWER, AND HE MAKES MY WAY PERFECT.
2 SAMUEL 22:32–33

IT MADE no difference to my dad whether I was in the A team at school or the F team, just as long as I did my best. He loved me for who I was, and for that I remain eternally grateful. He gave me the gift of affirmation.

We know also that our heavenly Father esteemed His Son greatly. He said, "This is My beloved Son, in whom I am well pleased" (Matt. 3:17). That must have given Jesus strength to press on.

Those in our care are not guaranteed to be with us forever. Our children are up and away and out of the home in no time at all. Our employees follow different career paths. Our friends and those we mentor can move on. So while we can, let's affirm them when they do something, no matter how big or how small it might be. Their level of success is not even the point. The point is to stand there with them, especially when they don't succeed. I think we sometimes don't understand how important a pat on the back or a "Well done!" can be.

Both of my sons excelled at sports. Sometimes I would only be able to make part of their soccer or rugby games due to work constraints, but the boys would always come home and ask their mom, "What did Dad think of the game?" It was so important to them to know what Dad thought.

If you want those in your charge to reach great heights, it's not going to be through extra lessons or extra coaching, but through affirmation.

PRAYER: God, thank You for entrusting me with those I care for. Please help
me to be a dependable encouragement in every aspect of their lives. Amen.

June 9
FALSE WITNESS

A FALSE WITNESS WILL NOT GO UNPUNISHED, AND
HE WHO SPEAKS LIKES WILL NOT ESCAPE.
PROVERBS 19:5

MY DAD always said when I was little that "whatever Angus says, you can cut in half." If I said it was a hundred, it was actually fifty. You could call that a "half-truth," but really, a lie is a lie—and harmful.

There was a couple in the Bible, Ananias and Sapphira, who told a famous lie. They were not unbelievers—they loved the Lord. They were good people who sold their land and brought the money to the apostles, but they kept back a portion for themselves while telling the apostles that they were giving the full amount. The apostle Peter asked Ananias why he had lied to the Holy Spirit. As soon as Peter stopped talking, Ananias took his last breath and died. They carried him out and buried him.

A while later his wife, Sapphira, who did not know what had happened to her husband, came along. Peter asked her how much they had made by selling their property. She lied and told him they had only received what they had given to the church. Again he asked Sapphira why she had lied to the Holy Spirit. She was struck down just like her husband, and was carried out and buried (Acts 5:1–11).

This may seem extreme, but it goes to show that we cannot lie to the Holy Spirit. If you have been convicted about something in your life, confess it and get it out of the way. The Bible says, "If we confess our sins, He is faithful and just to forgive us our sins and to cleanse us from all unrighteousness" (1 John 1:9).

PRAYER: Lord, it's useless to lie to You. Uncover any dishonesty
in my heart today and cleanse me from it. Amen.

June 10
THE ANOINTING OF GOD

ELIJAH SAID TO ELISHA, "ASK! WHAT MAY I DO FOR YOU,
BEFORE I AM TAKEN AWAY FROM YOU?" ELISHA SAID, "PLEASE
LET A DOUBLE PORTION OF YOUR SPIRIT BE UPON ME." SO HE
SAID, "YOU HAVE ASKED A HARD THING. NEVERTHELESS,
IF YOU SEE ME WHEN I AM TAKEN FROM YOU, IT SHALL
BE SO FOR YOU; BUT IF NOT, IT SHALL NOT BE SO."
2 KINGS 2:9–10

ELISHA WAS desperate for the power of God, and he was prepared to go as far as he could for the Lord. He was determined, at all costs, to inherit the spirit of the prophet Elijah.

The Lord was about to take Elijah up to heaven in a whirlwind. Three times Elijah said to Elisha, "Stay here, please," while he went to perform a task, and three times Elisha answered, "As the LORD lives, and as your soul lives, I will not leave you!"

Will you say with Elisha today, "No way! I want all that God's got for me. I want a double portion of His anointing"? Just as the people tried to convince Elisha to leave Elijah, there will be times when people try to persuade you not to follow the Lord. Elisha did not give up, and eventually Elijah asked him, "What may I do for you?" Elisha answered, "Please let a double portion of your spirit be upon me" (2 Kings 2:9).

Do you want more of the Lord? Do you want to serve Him better? Do you want to see more of the wonders of God? Then wait on God as Elisha did, and you will be richly anointed.

PRAYER: Dear God, I want to go where You go. Keep me
close to You—I refuse to go any other way. Amen.

June 11

ACTS

THEY SANG RESPONSIVELY, PRAISING AND GIVING THANKS
TO THE LORD: "FOR HE IS GOOD, FOR HIS MERCY ENDURES
FOREVER TOWARD ISRAEL." THEN ALL THE PEOPLE SHOUTED
WITH A GREAT SHOUT, WHEN THEY PRAISED THE LORD.
EZRA 3:11

I CANNOT face the day without first spending time with the Master. As an evangelist, I speak about Him and to Him all the time, but I also need an intimate, one-on-one time with Him. It is like spending time with your spouse—when you are together at a social gathering, it is fun, but there has to be time for just the two of you.

As a new believer I was taught a simple method of praying using the acronym ACTS.

A stands for *Adoration.* This is the time to adore the Lord for who He is; to give Him thanks for a new day; to praise Him for the beautiful new morning.

C stands for *Confession.* This is the time to repent before the Lord, to ask God to forgive your sins. Maybe you lost your temper with your family unintentionally; maybe it is something you have neglected to do; but the Lord forgives and cleanses.

T stands for *Thanksgiving.* We should thank God for His undeserved loving-kindness that gives us the opportunity to call ourselves His children. We can thank Him for our family and loved ones and for new opportunities in life.

S stands for *Supplication.* Bring all your requests before God concerning your life and your family's well-being and future.

Pray specifically, expectantly, and faithfully.

PRAYER: Lord, be with me in prayer as I engage with You through adoration, confession, thanksgiving, and supplication. Amen.

June 12
RECLAIMING YOUR JOY

THIS DAY IS HOLY TO OUR LORD. DO NOT SORROW,
FOR THE JOY OF THE LORD IS YOUR STRENGTH.
NEHEMIAH 8:10

A LADY named Betty had been in serious pain for more than ten years as a result of osteoarthritis and rheumatoid arthritis. She found it almost impossible to do the simplest of things, such as dressing herself, without her husband's help. Betty could not get out of a chair unaided or even lift her arms.

"I never had a day without pain," she testified. "Most of the time I was in absolute agony. Every bone in my body hurt." Betty loved attending her local church, and the ladies stood by her and helped whenever they could. Life, however, was difficult. The future looked very bleak.

One day Betty started reading the book *Faith Like Potatoes* and could not put it down. Faith arose in her heart as she read about the wonderful miracles God does. Healing, deliverance, provision—*Nothing is impossible with God*, she thought.

Betty decided enough was enough and told the devil her body was the temple of God. She commanded him to take his hands off her and began praising the Lord. One Wednesday morning Betty set off for her weekly ladies' meeting. "As I walked into the church, I realized that I had no pain. I could sit down and get up without assistance, and I could raise my hands and praise the Lord! It was wonderful. God had healed me." The ladies at her Bible study praised God for her healing.

Betty wants people in pain to know that they don't have to struggle by themselves. "Turn your faith loose and believe God," she says. All things are possible when we believe in God and take Him at His word.

PRAYER: God, You are the great healer. Thank You for answering prayer! Amen.

June 13

STAND FIRM

FOR IF YOU REMAIN COMPLETELY SILENT AT THIS TIME,
RELIEF AND DELIVERANCE WILL ARISE FOR THE JEWS
FROM ANOTHER PLACE, BUT YOU AND YOUR FATHER'S
HOUSE WILL PERISH. YET WHO KNOWS WHETHER YOU HAVE
COME TO THE KINGDOM FOR SUCH A TIME AS THIS?
ESTHER 4:14

WE ARE desperately in need of some modern-day Esthers who will risk life and limb for God. To be a Christian requires boldness: one needs to boldly stand up and call sin by its name, and be prepared to tell the truth at all costs! Today's verse reminds us that God does not share His power with those who do not step up to the plate. He'll raise another, and His work will go on. But don't despair if you think immediately of a time you shrank back. Just be prepared for the next opportunity to come your way.

If you are a shy person at heart, there is a way in which you can become bold in Christ: start spending time with Him and ask Him to give you a heart for the lost. When God gives you a heart of compassion for people, you'll find yourself becoming bold.

We must, of course, also be prepared to bear the consequences of speaking against sin, because we can become very unpopular, just as our Master was. He was ostracized for telling the truth, but it's the truth that will set people free (John 8:32). Ask the Spirit's guidance on when to speak and not to speak, and learn to listen to His gentle prompting. The truth, when spoken in love, wisdom, and with boldness, will bring peace, stability, and security.

PRAYER: God, thank You for placing me where I am for "such a time as this." Help me to speak boldly for You when the opportunity arises.

June 14

UNCONDITIONAL SURRENDER

THOUGH HE SLAY ME, YET WILL I TRUST HIM. EVEN
SO, I WILL DEFEND MY OWN WAYS BEFORE HIM.
JOB 13:15

AS AN evangelist, I have seen hundreds, if not thousands, respond to the gospel. Then months later I find that many have fallen by the wayside. Could it be that unconditional surrender is missing from those commitments?

The whole truth is that if He is not Lord of all, He is not Lord at all. There is danger in encouraging people to give their lives to Christ by bargaining with the Lord or applying conditions. In other words, saying, "Lord, You get me out of this tight spot and I'll serve You for the rest of my life," may not result in a long-lasting faith. There is no record in the Bible of the Lord encouraging that type of shallow commitment.

What He does say is, "If anyone desires to come after Me, let him deny himself, and take up his cross daily, and follow Me" (Luke 9:23). The Lord is looking for men and women who are prepared to surrender their lives unconditionally to Him.

It is not commitment to serve the Lord for what we can get from Him, or even what we can give Him. We should serve Jesus Christ for one reason only—because of who He is. Yes, He helps us and provides for us, but we serve Him because He is a magnificent and loving God—not because of what He does for us. His goodness is enough. So when you tell God you love Him, show Him too. It takes continual daily surrender of our lives and will.

PRAYER: Dear God, I surrender to You. Help me to give over to You fully. Amen.

June 15

PRESS ONWARD

GOD IS OUR REFUGE AND STRENGTH, A VERY
PRESENT HELP IN TROUBLE.
PSALM 46:1

PSALM 34:19 says, "Many are the afflictions of the righteous, but the LORD delivers him out of them all." Every time I've faced a huge challenge, there's always been an amazing outcome. If I look back on my career over the past forty years, my fondest memories are of the tough times, because God brought great blessing out of those times.

The greater the battle, the greater the victory! Be encouraged to keep pressing on. You may not know what tomorrow holds, but remind yourself who holds tomorrow.

When you're looking defeat in the face, with your back up against the wall and commitments to meet, accounts to pay, and answers to give—that's when you need to give it your all. Victories are won by people who are prepared to face challenges. We do the battle, and God has promised us that He will deliver us out of every affliction. Therefore, as Paul said, "Let us not become weary in doing good, for at the proper time we will reap a harvest if we do not give up" (Gal. 6:9 NIV).

We have to face the enemy, whether it be poverty, inflation, or the elements. I have yet to meet a person worth their salt who has not been through a fiery trial. As John Bunyan wrote, "In times of affliction we commonly meet with the sweetest experiences of the love of God."

PRAYER: God, help me to press on through trial and discouragement.
I pray You'll let me feel that You're near. Amen.

June 16

ANXIOUS FOR NOTHING

BE ANXIOUS FOR NOTHING, BUT IN EVERYTHING BY
PRAYER AND SUPPLICATION, WITH THANKSGIVING,
LET YOUR REQUESTS BE MADE KNOWN TO GOD.
PHILIPPIANS 4:6

TODAY'S VERSE is an encouraging word that I believe God wants to give each one of us. If ever we needed faith, it is now. The Lord is never late. He is on time, and He will undertake for us. God will never fail us. Take your requests to Him, and He will answer every one—not always in the way you want, but He will give you peace, something that the world is desperately seeking.

If you keep your eyes fixed on the Lord and not on your circumstances, you will sail through those anxious moments. You will be able to look back in years to come and count your blessings.

Start to live one day at a time, knowing that the Lord will take care of you as long as you are walking in His ways. Half the things that you and I worry about are not going to happen anyway, and all it will do is give us ulcers and sleepless nights. Rather, pray about your situation and take it to the Lord. Leave your worries in His hands.

As the writer J. A. Bengel said, anxiety and prayer are as opposed to each other as fire and water. By spending more time with the Lord and enjoying what He has given to us, we will cease to be anxious and start thinking more clearly.

PRAYER: God, I leave my anxieties with You. As they push into my mind during the day, help me to bring them back where they belong—in Your hands. Amen.

June 17
GOD'S PROMISE OF BLESSING

GOD BE MERCIFUL TO US AND BLESS US, AND
CAUSE HIS FACE TO SHINE UPON US.
PSALM 67:1

GOD BLESSES His own people; He always multiplies what He sows. We are all children of promise, not because of what we have done, but because of God's covenant with Abraham (Gen. 17). Let us never forget that the blessings we receive are not because of our own doing, but because of God's promise to Abraham.

Let's not allow blessings to pass us by through neglect, a willingness to compromise, or a plain couldn't-care-less attitude. Esau sold his birthright for a plate of food and lost his blessing (Gen. 25:29–34). Instead, let's keep our priorities in check. We cannot put God's blessings on hold; what He says He will do, He will bring to pass—you can be assured it will be done. God's word was good enough for Abraham, and it is good enough for us.

The Father has blessed each one of us with a special gift: to preach, to teach, to be a good friend, etc. We must aim to use our gift according to His will, and to be mature and steadfast in the faith.

God's blessings are so precious in life, and even when it might appear as though all is lost, the Lord still blesses us. Look at Isaac. He was removed from his land, banished numerous times, and yet the very people who chased him away later came back to make peace because they saw how God had blessed him and his family (Gen. 26).

Thank the Lord for His blessings on your life today!

PRAYER: Lord, I am unimaginably blessed. Thank You for all You've given! Amen.

June 18

SOUND THE ALARM!

YOU SHALL NOT BE AFRAID OF THE TERROR BY NIGHT,
NOR OF THE ARROW THAT FLIES BY DAY, NOR OF THE
PESTILENCE THAT WALKS IN DARKNESS, NOR OF THE
DESTRUCTION THAT LAYS WASTE AT NOONDAY. A THOUSAND
MAY FALL AT YOUR SIDE, AND TEN THOUSAND AT YOUR
RIGHT HAND; BUT IT SHALL NOT COME NEAR YOU.
PSALM 91:5–7

THE NEWSPAPERS are filled with stories of intolerance and the irrational fear and hatred of other peoples, groups, and races. This hatred has led to countless deaths and bloodshed around the world and within the borders of our own country. The enemy is on the prowl and inciting people to do what they like. In order for evil to prosper, all that good people have to do is nothing!

As Christians we must take up our position as watchmen, blow the trumpet, and sound the alarm. Ezekiel 33:6 says, "But if the watchman sees the sword coming and does not blow the trumpet, and the people are not warned, and the sword comes and takes any person from among them, he is taken away in his iniquity."

The church, you and I, are the conscience of the nation! We, the watchmen, must blow the trumpet and warn the people of the ensuing danger. We need to become more vocal, to call sin by its name, and to stand up for the poor, the innocent, the young, and the vulnerable, and to tell society that Jesus Christ is a holy and righteous God who will not tolerate sin of any description. When this nation turns back to God wholeheartedly, then we will see revival; and that alone will put an end to the chaos that prevails in the world today.

PRAYER: Lord, give us all the bravery to blow the trumpet and
call for righteousness, loudly, in every way we can. Amen.

June 19

GOING IT ALONE

MY BRETHREN, COUNT IT ALL JOY WHEN YOU FALL INTO VARIOUS
TRIALS, KNOWING THAT THE TESTING OF YOUR FAITH PRODUCES
PATIENCE. BUT LET PATIENCE HAVE ITS PERFECT WORK, THAT
YOU MAY BE PERFECT AND COMPLETE, LACKING NOTHING.
JAMES 1:2–4

THERE COMES a time in everyone's life when he or she needs to "go it alone." We might have been taught and shown many things, but at some stage we have to pick up the reins, get on that horse, and kick in our heels. We can go to lectures and courses to learn how how to ride a horse, but it's only when we get on the animal's back that we truly learn.

God will give you sufficient strength for the job at hand. As you step out and "walk on the water," He will support you. All you need to do is take that first step of faith. When I look back on my own life, I see that I have only really matured during the difficult times. I didn't grow through times of success, blessing, or opportunity. I grew through hard times, through personal tragedy, through setbacks.

Don't be afraid to put your trust in God during these times. He will enable you to mature and rise to the occasion. Don't worry about pleasing your former teachers and mentors. Look to God and continue to press through. If your teacher or mentor has taught you well, you should excel and be able to persevere.

PRAYER: Jesus, thank You for letting me step into my future.
Help me to rise to whatever is before me today. Amen.

June 20
MUTUAL RESPECT

HONOR ALL PEOPLE. LOVE THE BROTHERHOOD.
FEAR GOD. HONOR THE KING.
1 PETER 2:17

OSWALD CHAMBERS wrote: "We slander God by our very eagerness to work for Him, without knowing Him." Put another way, we can't tell others about the Lord Jesus without getting to know Him first. If we don't spend time with God, how can we tell others what Jesus means to us personally? Knowing Him should be our heart's desire.

The same thing goes for the people we work with; we can't produce anything good together without knowing them. It takes time to learn what makes them tick, but you'll find that the business operation will become more profitable and effective as a result. Job satisfaction is vital in any workplace. You may be an expert in your field, but unless you can get those who work with you to do the job well, you cannot succeed. Mutual respect is critical. We need to love and respect one another, and this only happens when we spend time together.

A fair day's pay for a fair day's work is a biblical teaching for employers, and diligent work is a biblical principle for employees. But we can all go over and beyond that, genuinely caring for people as a whole; it will mean so much to them, and you will all soon reap the rewards. One of the most effective ways of doing this is to spend time in prayer with your colleagues before the workday begins. Another is being there to help them in times of trouble, even outside the confines of the workplace. From personal experience, I can tell you that doing this daily will transform the entire attitude and work ethic of the staff.

PRAYER: Dear God, thank You for those with whom I work.
Show me how to know and bless them today. Amen.

June 21
HUMBLE STRENGTH

UNLESS THE LORD BUILDS THE HOUSE, THEY LABOR IN
VAIN WHO BUILD IT; UNLESS THE LORD GUARDS THE
CITY, THE WATCHMAN STAYS AWAKE IN VAIN.
PSALM 127:1

EVERYTHING THAT we do in this life has God's fingerprint on it. We go to work and put in long hours, but it is God who turns our hard work into success.

Humility is one of the greatest virtues of any great man or woman of God. In Scotland two hundred years ago, there was a young preacher by the name of Robert Murray MacCheyne. He was an extremely humble man who died before his thirtieth birthday, his work on earth complete.

Of the revival that had started in Dundee, Scotland, he wrote, "Lord, I thank thee that thou hast shown me this marvelous working, though I was but an adoring spectator, rather than an instrument." With that kind of attitude, God can use us to move mountains. We just need to acknowledge where our strength comes from: God alone.

Whatever venture you and I enter into, let us be quick to understand that unless God blesses it, we will not accomplish much. Seek the face of the Lord and find out what it is that He wants you to do. Once it succeeds, don't be slow in acknowledging that the Lord Jesus Christ made it possible.

PRAYER: God, You are the power behind every venture we
undertake. We praise and honor You first. Amen.

June 22

THE BURDEN

THE FEAR OF THE LORD IS THE BEGINNING OF KNOWLEDGE,
BUT FOOLS DESPISE WISDOM AND INSTRUCTION.
PROVERBS 1:7

IT'S EASY to criticize and point fingers at young people who get caught up with drug addiction, perversion, and other evils. The world beckons them, and we fail to realize that most of these young people are actually searching for a vision and a purpose for their existence here on earth.

What they're missing is a burden. A burden from God is carried in our hearts and gives us a reason to live. It arouses excitement, desire, and passion. When we receive a burden from God, He will give us vision and direction.

John Knox had a burden. He cried out to God, "Give me Scotland or I die." God gave him Scotland. Knox was so passionate for his countrymen that nothing could stop him from bringing revival to that nation. Mary, Queen of Scots, said of him, "I fear the prayers of John Knox more than all the assembled armies of Europe!"

So the next time you see an aimless young person (or feel aimless yourself), pray that God will produce a burden within. The world is full of needs, and there is one that each person is perfectly suited to meet.

PRAYER: Dear Lord, I pray that each of us would have the gift of a burden. Introduce this passion into the lives of the confused and aimless today. Amen.

June 23

LEAVING A LEGACY

A GOOD MAN LEAVES AN INHERITANCE TO HIS
CHILDREN'S CHILDREN, BUT THE WEALTH OF THE
SINNER IS STORED UP FOR THE RIGHTEOUS.
PROVERBS 13:22

IN ECCLESIASTES 3, Solomon talks about seasons. There is a time to live, a time to die, a time to rejoice, and a time to mourn. There is also a time to step aside and let others climb the ladder you have built. This is one of the most difficult things you can do, especially if you started with nothing. However, there's a season to teach your successor the ropes, there's a season to walk with him, and then there's a season to hand over the reins.

One of the most effective outcomes of the Mighty Men phenomenon has been passing the reins to the next generation. I don't know how many men I've met who, with joy and a tear in their eye, have told me that they've finally handed over their business to their children.

You will not live forever, and you cannot continue your work in perpetuity. So do it in a way that will allow you to leave a lasting legacy. And eventually, give your successors the opportunity to show you and, more importantly, God, what they can do with what you've given them. You may not be a business owner, but there may be new seasons in your relationship with those you lead where they might need to stretch their wings and fly.

PRAYER: Dear God, keep me from becoming too attached
to what we've built together. Allow it to live beyond me,
in the capable hands of my successors. Amen.

June 24

BE OF GOOD COURAGE

WAIT ON THE LORD; BE OF GOOD COURAGE, AND HE SHALL
STRENGTHEN YOUR HEART; WAIT, I SAY, ON THE LORD!
PSALM 27:14

IN ALL my years of farming, I have learned that an impatient person will never make a successful farmer. I've seen them come—and I've seen them go. Farmers have to wait for the rain, we have to wait for the harvest, we have to wait for the calves to be born, we have to wait for the chickens to grow . . . we have to wait. And the way to do this is to apply the lessons of the Bible in our lives.

We are in a long-distance race in this life, not a sprint. And if we refuse to take in spiritual sustenance, we are going to fall short. I encourage you to pause, refresh, and take a breath before you make a drastic decision such as changing your job or giving up on a business venture. In short, when in doubt, don't do anything in haste. More often than not, things will turn around.

A farmer doesn't pick fruit that's still green. We wait for it to ripen properly before harvesting. This principle can be applied in many other ways too. If you say that you've prayed, but the Lord has not answered your prayers, perhaps His answer is "no" or "wait." So let us wait on the Lord. He will give us direction, renew our strength, and supply our hope.

∞

PRAYER: Lord, give me the patience and fortitude
to see You working in my life. Amen.

June 25

STAYING THE COURSE

LET US NOT GROW WEARY WHILE DOING GOOD, FOR IN DUE
SEASON WE SHALL REAP IF WE DO NOT LOSE HEART.
GALATIANS 6:9

GOD WILL use any person prepared to stay the course, to run the race, to never let go of his or her vision. If we revisit history we'll see that God doesn't always use the best; He uses those who are available.

When He told Moses to take the Israelites out of Egypt, for example, Moses complained that he couldn't speak properly because he stuttered. God helped him with this issue (Ex. 4). And we remember that Jesus used Peter, an uneducated fisherman, to head up the church when Christ returned to heaven after the resurrection (John 21:15–19).

Some of the most successful people I've ever met don't have university degrees. They're disciplined individuals who get up in the morning and work hard, who don't back down or let discouragement defeat them.

Today's verse is one of my favorite passages in the Bible. We will be rewarded if we do not lose heart, says the Lord. We need to keep up our standards, treat everyone with dignity and fairness, and lead by example. I see tremendous possibilities, and what wonderful opportunities you have to make a difference. Go out and do your part, no matter how insignificant it may seem.

PRAYER: God, thank You for using people who show up. I am available!
Please allow me to be part of what You are doing on this earth. Amen.

June 26

BIRDS OF A FEATHER

AS IRON SHARPENS IRON, SO A MAN SHARPENS
THE COUNTENANCE OF HIS FRIEND.
PROVERBS 27:17

"**YOU WILL** never see an eagle flying with a flock of turkeys." This expression conjures up an image that might make us smile, but at the same time there is a lot of truth in it.

We are always associated with the company we keep. That is why it is very important to know the person whom you vouch for very well. Someone will give him a job or opportunity on your recommendation, thinking that if he is a friend of yours then he must be trustworthy. Your reputation is at stake, so recommend wisely. George Washington said, "Associate yourself with men of good quality if you esteem your own reputation; for it is better to be alone than in bad company."

As Christians we need to keep good Christian company. In that way we sharpen each other and challenge each other to live like Jesus. But it is also true that we cannot isolate ourselves from non-Christians. We must operate in the world because that is where the harvest field is! The balance is found in being "in the world, but not of the world" (see Matt. 13:49).

Jesus said, "He who is not with Me is against Me, and he who does not gather with Me scatters abroad" (Matt. 12:30). Let us make sure that we are keeping company with our greatest and best Friend of all. Fly with the eagles and you will find yourself soaring to great heights!

PRAYER: God, bring me into a good flock, where I can be with
people who inspire greatness and faithfulness. Amen.

June 27
THE WAY WE OUGHT TO LIVE

THE FLOWERS APPEAR ON THE EARTH; THE TIME OF SINGING HAS
COME, AND THE VOICE OF THE TURTLEDOVE IS HEARD IN OUR LAND.
SONG OF SOLOMON 2:12

I ONCE drove in the beautiful and majestic Drakensberg mountains in South Africa. I had to pull over to the side of the road because there was a huge herd of cattle walking up the road to another grazing point. As I sat there, it was as if the Holy Spirit said to me, "You see, Angus, this is what Christianity is like."

As these beautiful animals walked past, I saw that they were absolutely immaculate, all large and healthy and a beautiful deep red color. Their conformation was impeccable. They were well fed, and their coats were shining in the beautiful autumn sun.

Then came young oxen, walking up together, and right at the back of the herd came the bull. He held his head high; it seemed as if he was so proud of his herd. As they walked past me, I realized that it is so easy when we are involved in the work of the Lord to miss the Lord of the work. I saw Jesus in those magnificent animals; I saw His hand of creation in the countryside.

Sometimes we feel alone, striving to serve the Lord frantically or to get through the storms of life. But really, we are part of a majestic herd, led by the Author of the gospel and the Artist behind creation. Let us spend more time resting and taking in God's beautiful earth, enjoying the order and setting He has constructed for us.

PRAYER: Dear God, Your creation is magnificent. Thank
You for my place in it and in Your herd. Amen.

June 28

EXTRAVAGANT FEATS

THE SPIRIT OF THE LORD SHALL REST UPON HIM, THE SPIRIT OF
WISDOM AND UNDERSTANDING, THE SPIRIT OF COUNSEL AND
MIGHT, THE SPIRIT OF KNOWLEDGE AND OF THE FEAR OF THE LORD.
ISAIAH 11:2

HOW WAS it that David, a young boy with a leather sling and five stones, could slay a powerful giant and seasoned warrior (1 Sam. 17)? How was it that a shepherd could go to the pharaoh, who was regarded as a god, and tell him to let God's people go (Ex. 5)? How was it that Moses was able to take the Israelites through the desert and open the sea when they needed to get across to escape the Egyptians (Ex. 14)? They were able to do these things because they believed God's Word.

What is the difference between them and us? Absolutely nothing! The same blood that flowed through their veins flows through yours. There's nothing stopping you from being used by God to perform similar miracles; all you have to do is believe and follow Him.

Scripture has the power of an atom bomb, fueled by the will of God. If your vision doesn't scare you, it's not big enough! We are called to attempt something so big that apart from the power of God, it will fail. Charles Studd wrote, "Real Christians revel in desperate ventures for Christ, expecting from God great things and attempting the same with exhilaration."

PRAYER: Lord, fill my heart with passion to attempt
something outrageous for You! Amen.

June 29

THE LAMPSTAND

THUS SAYS THE LORD: "I REMEMBER YOU, THE KINDNESS OF
YOUR YOUTH, THE LOVE OF YOUR BETROTHAL, WHEN YOU WENT
AFTER ME IN THE WILDERNESS, IN A LAND NOT SOWN."
JEREMIAH 2:2

OFTEN THE Holy Spirit is represented by the symbol of oil. When we pray for the sick at Shalom, we always anoint them with oil and remind them that it represents the Holy Spirit. There is no power in the oil itself; it is purely a symbol of the Holy Spirit.

The Holy Spirit is the oil that lights your lamp. If you want your lampstand to burn brightly and light up your life, be full of the Holy Spirit. He gives us the strength and power to accomplish whatever God has called us to do. If you are feeling very weary, as if you have nothing left to give, or if you don't feel like getting up in the morning, your oil supply is running low. If Jesus is not enough in your life, then you are going to dry up and burn out. That's because we give of our overflow of Spirit—not from our very substance. Of course, the overflow comes from the time we spend with Jesus.

In order for us to be the light of this dark world, we need to burn steadily for many long hours. That can only happen when we yield our lives to the Holy Spirit's unlimited power and strength by spending time with God.

Do not wait until your oil runs out. Repentance and returning to your first love, Christ, will bring you to a place of restoration. The Lord will restore joy and excitement in your heart, and your lampstand will be refilled.

PRAYER: God, thank You for the never-ending supply of fuel You offer.
Fill me up today, so that I can keep shining brightly. Amen.

June 30

THE LORD WILL PROVIDE

FOR THE LORD WILL NOT CAST OFF FOREVER. THOUGH HE
CAUSES GRIEF, YET HE WILL SHOW COMPASSION ACCORDING
TO THE MULTITUDE OF HIS MERCIES. FOR HE DOES NOT
AFFLICT WILLINGLY, NOR GRIEVE THE CHILDREN OF MEN.
LAMENTATIONS 3:31–33

NIGEL BUTLER organized a UK campaign we held some years back. It was his task to hire a large venue, and the Lord met the expenses in a most remarkable way. Nigel described it like this: "It all started when I received a copy of Angus's book *Faith Like Potatoes*. I finished it at midnight with tears in my eyes and immediately knew that I had to share this book with the other farmers in our prayer chain."

Nigel ordered one hundred copies of the book and distributed them as soon as they arrived. "Within a few days I was contacted by a fellow farmer who told me that he was organizing for Angus to visit and asked if I would like to arrange a venue. . . . I knew it was God's perfect timing. I contacted the biggest venue in Newbury—the Corn Exchange—and made a tentative booking. Then the bills started to arrive.

"The very next morning there was a knock on our front door. A man from British Telecom stood on our doorstep. 'You are due for a way-leave for some telegraph poles on your farm,'" he said. The telephone company owed him money for placing poles in his property.

"I stared at him in amazement. He explained that, due to an act of Parliament, I would get one hundred pounds per pole." When he left, Nigel counted his poles and found he had thirty-two on his farm. It was the exact amount he needed.

God always pays for what He orders!

PRAYER: Dear God, You are a worker of miracles. I trust in You to bring about what is needed so Your will can be done! Amen.

JULY

July 1

A LIVING SACRIFICE

PRESENT YOUR BODIES A LIVING SACRIFICE, HOLY, ACCEPTABLE
TO GOD, WHICH IS YOUR REASONABLE SERVICE.
ROMANS 12:1

ONE OF the biggest influences in my life was my aunt Peggy. She was a dear old lady who lost her leg to diabetes, had blood pressure problems, and suffered from other physical ailments, but even to the end she had fire in her eyes. I will never forget going to her seventieth birthday party. With her whole family present, she said she would be going full time for Jesus, and was moving out to the farm to join us at Shalom Ministries. She would accompany the ministry team into rural Africa and live with us younger folk in the most primitive conditions, often for weeks on end on our evangelistic tours. She was truly a modernday saint; never once did we hear a complaint come from her mouth.

The day before she passed away I visited her and she was still as much in love with Jesus as ever. When we spoke about death and going home to be with Jesus, her eyes shone with excitement. Yes, the old lady was more than ready to face her Maker. She had truly offered herself up to the Lord.

When you offer yourself up to Jesus, it is unconditional. It is not a temporary emotional undertaking but a daily reality. Say to the Lord, "I am giving You my life. I am putting it all on the altar, Lord. I am in it until the end." It doesn't matter if the body you present as a "living sacrifice" is weakened, ill, or beset with problems like my aunt's was. You offer yourself up—body and soul—come what may. When you do this, God will purify you with fiery trials, so that when tests come in your life, as they did in Aunt Peggy's, you will be able to cope.

PRAYER: Dear God, my body and soul belong to You. I am a
living sacrifice; take my all, and do Your will! Amen.

July 2
THE WELL-BEATEN PATH

DO NOT BE DECEIVED: "EVIL COMPANY CORRUPTS GOOD HABITS."
AWAKE TO RIGHTEOUSNESS, AND DO NOT SIN; FOR SOME DO NOT
HAVE THE KNOWLEDGE OF GOD. I SPEAK THIS TO YOUR SHAME.
1 CORINTHIANS 15:33–34

YOU MIGHT be starting something new and feel nervous and afraid of what the crowd might say. But being timid or self-conscious, or giving in to peer pressure, is not from God. It doesn't matter what people say; what matters is what God says about you. Jesus was never influenced by the crowd—He always did exactly what His Father said.

Many young people make big mistakes in their lives, not because they are "bad," but because they buckle under the pressure. They often behave irresponsibly, not because they want to, but because all of their friends at school say it's cool. The pain that can result from this is immense, something that young people often underestimate: drug addiction, alcoholism, unplanned parenthood, emotional suffering, or even death. Remember, God gave us rules for our own good—He wants us to avoid this kind of suffering. It's just not worth the price of popularity.

The same thing goes for adults. If you work in an office, for instance, and you know that there are irregularities and possibly fraud, speak up—otherwise you will be a part of the problem. Remember the saying, "Don't think you're on the right road just because it's a well-beaten path." Instead of giving in to the crowd, stand up for God, and the Lord will bless you.

PRAYER: Lord, peer pressure sneaks into my life in subtle ways
and with unintended consequences. Please make me discerning
and strong enough call it out and stand against it. Amen.

July 3

REVIVAL IS CONTAGIOUS

"I DWELL IN THE HIGH AND HOLY PLACE, WITH HIM WHO HAS A
CONTRITE AND HUMBLE SPIRIT, TO REVIVE THE SPIRIT OF THE
HUMBLE, AND TO REVIVE THE HEART OF THE CONTRITE ONES."
ISAIAH 57:15

JOHN WESLEY, a renowned English revivalist, reportedly said the definition of revival is "a people saturated with God." I think you'd agree that the world needs a re-awakening of religious fervor.

Preacher and author John Blanchard once said, "Man can no more organize revival than he can dictate to the wind." A revival has no boundaries, it has no racial groupings, it has no favorites—it is exactly like a bushfire. Revival is contagious.

Just a few weeks ago I saw something I never would have believed possible in my lifetime, when multitudes of men from every walk of life, from miners to farmers, businessmen to professional sportsmen, teachers to government ministers, came together, as ordinary people, to seek the face of God. Often it's much easier to attract women and children to hear the Word of God, but to my amazement, this crowd was only men. And God did not fail us. I have never seen so many tears and so much repentance in my life! We were challenged to be watchmen over the house, over our community, and over our nation. It was a true revival, and still continues today.

God moves in ways that we will never understand, and He will not be put in a box. I believe that God will touch every corner of the world, every sector and ethnic group, and bring the peace we so desperately need.

PRAYER: God, the spirit of revival is so mysterious,
yet so needed. Please bring it today! Amen.

July 4

THROUGH EVERY CIRCUMSTANCE

WE DO NOT LOOK AT THE THINGS WHICH ARE SEEN,
BUT AT THE THINGS WHICH ARE NOT SEEN. FOR THE
THINGS WHICH ARE SEEN ARE TEMPORARY, BUT THE
THINGS WHICH ARE NOT SEEN ARE ETERNAL.
2 CORINTHIANS 4:18

THE ISRAELITES lived an up-and-down existence when they were in the desert. They complained because they did not have water and food, so God gave them water and manna. One minute they stood in awe as God parted the Red Sea; the next minute they wished they were back in Egypt. Their faith was dependent on their circumstances, and this is certainly not the kind of faith that God wants us to have.

So many times in my career I have seen a potentially disastrous situation turn around. Many years ago, we were in financial difficulty on our farm, and we asked the Lord what to do about it. Most farmers experience this kind of difficulty at one time or another in their lives. A few of our cattle had won prizes at show, but due to our lack of funds, we reluctantly decided to offer up the whole herd for sale. We really believed that the Lord wanted us to get out of debt, and we got top prices for our animals, even though it broke our hearts to sell them. Just two weeks later, foot-and-mouth disease broke out, and you could not give your cattle away.

I really believe that the Lord undertook for us because we sought His face for direction. Sometimes you have to cut your cloth according to your pocket, and again you need to seek God for direction to know how much and when to cut. Seek confirmation from Him, and His shalom—His peace—will guide you on the right path.

PRAYER: Lord, give me faith to seek You daily, despite my circumstances. Amen.

July 5

A LESSON ON HUMILITY

THE KING SPOKE, SAYING, "IS NOT THIS GREAT BABYLON,
THAT I HAVE BUILT FOR A ROYAL DWELLING BY MY MIGHTY
POWER AND FOR THE HONOR OF MY MAJESTY?"
DANIEL 4:30

ONE OF the greatest and most successful leaders who ever lived was Nebuchadnezzar, the ruler of Babylon. They say that the Hanging Gardens, which he built for his wife, was one of the seven wonders of the ancient world. However, he boasted about his notable accomplishments, taking all the glory for himself.

Then, one day as he was standing on the balcony of his royal palace admiring all his incredible feats, he heard a voice from heaven saying, "King Nebuchadnezzar, to you it is spoken: the kingdom has departed from you! And they shall drive you from men, and your dwelling shall be with the beasts of the field . . . until you know that the Most High rules in the kingdom of men, and gives it to whomever He chooses" (Dan. 4:31–32).

Nebuchadnezzar went from being the most powerful leader in the world to going temporarily insane—acting like an ox in the field eating grass. As we read this account, it is clear that we really do walk a tightrope in this life. One minute we can be millionaires and the next minute paupers. It takes a mighty man or woman to never steal God's glory.

After seven seasons the Lord restored Nebuchadnezzar to his former position, simply because he praised and honored the King of heaven. There's nothing I love to see more than a successful person who remains humble. When asked about the three greatest virtues of religion, Saint Augustine replied, "First humility, second humility, third humility."

PRAYER: God, please make my heart humble and my motivations pure. Amen.

July 6
THE LORD IS OUR DEFENDER

THE LORD SHALL PRESERVE YOU FROM ALL
EVIL; HE SHALL PRESERVE YOUR SOUL.
PSALM 121:7

PEOPLE CAN be extremely unpredictable when the heat is on, and quick to change their loyalties depending on which way the wind is blowing. In such times it is crucial that we follow the same instructions Moses gave to the Hebrews when they were escaping Egypt: to stand still and watch the glory of God unfolding as He protects His people: "And Moses said to the people, 'Do not be afraid. Stand still, and see the salvation of the LORD, which He will accomplish for you today'" (Ex. 14:13).

Any person or group of people who tries to raise their hand against our heavenly Father or His children will always lose. Even the devil himself will fail when he attacks God's children. Why? Because if we walk with God, He will always act for us.

Exodus 14:14 says, "The LORD will fight for you," and Psalm 55:22 reads, "Cast your burden on the LORD, and He shall sustain you; He shall never permit the righteous to be moved." So we need not be afraid, for our heavenly Father is always with us.

PRAYER: God, thank You that Your victory is utterly dependable,
and that You guarantee final victory for Your children! Amen.

July 7

BLESSINGS FROM GOD

"AND IT SHALL COME TO PASS AFTERWARD THAT I WILL
POUR OUT MY SPIRIT ON ALL FLESH; YOUR SONS AND YOUR
DAUGHTERS SHALL PROPHESY, YOUR OLD MEN SHALL DREAM
DREAMS, YOUR YOUNG MEN SHALL SEE VISIONS."
JOEL 2:28

JESUS SAID, "The Spirit of the LORD is upon Me, because He has anointed Me to preach the gospel to the poor; He has sent Me to heal the brokenhearted, to proclaim liberty to the captives and recovery of sight to the blind, to set at liberty those who are oppressed" (Luke 4:18). This anointing fueled everything Jesus did.

And this anointing of the Holy Spirit is absolutely critical for Christians to fulfill the calling of God on their lives. Without it, we operate like history teachers. We know the Word of God, we memorize scriptures, we know the stories in the Bible, but there is no power evident in our lives.

Elisha recognized the importance of the anointing (2 Kings 2). You'll remember that Elisha wanted only one thing—a double portion of Elijah's anointing. He persevered and never gave up until Elijah had blessed him. If you study the Word of God, you will observe that Elisha performed twice as many miracles as Elijah. God answers prayer. If Jesus Christ is at the center of your life, you will receive the power of the Holy Spirit and be an effective witness for Him in the world. Yes, Jesus is more than enough for those who will take the time to wait on Him for the anointing of the Holy Spirit.

PRAYER: Father, I pray for Your anointing; I long for the holy vision You rained down on Elisha and on Christ—the kind that produces real life! Amen.

July 8
LIVING YOUR VISION

"WRITE THE VISION AND MAKE IT PLAIN ON
TABLETS, THAT HE MAY RUN WHO READS IT."
HABAKKUK 2:2

I LOVE reading biographies and autobiographies, especially those about men and women who have completed their lives here on earth and have finished strong. It is a huge statement that we make to the world when we complete a task we set out to do. Of course, it works the other way around too: when we don't finish what we set out to accomplish, it's a tremendous discredit to us and our Lord.

At so many Christian conferences I've attended the speakers are fantastic, the ideas are wonderful—life-changing even—but when the conference is over, everybody goes back and carries on as they did before. Instead, let's take a cue from today's verse and write down our vision, to make it plain and bring it to life.

The next step is to complete the task—to knuckle down and get things done. Then we can be a testament of follow-through to this dying world. We could show this by being disciplined in our eating habits, in our sleeping habits, in our physical training habits, and most importantly, in spending time in the presence of God.

PRAYER: Lord, there is always need for more discipline and clearer vision in my life. Guide me as I write down what You've asked me to do, and as I act on it consistently. Amen.

July 9

FIGHT YOUR FEAR

"FEAR NOT, FOR I AM WITH YOU; BE NOT DISMAYED, FOR I AM
YOUR GOD. I WILL STRENGTHEN YOU, YES, I WILL HELP YOU,
I WILL UPHOLD YOU WITH MY RIGHTEOUS RIGHT HAND."
ISAIAH 41:10

MY WIFE and I went on holiday once near a beautiful mountain. I wanted to climb to the top, so I started along the contour path at its base. The higher I got, the narrower it became. Eventually I came to a place where the mountain fell away in a sheer drop on one side of me. Fear took over. I looked up and saw that I only had another forty yards or so to go in order to reach the top of the mountain. But I was frozen in place, unable to move. I had to make a choice: let the spirit of fear overcome me or press on in faith.

Eventually I decided to continue. I asked the Lord to give me strength and I carried on walking, just putting one foot in front of the other. Within fifteen minutes I was standing on the top of the mountain, absolutely exhilarated. I felt as if I were standing on top of the world!

When I had spent some time on top of the mountain and got used to the height, I walked down past the place where I had frozen as if out for a Sunday afternoon stroll. It was still the same path, but I had changed. I had won. We can thank God that He "has not given us a spirit of fear, but of power and of love and of a sound mind" (2 Tim. 1:7). He allows us to walk past our fears one step at a time.

PRAYER: God, thank You for taking away our fear. When I panic or freeze, help me to keep going, trusting in Your provision. Amen.

July 10

RELENTLESS LOVE

THE LORD YOUR GOD IN YOUR MIDST, THE MIGHTY ONE, WILL SAVE;
HE WILL REJOICE OVER YOU WITH GLADNESS, HE WILL QUIET YOU
WITH HIS LOVE, HE WILL REJOICE OVER YOU WITH SINGING.
ZEPHANIAH 3:17

THE CROSS and the Switchblade is the story of David Wilkerson and Nicky Cruz. Wilkerson was a preacher who started a ministry in New York after reading a report on the young boys involved in the city's gang problem.

Cruz was the leader of a notorious gang and was feared even by the police. His home background couldn't have been much worse: he grew up with seventeen siblings to parents who practiced witchcraft. Cruz endured severe mental and physical abuse, which filled him with rage. By age fifteen he was living on the streets.

Wilkerson felt a great burden for Cruz, even though Cruz spat on him, beat him up, and even threatened his life. Wilkerson told Cruz, "You could cut me in a thousand pieces and lay them out in the street and every piece would love you." Wilkerson risked his life to show Nicky something he'd never known before: relentless love.

Nicky said that for weeks he couldn't stop thinking about it. One night he showed up at one of Wilkerson's crusades and gave his life to the Lord. Cruz left the gang, enrolled in Bible college, and has spent his life working with troubled youth.

Let us not judge people by their present performance. Never close the door on them. The Lord seems to delight in turning big troublemakers into powerful men and women of God.

PRAYER: Jesus, thank You for Your redeeming, relentless love. Show me how to pass it on to the ones who are desperately in need of it. Amen.

July 11

SLAY YOUR GIANT

"I AM WITH YOU, SAYS THE LORD."
HAGGAI 1:13

KING SAUL and his warriors were completely intimidated and hypnotized by the giant Goliath. The more Saul and his soldiers focused on Goliath, the more convinced they became that he could not be defeated.

David, a ruddy-faced, teenage boy with a sling, was totally unaffected by the huge bully. This young man had been spending time with God on the mountain as he looked after his father's sheep, and he knew God could defeat any enemy. He took his sling and five stones and, rejecting the king's armor, walked fearlessly down the valley. There he faced Goliath, showing him no respect whatsoever. He taunted, "Who is this uncircumcised Philistine, that he should defy the armies of the living God?" (1 Sam. 17:26).

At that very moment, I believe, the battle was over. Before David flung the first stone, Goliath was already dead.

How big is the giant in your life today? It doesn't matter what form it takes: it could be financial trouble, your health, your marriage, or trouble with one of your children. God is bigger than any problem you might have. Keep going. It takes courage, but God says, "Fear not, for I have redeemed you; I have called you by your name; You are Mine" (Isa. 43:1).

PRAYER: Lord, the giants in life can be so terrifying. Give me boldness like David today, and confidence that You have already defeated them. Amen.

July 12

UNEXPECTED FAVOR

"REJOICE GREATLY, O DAUGHTER OF ZION! SHOUT, O
DAUGHTER OF JERUSALEM! BEHOLD, YOUR KING IS COMING
TO YOU; HE IS JUST AND HAVING SALVATION, LOWLY AND
RIDING ON A DONKEY, A COLT, THE FOAL OF A DONKEY."
ZECHARIAH 9:9

ONE OF the lowliest creatures in the animal kingdom is the donkey. He has a cross imprinted on his back—dark fur in a line down his spine and across his shoulders. The animal that God chose to carry His Son into Jerusalem is, therefore, a very noble beast, even though he is lowly.

I'll never forget an elderly gentleman who would sometimes catch a lift with me years ago. Whenever we passed a group of donkeys, he'd raise his hat and salute them. When I asked him why he did that, he replied, "Son, because that animal is the one that carried my Savior into Jerusalem."

All God wants us to do is to trust Him. We may feel weak and lowly, like the donkey, but God has a plan for us, and He is the one who enacts it—not us. We often have to be made very low in order to realize God's true power to work through weakness. I don't believe that God brings devastation upon people, but He does allow devastation to come upon us sometimes so we might take notice of where we are. If you're going through hard times at the moment, take heart, be patient, and trust God to make use of it all.

PRAYER: Lord, I'm amazed at the way You redeem what
the world would look over. Even when I'm laid low, I pray
that You'll lift me up as a vessel for You. Amen.

July 13
THE FAITH TO SAY NO

"LET YOUR 'YES' BE 'YES,' AND YOUR 'NO,' 'NO.' FOR WHATEVER
IS MORE THAN THESE IS FROM THE EVIL ONE."
MATTHEW 5:37

I ALWAYS thought that it took courage to say yes to God's call to give our possessions to the poor or go into the mission field. However, as I get older I realize it takes more faith to say no sometimes. It takes immense courage to swim against the current, to stand up and say, "No, not me and my family; we don't do that, we serve the Lord." We often shake under the fear of man. Such fear might persuade you not to speak out against evil and to instead go with the flow. But the brave stand has eternal benefits!

I was invited to hold a Christian campaign a few years back where a very important rugby match was due to take place. One of the teams wanted to come to the outreach meeting, which was happening at the same time as the match. These young men told the management that they wanted to play on Friday evening so they could attend the meeting on Saturday. They stood their ground, and the match, which was set in stone months before, was changed. A great victory!

Before the meeting started, I asked the team in question to stand. I said, "Chaps, that score will be forgotten about a week from now, but the stand you took will never be forgotten."

PRAYER: Jesus, I pray for the discernment and bravery to say no when I am being sucked down a path that is not Your will. Please remove distractions from my line of sight, and show me when to put my foot down. Amen.

July 14
SEA OF FACES

"TO YOU WHO FEAR MY NAME THE SUN OF RIGHTEOUSNESS
SHALL ARISE WITH HEALING IN HIS WINGS; AND YOU SHALL
GO OUT AND GROW FAT LIKE STALL-FED CALVES."
MALACHI 4:2

WHEN PREACHING, I regularly see miracles, signs, and wonders. I witness incredible healings take place, for which I am eternally grateful to God. I've seen people get out of wheelchairs and walk. I've seen the sick healed. I hear the beautiful music, and see wonderful praise and worship with people dancing in the stands. For me, however, the climax is the altar call.

Sometimes even before I finish speaking, people are already coming forward in search of God. It's so moving to see hundreds of people standing at the altar weeping, carrying heavy burdens. But after we pray the Sinner's Prayer and I look into their faces, I see a completely different crowd. One moment the sea of faces shows pain, suffering, and turmoil; the next moment elation, peace, joy, hope, and a new beginning. People are laughing and smiling and crying with joy because Jesus has taken away their burdens. And that is the reason why I preach the gospel of Jesus Christ—to see lives transformed in the twinkling of an eye.

I would exhort anyone who's given their life to the Lord to go and tell at least three people as soon as you can. There is just as big a sea of faces in your life, and you could be the witness that turns them from weeping to joy. Let us nail our colors to the mast, not being ashamed of who we are in Christ.

PRAYER: Lord, only You have fully transformative power. I long to
see You act in the lives of those I encounter today. Amen.

July 15

INVEST IN HEAVENLY THINGS

"DO NOT LAY UP FOR YOURSELVES TREASURES ON
EARTH, WHERE MOTH AND RUST DESTROY . . . BUT LAY
UP FOR YOURSELVES TREASURES IN HEAVEN."
MATTHEW 6:19–20

THERE WAS once a wealthy church lady who had an estate with a garden, a swimming pool, and an exquisitely furnished house. Her housekeeper had little, and she lived in a tiny room at the back of the mansion. But she was a grateful woman who spent much of her time in prayer for her mistress, her nation, her family, and the lost.

One day the housekeeper died and went to heaven, and a few years later her mistress followed. Saint Peter met her at the gate. Near the gate the streets were paved with gold and lined with large mansions. The trees beside by the beautiful river were heavy with fruit. Saint Peter pointed out the most magnificent home and said, "That is where your old housekeeper now lives." The lady was so excited, thinking that hers would be even greater.

They carried on walking. Soon the houses grew smaller and smaller, and the gold road became silver, then tarmac, then gravel, then a rustic track. There were quaint little dwellings on either side of the road.

Eventually Saint Peter stopped in front of a small, cozy house. Still, the lady was devastated. "How is my housekeeper living in a mansion when I have this?" Saint Peter replied, "This is all the material you sent up to heaven with which we could build your home here. Your housekeeper invested in things that moths cannot destroy, but you sent me very little."

PRAYER: Lord, in each decision I make, help me to invest in heavenly
things, and not in things that rust and fade away. Amen.

July 16

LIVING IN UNITY

BEHOLD, HOW GOOD AND HOW PLEASANT IT IS FOR
BRETHREN TO DWELL TOGETHER IN UNITY!
PSALM 133:1

ONE SUNDAY afternoon, my youngest son was short-staffed but needed to bring in a large herd of cattle from an outlying field. He asked me to help him, and of course I said I'd give him a hand. As I saddled up my horse, I saw my young grandson Josiah, just four years old, being mounted on a horse for his first ride on his own. His huge horse stood approximately sixteen hands high, and this little fellow was on its back, showing no fear. My son was so proud of him! The three of us went out together and brought in that large herd of cattle.

Later, the Lord laid the following on my heart: the importance of family, the importance of teamwork, and the importance of prayer. (After all, the family that prays together stays together.)

If we get these things right, each working together and supporting each other in our roles, we will see prosperity. Unity and teamwork in our family speaks volumes to those who observe us. Let us be thankful for our families, for friends, and for our blessings. Of course, there will always be challenges to face, but God has given us people to help us, and He is training us for future endeavors.

Jesus said, "These things I have spoken to you, that in Me you may have peace. In the world you will have tribulation; but be of good cheer, I have overcome the world" (John 16:33). This means we can take heart, be positive, work hard, and continue to faithfully do our best to honor God in everything we do.

PRAYER: God, thank You for placing us in communities. Show me when
to give and ask for help from the precious ones in my life. Amen.

EVERLASTING LIFE

IN HIM WAS LIFE, AND THE LIFE WAS THE LIGHT OF MEN.
JOHN 1:4

RICK WARREN said, "Life on earth is a temporary assignment." I believe that. Death awaits us all. However, for the believer, it is just passing on to a better place, to the reward that Jesus has waiting for us. He says in His Word, "In My Father's house are many mansions; if it were not so, I would have told you. I go to prepare a place for you" (John 14:2).

Just consider these beautiful words from Eliza Hewitt:

Sing the wondrous love of Jesus,
Sing His mercy and His grace;
In the mansions bright and blessed
He'll prepare for us a place.
When we all get to heaven,
What a day of rejoicing that will be!
When we all see Jesus,
We'll sing and shout the victory!
While we walk the pilgrim pathway,
Clouds will overspread the sky;

But when trav'ling days are over,
Not a shadow, not a sigh.
Let us then be true and faithful,
Trusting, serving every day;
Just one glimpse of Him in glory
Will the toils of life repay.
Onward to the prize before us!
Soon His beauty we'll behold;
Soon the pearly gates will open;
We shall tread the streets of gold.

PRAYER: Lord, my heart longs for my home in heaven. Please guide me as I walk in faith toward the day when I meet You there. Amen.

July 18
BURY YOUR DIFFERENCES

HATRED STIRS UP STRIFE, BUT LOVE COVERS ALL SINS.
PROVERBS 10:12

CARRYING OFFENSES with us is like carrying a 110-pound bag of cement on our backs all day long. It doesn't affect the person who has caused the offense; instead, it hurts us. The way we overcome offense is by love.

Love covers all sin. First Corinthians 13 speaks very clearly of the power of love: It never gives up. Love never loses faith. Love is always hopeful, giving the benefit of the doubt. Love endures through all.

If you're having a problem with your spouse, with your children, or with your parents, dig that hole, bury the offense, and walk away. Love unconditionally. The time we have on earth is too short to carry grudges.

It can help to look at things from the others' point of view. This would at least help you understand why they behave the way they do. Often it's due to fear, and they're taking it out on the ones they love. The correct way to respond is not by throwing more fuel on the fire and retaliating. Instead, be understanding and forgiving. That will defuse the situation, and you'll earn their respect.

PRAYER: Dear God, help me to respond to offense in a way that honors You. Please heal the wounds, and give me the strength to walk away. Amen.

July 19
SAVED BY THE LAMB

"BEHOLD! THE LAMB OF GOD WHO TAKES
AWAY THE SIN OF THE WORLD!"
JOHN 1:29

THE WHOLE gospel message comes down to one very important act: the Lamb of God died to take away the sins of the world. Jesus came to earth and lived like one of us. He was persecuted, tortured, and hung on a cross by the hand of man. He suffered and died in order to save us, to give us eternal life. Isn't that incredible? The Son of God died to save you and me!

We cannot save or sanctify ourselves, and we cannot redeem the world; that is the sovereign work of God. Therefore we must focus on what God has done for us and not our earthly experiences.

Our walk with Jesus is not a gradual relationship, but rather one of obedience. We commit ourselves to believing and obeying His ways because He makes us totally forgiven and free. Our relationship with Jesus is not based on philosophy or reasoning, but rather simple obedience and belief in the Lord Jesus Christ as our Savior.

However, if we turn away from God, if only for a second, sin can move in again. Therefore we must be careful of becoming wise and arrogant. We must not think ourselves clever or better than others, because it is only by God's divine grace that we can have faith in Him.

PRAYER: God, thank You for Your miraculous sacrifice for us. Guide my relationship with You to grow in trust each day. Amen.

July 20

MENTORS

YOU, BELOVED, BUILDING YOURSELVES UP ON YOUR
MOST HOLY FAITH, PRAYING IN THE HOLY SPIRIT, KEEP
YOURSELVES IN THE LOVE OF GOD, LOOKING FOR THE MERCY
OF OUR LORD JESUS CHRIST UNTO ETERNAL LIFE.
JUDE VV. 20–21

AN INTERESTING incident took place at a game reserve in South Africa some years ago. Young bull elephants were running riot, attacking other animals and generally causing havoc. It did not take long for the authorities to realize that the reason for their behavior was because they had been relocated to the reserve without any mature males to teach them how to behave. They had no role model—no one to follow and emulate. The old patriarchs were brought in, and the young elephants settled down before long.

I cannot overstate the urgent need in the Christian world for mentors, men and women of God who are prepared to stand up and be counted, to take on our responsibility, whatever the cost. The goalposts are continually being moved and the rules being bent, and our young people are confused. There are few today who can say with the apostle Paul, "Imitate me, just as I also imitate Christ" (1 Cor. 11:1).

My prayer is that the Holy Spirit would make Christian men and women aware of the vital role they play in teaching and guiding the younger generation. May God have mercy on us if we lead them astray. We have an awesome responsibility to lead by example. Younger men and women watch us closely. We must never buckle under pressure, always being aware that we represent our Lord and Master, Jesus Christ.

PRAYER: Lord, please point out to me how I may be consciously
and unconsciously mentoring the younger generation. Show
me how to be an intentional good example. Amen.

July 21
THE RIGHT MIND-SET

THEREFORE HUMBLE YOURSELVES UNDER THE MIGHTY HAND
OF GOD, THAT HE MAY EXALT YOU IN DUE TIME, CASTING
ALL YOUR CARE UPON HIM, FOR HE CARES FOR YOU.
1 PETER 5:6–7

YOU CAN have the right job, a good income, and a loving family, but if you don't have the right mind-set, you're in trouble.

You see, the devil is hell-bent on making you panic. He wants to force you onto the back foot and have you functioning in crisis mode. He wants you going from one problem to another, instead of sitting down and saying, "Stop! This far and no further!" He doesn't want you to take a deep breath, study the situation more closely, and go to your friends and ask them for good godly counsel before making your decision.

You'll never achieve anything if you're constantly racing around, dealing with emergencies. A good friend who will sit down, have a cup of tea with you, and listen to your woes is so valuable. Share your burden. Spend time with and invest in genuine, godly friends.

Always bring along your life manual—your Bible. All the answers are in there, even regarding your health, peace of mind, loved ones, and self-esteem. So let's get our priorities right with the help of God's instruction manual and our Christian friends.

PRAYER: God, show me how to invest in my friends and
the things that make us strong for You. Amen.

July 22
A LIFESTYLE OF WORSHIP

"GOD IS SPIRIT, AND THOSE WHO WORSHIP HIM
MUST WORSHIP IN SPIRIT AND TRUTH."
JOHN 4:24

WORSHIP IS a lifestyle. It is not just singing worship songs to the Lord on a Sunday morning for half an hour, then again at a midweek meeting. That is only the tip of the iceberg.

We worship God by the way we live. Men and women have dedicated their lives to Jesus throughout the ages, leaving their comfort zones and their homes. They have gone into the mission field because they love God, and they have done it as an act of worship.

We founded our home for children as an act of worship to the Lord, and the fragrance of Jesus permeates the place. We receive such love from God through those precious children, and we see Jesus responding to our worship through them.

We cannot out-bless the Lord. We are called by God to worship Him in spirit and in truth. When we do that, the Lord speaks back to us in more ways than one. An act of worship is done out of love for Him, not so that you may receive something. You worship God by the way you treat your spouse, by the way you sow money into the kingdom, by acts of grace, by forgiving people who've hurt you, by praying, and by taking up your cross daily and following Him.

Worship is saying thank You to Jesus for dying on the cross for sinners like us. Worship is not determined by circumstances or situations, because it is an expression of your personal relationship with Him.

PRAYER: God, make my life a constant worship service
for You. Your love is magnificent! Amen.

July 23
A NEW BEGINNING

HE SHALL COME DOWN LIKE RAIN UPON THE GRASS BEFORE
MOWING, LIKE SHOWERS THAT WATER THE EARTH.
PSALM 72:6

WHEN THE grass in our gardens gets long, we take the lawn mower and cut the lawn. After this, the grass sometimes looks as though it is absolutely devastated. But if we fertilize it right away, and if the rain comes down from heaven, new growth comes up and looks so much better than before.

Sometimes we feel like freshly mown grass that doesn't look so good. Maybe you have just been diagnosed with a terminal disease. Maybe you have lost a loved one and you don't know if you can carry on anymore. Trust that the Lord is going to send rain from heaven. It will stimulate you to live again. In fact, you will live better than before.

When we go through a testing time and we think we will never recover from it, God reassures us that we will. Mowing and fertilization may feel violent and unpleasant, but in due season God will send refreshing, invigorating rain from heaven, rain full of goodness and grace. Just keep talking to Him and keep the door open.

Remember that our God is a good God. He is for you, not against you. So go out today and say, "Lord, I am expecting a new beginning!"

PRAYER: Jesus, I rely on You to bring freshness and new growth. When I am dry and withering, I wait dependently on Your miraculous mercy. Amen.

July 24

ONE WHO TELLS THE TRUTH

THEN JESUS SAID TO THOSE JEWS WHO BELIEVED HIM, "IF YOU
ABIDE IN MY WORD, YOU ARE MY DISCIPLES INDEED. AND YOU SHALL
KNOW THE TRUTH, AND THE TRUTH SHALL MAKE YOU FREE."
JOHN 8:31–32

WHAT IS the moral temperature of our nation? One only has to turn on the television to see ordinary commercials that border on soft pornography. A few years ago those advertisers would have been summoned to court and prosecuted for the blatant immorality that they display on television. And I am not even taking movies into consideration!

I think the blame must be put fairly and squarely at the door of the church, because we're not telling the whole truth. We're not shooting straight, as they say. We're acting as if anything goes—for example, that what we watch on television doesn't affect us—leading people to believe that all roads lead to heaven. But, the Bible is very clear: Jesus says that He is the *only* way, the truth and the life, and that no one gets to the Father except through Him (John 14:6).

We must get back to basics by telling the truth as the Lord Jesus Christ told it. There is no other god, save the God of Israel. There is no other way, save the way of Jesus.

God's not asking us to make as many friends as we can. He is asking us to be upstanding, so that when people come to us they hear the truth, even when they don't like it. The object of our walk on earth is to be ambassadors for Jesus Christ, and a good ambassador is one who tells the truth.

PRAYER: Lord, I want no part of watered-down truth. Help me to tell
it like it is, with love, and without fear or equivocation. Amen.

July 25
DELEGATED POWER

"DO YOU NOT KNOW THAT I HAVE POWER TO CRUCIFY YOU?" . . .
JESUS ANSWERED, "YOU COULD HAVE NO POWER AT ALL
AGAINST ME UNLESS IT HAD BEEN GIVEN YOU FROM ABOVE."
JOHN 19:10–11

TO HAVE authority, one needs to be under authority. Think of the story of the centurion who sent someone to Jesus to ask Him to pray for his servant who was sick. Jesus sent back the reply that He was coming, and the centurion replied not to come; Jesus could just say the word and his servant would be healed. The Lord said He had never seen faith like that in all of Israel (Luke 7:9). Because the centurion was himself a man of authority, he understood the power of authority.

Authority doesn't just come with a certain rank. It comes when people respect you—and in order to gain respect, you have to be able to do your job. The same thing applies in the home. There is no point in telling your children not to drink alcohol when you drink, or not to smoke when you smoke forty cigarettes a day. They'll disregard what you say, and the chances are good that they'll end up smoking and drinking just like you.

Put things in perspective by understanding where our authority ultimately comes from. If God has placed you in a position of authority, exercise it in a godly manner. When people love you and respect you, they will do anything for you.

It is also advisable to have people in place who can correct or redirect you if necessary—to give you some accountability. Submit yourself to others who can direct you. This will keep you grounded.

Remember, if you want to have authority, you must operate with a humble spirit.

PRAYER: Lord, cause me to recognize and use wisely the
authority You've given me, whatever it may be. Amen.

July 26
A CHOSEN VESSEL

THE LORD SAID TO HIM, "GO, FOR HE IS A CHOSEN
VESSEL OF MINE TO BEAR MY NAME BEFORE GENTILES,
KINGS, AND THE CHILDREN OF ISRAEL."
ACTS 9:15

THE MORE Paul preached, the more trouble came his way—especially toward the end of his ministry. He was persecuted by the temple priests; stoned, whipped, and left for dead; shipwrecked, jailed, misrepresented, and betrayed. Yet he kept going.

There are times when I don't feel like fulfilling my call. Circumstances, financial pressures, frayed relationships, increased responsibilities, and expectations from people can wear a person down. Sometimes it feels as if people are asking for something all the time, and I always seem to be on the giving end. I'm sure you have experienced the same thing.

As the pressure mounts, let's remember that the sole reason we live for Christ is because of our relationship with Him. Jesus must be enough, otherwise we are not going to follow through to the end.

Perhaps you are struggling with a tremendous task. Some of you might be in the middle of a difficult marriage and you just don't feel like going on with it. Remember your covenant to God. You must see it through. You may have laid down everything for the Lord and it hasn't turned out the way you thought it would. Your ministry is not bearing fruit. You feel like throwing in the towel. Don't do it. Just around the corner is the most incredible victory you have ever dreamed of.

We must look to Jesus, the Author and Finisher of our faith. When we do everything as "unto Him," we will be able to overcome any problem.

PRAYER: Dear God, I am honored that You've chosen me as Your vessel, though I am broken, tired, and sometimes empty. Please keep me going for You. Amen.

July 27

WALK IN FORGIVENESS

"BLESSED ARE THOSE WHOSE LAWLESS DEEDS ARE
FORGIVEN, AND WHOSE SINS ARE COVERED; BLESSED IS
THE MAN TO WHOM THE LORD SHALL NOT IMPUTE SIN."
ROMANS 4:7–8

GOD TELLS us to forgive. Why? This is not for anyone else's sake, but for ours. Unforgiveness has dreadful side effects. It leads to bitterness, hatred, and death.

There is not a man or woman of God who has not been hurt by other Christians, organizations, or people in general. If we want God to use us, we have to learn to forgive. All of us "have sinned and fall short of the glory of God" (Rom. 3:23). Therefore, forgiveness is essential.

The Holy Spirit often prompts me to ask people who come for prayer whether they are harboring unforgiveness towards someone. I've seen people freed from many physical ailments once they have learned to forgive. As we are forgiven, so we must learn to forgive in order for our daily lives and relationship with Jesus Christ to flourish.

It may seem like an impossible task, but we can do all things through Christ who strengthens us (Phil. 4:13). He can restore that which the "locusts" have tried to destroy if we put Him first in our lives (see Joel 2:25). Jesus can make a relationship sweeter than it was before. If you feel you cannot trust your loved ones because of what they have done to you, trust Jesus to make the difference.

PRAYER: Dear Lord, please point out any unforgiveness that lies dormant in my heart. Show me what to bring to You today, that I might be freed. Amen.

July 28
PATIENT AND FAITHFUL

WE OURSELVES BOAST OF YOU AMONG THE CHURCHES OF GOD
FOR YOUR PATIENCE AND FAITH IN ALL YOUR PERSECUTIONS AND
TRIBULATIONS THAT YOU ENDURE . . . THAT YOU MAY BE COUNTED
WORTHY OF THE KINGDOM OF GOD, FOR WHICH YOU ALSO SUFFER.
2 THESSALONIANS 1:4–5

NOWHERE IN the Bible does the Lord promise that the going will be easy when we
follow Him. On the contrary, He says, "If anyone desires to come after Me, let him
deny himself, and take up his cross, and follow Me" (Matt. 16:24). However, God is
faithful, and we may confidently trust in His promise to see us through.

Our faithfulness and patience go hand in hand. In the twenty-first century,
many people are not prepared to wait for God to fulfill His promises in their lives.
Taking things into our own hands will yield disappointing results, but patience will
show us a plan far beyond what we could imagine ourselves.

David Livingstone, who helped abolish the slave trade, knew about waiting for
God and trusting His faithfulness. Although he personally led very few people to
Christ, he stood on Psalm 126:5–6, which reads, "Those who sow in tears shall
reap in joy. He who continually goes forth weeping, bearing seed for sowing, shall
doubtless come again with rejoicing, bringing his sheaves with him."

Livingstone knew that his work would one day yield a beautiful harvest.
Without the sowing, there can be no reaping; so we must be patient and rely on
God through our trials.

PRAYER: God, though I sow in tears, may I reap in joy. Help
me have patience and faith in Your larger plan. Amen.

July 29
EVERYDAY GODLINESS

KEEP BACK YOUR SERVANT ALSO FROM PRESUMPTUOUS SINS; LET
THEM NOT HAVE DOMINION OVER ME. THEN I SHALL BE BLAMELESS,
AND I SHALL BE INNOCENT OF GREAT TRANSGRESSION.
PSALM 19:13

CHRISTIANS ARE under a huge magnifying glass. The whole world is watching us to see what our next move will be. That is exciting, but at the same time it can be a bit daunting, don't you think? Nonbelievers can do whatever they like and nobody cares, but as soon as a believer does something remotely questionable, it's in the headlines.

It's so important to take precautions for godly living. When I travel overseas and I speak at big meetings, I never travel alone. I learned that from Billy Graham. He only ever met with women, other than his wife, in a public place—never in private. It's the honorable thing to do. I also don't touch any of the funds that come into our ministry. Other people take care of the finances.

If you are going out to do God's work, go two by two. Why? So you can watch out for, encourage, and pray for one another. Don't go into the lions' den alone; that's why you have the body of Christ.

Every time I start a meeting, whether in a big stadium or a small church, I get on my knees and I pray because I want my words to be godly. Lift up the name of Jesus and He will draw people to Himself. If we remain humble, we allow the Holy Spirit to pour over us and do the work of saving lives.

PRAYER: Lord, show me how to be blameless in daily life.
Though I'm only human, help me use the tools You've put in
place so I can be a shining example to others. Amen.

July 30
CONTROL YOUR CHARACTER

MANY ARE THE AFFLICTIONS OF THE RIGHTEOUS, BUT
THE LORD DELIVERS HIM OUT OF THEM ALL.
PSALM 34:19

WE SUFFER for different reasons—sometimes for our poor decisions, but not always because of sin in our lives. Our Lord Jesus Christ Himself suffered greatly, and there was absolutely no sin in His life. So we too, as His creation, must be prepared to suffer if we are to grow.

When we go through unfortunate or difficult times, we sometimes lose our standing with the people around us. They may judge us and accuse us of causing our own suffering through our sin. But if we compromise our standing with God during our time of suffering just so that we can keep the favor of the world, then we may lose everything. One cannot both run with the hares and hunt with the hounds. Circumstantial failure does not disqualify us; it is character failure that disqualifies us.

We cannot control or hope to control our circumstances, but we can control our character and the choices we make during times of difficulty. It is in times of great trial that our character is truly put to the test. We need to stand strong as children of God and remain firm in our faith. The Bible says, "We know that all things work together for good to those who love God, to those who are the called according to His purpose" (Rom. 8:28).

PRAYER: God, when things are at their worst and I come up
against embarrassment, please help me to keep my character
and dignity. I believe You'll get me through it. Amen.

July 31

THE FAMILY OF GOD

FOR THERE IS NO DISTINCTION BETWEEN JEW AND GREEK, FOR
THE SAME LORD OVER ALL IS RICH TO ALL WHO CALL UPON HIM.
ROMANS 10:12

A FEW years ago my wife, Jill, and I had the privilege of going to Israel. There we drove up to the Mount of Beatitudes, where Jesus delivered His incredible Sermon on the Mount found in Matthew 5–7.

After spending some time there, we started walking back toward the car park. Near the big gates was a little portable shop. The vendor was a man probably in his midsixties with dark brown skin. He had a long, snow-white, drooping moustache and a hook nose. He asked where we were from, and we told him South Africa.

Not knowing whether he was an Arab or a Jew, I asked him, "Sir, what nationality might you be?" He looked at me through big brown eyes and said, "I am a believer."

You see, when "anyone is in Christ, he is a new creation; old things have passed away; behold, all things have become new" (2 Cor. 5:17). When we follow Jesus Christ, we become one people, one nationality, one race group, one family. That's what the man in the little stall was trying to tell me.

God says that we must pray for His people, and His people are Chinese, isiZulu, Scottish, Russian, Indian, Scandinavian, Swiss, Masai, female and male, young and old, rich and poor. All who profess Jesus Christ as Lord and Savior belong to the family of God.

PRAYER: Lord, remind me to pray for my brothers and sisters in Christ
across the world. May I never forget that our faith makes us family. Amen.

AUGUST

August 1

GOD BLESSES PEOPLE, NOT PROGRAMS

THOUGH I HAVE THE GIFT OF PROPHECY, AND UNDERSTAND
ALL MYSTERIES AND ALL KNOWLEDGE, AND THOUGH I HAVE
ALL FAITH, SO THAT I COULD REMOVE MOUNTAINS, BUT HAVE
NOT LOVE, I AM NOTHING. AND THOUGH I BESTOW ALL MY
GOODS TO FEED THE POOR, AND THOUGH I GIVE MY BODY TO
BE BURNED, BUT HAVE NOT LOVE, IT PROFITS ME NOTHING.
1 CORINTHIANS 13:2–3

I AM all in favor of a disciplined church life and of being a good timekeeper (although I battle with this myself). For Nelson Mandela, the first black president of South Africa who spent twenty-seven years in jail, time was not his master. He always had time to talk to people, to ask someone how they were, to inquire after their family.

Programs never governed Jesus—He always had time for people. To make time for others is to show them love. Likewise, it is important for Christians to spend time with Jesus Christ in order to share His heart. Merely staying busy with a church program will not carry you to your destination; only your relationship with Jesus will do that.

May we let the Lord Jesus Christ be God, not only in our lives, but also in our homes, businesses, and churches. I have learned not to put God on a schedule. I am not suggesting for one moment that there is no order in the kingdom of God. Our God is indeed an orderly God. But, at the same time, as we make our programs, schedules, and plans, we must be flexible and allow the Lord to do whatever He wants with our time.

PRAYER: Lord, as I endeavor to be disciplined and organized, keep me attuned to You so that I may show love to others with the time I've been given. Amen.

August 2
LISTENING TO GOD'S VOICE

NOW THE DONKEY SAW THE ANGEL OF THE LORD STANDING IN THE
WAY WITH HIS DRAWN SWORD IN HIS HAND, AND THE DONKEY
TURNED ASIDE OUT OF THE WAY AND WENT INTO THE FIELD. SO
BALAAM STRUCK THE DONKEY TO TURN HER BACK ONTO THE ROAD.
NUMBERS 22:23

PERHAPS YOU'VE heard the outrageous Bible story about Balaam's donkey. King Balak wanted Balaam to curse the Israelites so that he would be able to defeat them. But the Lord said to Balaam, "You shall not go with them; you shall not curse the people, for they are blessed" (Num. 22:12).

However, Balaam didn't listen. He was on his way to Balak when the donkey he was riding refused to continue along the road, for an angel had appeared. Balaam couldn't see the angel and beat the donkey with a stick when she wouldn't move the way he wanted her to. Eventually the Lord opened the donkey's mouth, and she asked Balaam, "What have I done to you, that you have struck me these three times?" (v. 28). The donkey was simply obeying the Lord.

Some of us are so hard of hearing that God allows catastrophe in our lives to make us wake up and pay attention. Why must we learn the hard way? God may forgive us, but we will always carry those scars. Developing a sensitivity to God's warnings is one of the most valuable things we can do.

Balaam eventually listened to God. Balak offered Balaam gifts to prophesy that the nation of Israel would fall. And you know something? Balaam wouldn't. I aspire to be like Balaam and turn from stubbornness to obedience.

PRAYER: Lord, if I am going the wrong way, please do whatever
You must to get me back on track! Give me the grace to take
correction and the wisdom to alter course. Amen.

August 3
THE FRAGRANCE OF CHRIST

WE ARE TO GOD THE FRAGRANCE OF CHRIST AMONG THOSE WHO
ARE BEING SAVED AND AMONG THOSE WHO ARE PERISHING.
2 CORINTHIANS 2:15

WHEN SPRING comes to our farm, I can smell the orange blossoms in the orange grove, the aroma of the bush. And when we have a bit of gentle rain, the smell of the earth gives off a fragrance that is so invigorating.

We too, as believers in this dry and dusty world where the love of Christ seems so sparse, are asked by God to give off the fragrance that comes in the form of hope, joy, and faith in God. This is what a dying world is looking for: hope in Jesus and hope for the future.

In order to be that fragrance, we must be prepared to be crushed. It's only when one is crushed, as the petal of a rose is crushed, that the strongest fragrance is released. We have to be honest about our struggles is in order to be the perfume of God to the world.

People are looking for the truth. So often, however, because we fear man's response, we are not prepared to tell the truth as it is written in the Word of God. When this happens, our fragrance dissipates and becomes inconsequential.

Paul said that to one we are the aroma of death, while to another we are the aroma of life (2 Cor. 2:16). To one who denies Christ, the gospel judges; but to another, it saves. When you start to live and preach the truth of Christ, the ones who are ready to hear the Word will catch the fragrance.

PRAYER: Lord, help me to give off the aroma of
Your Spirit in everything I do. Amen.

August 4
YOUR HEAVENLY HELPER

I WILL LIFT UP MY EYES TO THE HILLS—FROM WHENCE
COMES MY HELP? MY HELP COMES FROM THE LORD, WHO
MADE HEAVEN AND EARTH. HE WILL NOT ALLOW YOUR FOOT
TO BE MOVED; HE WHO KEEPS YOU WILL NOT SLUMBER.
PSALM 121:1–3

WHO IS your helper? When you turn on the television and you listen to the news, what do you see and hear? There is a meltdown taking place in the world today— economically, environmentally, politically. You start to wonder if there is a future for your children. What hope is there left for the world?

I am just a simple farmer, but I want to tell you that the Lord Jesus Christ, the greatest Friend who has ever lived, has been with me in my darkest times. Today He says, "Fear not, for I am with you; be not dismayed, for I am your God. I will strengthen you . . . I will uphold you with My righteous right hand" (Isa. 41:10).

Jesus Christ has never let me down. He is more than my Helper; He is my Protector. He is the one who looks after my wife when I am away overseas preaching. I know that she is safe because He stations His angels around our home. I want to encourage you today to start concentrating on what Jesus says about you and not on what is going on in a world gone mad.

Let's pray and refocus. I am so excited to be alive, because the best is yet to come—the Master is coming in all His glory. So take heart, be of good cheer, because the Lord has promised never to abandon us.

PRAYER: Lord, I know there has been discord on this earth
every day since the Fall in the garden. Help me to look
forward to a day when all is made right again. Amen.

August 5

UNKNOWN FRONTIERS

HE SAYS: "IN AN ACCEPTABLE TIME I HAVE HEARD YOU, AND IN
THE DAY OF SALVATION I HAVE HELPED YOU." BEHOLD, NOW IS
THE ACCEPTED TIME; BEHOLD, NOW IS THE DAY OF SALVATION.
2 CORINTHIANS 6:2

THE DICTIONARY definition of a *frontier* is the limit of knowledge in a particular field. In other words, when you move beyond the known, you are stepping into frontier territory.

An unknown frontier can be a scary place. It can make you feel vulnerable. That is a good thing, because when we are vulnerable, we run to God.

Life is full of challenges. Children of three or four years of age face a huge challenge when they set off for preschool. Leaving their mother for the first time is a tremendous frontier. Old age is a challenge. So is starting an apprenticeship, receiving a retirement package, or getting married.

How do we face new frontiers? How do we face unknown territory in this life? The answer is very simple: by putting our hand in the hand of the Lord, living one day at a time, and realizing that Jesus is all we need.

We can carry on doing what Jesus has told us to do, knowing full well that our reward is not here on earth, but is awaiting us in glory. So keep on keeping on, rejoicing in the fact that our names are written in the Lamb's Book of Life. There is no frontier, no unknown, no uncharted territory we need to fear if we know that Jesus Christ is with us.

Make sure you are walking with your hand in the hand of the greatest Conqueror who ever lived.

PRAYER: Dear God, when I embark on a new journey into unknown territory, please lead me through my fear and on to the promise You've given. Amen.

August 6
MAKING DECISIONS

COMMIT YOUR WORKS TO THE LORD, AND YOUR
THOUGHTS WILL BE ESTABLISHED.
PROVERBS 16:3

WHEN YOU make a decision, there are three powers involved—the Lord, the devil, and human nature. The devil will try everything in his power to lead you astray and defeat you, preying on your human failings. Accordingly, when you make a decision, make sure you always consult the Lord first.

The devil will tell you that you will never amount to anything, that you are useless and have no hope. Combat that lie by knowing who you are in the Lord and begin to think of yourself the way He does. In Him you are beloved, treasured, and holy. If you know who you are in Christ and you know who the devil is, then you will be prepared for attacks. Be cautious because he is the father of all lies. He might try to make you think that something is the Lord's will when really it is his.

When you make a decision, ask yourself one question: What would Jesus do? The only way to know for sure whether it is the Lord telling you to do something is to spend time with Him in the Word every day. Eventually, if it is the Lord, you will have peace in your heart. You will be certain because you know that this is what God has called you to do. Once you have your answer, do it with all your heart. If God tells you to do something—once you are sure the instruction is from Him—act confidently.

PRAYER: Dear God, I ask that You grow my decision-making
ability and make it attuned to Your will. Amen.

August 7

THE BADGE OF THE BELIEVER

WALK IN LOVE, AS CHRIST ALSO HAS LOVED US AND
GIVEN HIMSELF FOR US, AN OFFERING AND A SACRIFICE
TO GOD FOR A SWEET-SMELLING AROMA.
EPHESIANS 5:2

THE BADGE that you and I wear as believers is summed up in one word: *love*. And we have access to the most powerful element in the world: endless, perfect love. Perfect love casts out all fear (1 John 4:18). The Bible says that ordinary people will love somebody who loves them, but Christians are to love those who hate them (Matt. 5:44). That's another thing entirely—something that can only happen through the power of God in our lives.

Let me tell you the story of Billy Bray. He was a miner and a tough boy. Billy became a Christian, then went on to build three churches in Cornwall, England. He used to stand on a stone wall at the market and preach. The story goes that one day a big, tough miner came up to him and told him to stop preaching, otherwise he would punch him. Billy told him that Jesus loved him, and that he could be saved by grace. With that, the man knocked Billy off the wall.

Billy got up, his mouth full of blood, and spat out some teeth. He got back on the wall and starting preaching with more fervor, more power, and more courage. The man hit him a second time. Billy got back on the wall and told the man, "Jesus still loves you."

The big miner couldn't take it anymore; he fell to his knees. "Billy, tell me about your Savior," he said. That day another man was saved for the kingdom. There is no power on earth more powerful than love.

PRAYER: God, I crave more of Your love. Thank You for the endless supply
You give us, and help me to show it to others in sacrificial ways. Amen.

August 8
LOOKING FOR A HERO

THE THINGS WHICH YOU LEARNED AND RECEIVED AND HEARD AND
SAW IN ME, THESE DO, AND THE GOD OF PEACE WILL BE WITH YOU.
PHILIPPIANS 4:9

WHAT ARE the characteristics of a hero? Young people especially look for a hero who is a winner, someone who is successful in his or her field. But a true hero should be humble and meek, since meekness is controlled strength. He must know where he's going and be prepared to get there whatever the cost. He must also be holy—honest and reliable; sincere and dependable. He is an overcomer; one who rises to the challenge; and one who is fearless, irrespective of the mountain before him.

One significant characteristic of a hero is a willingness to lay down his life for others. You have probably heard the story of the little boy whose sister was dying of leukemia. She had a rare blood type, and he was the only match that could be found. After being asked if he would donate his blood, he asked for some time to think. He agreed to the procedure in order to save his sister's life. As the doctor began, the little boy asked, "How soon until I start to die?" He thought that giving his blood to his sister would kill him.

I have walked this earth for some years now, and I have never found a hero who comes close to Jesus. He has redeemed me and given me a brand-new life. He has washed away my sins and healed me physically, spiritually, and emotionally. Let us, as men and women of God, emulate Jesus and be the heroes and heroines that the world so desperately needs.

PRAYER: God, shape in me a hero's heart today. Amen.

August 9

A PURPOSE FOR LIVING

KNOW THAT THE LORD, HE IS GOD; IT IS HE WHO
HAS MADE US, AND NOT WE OURSELVES; WE ARE HIS
PEOPLE AND THE SHEEP OF HIS PASTURE.
PSALM 100:3

DO YOU have a purpose in life? Your purpose is what should get you out of bed in the morning. If you have no reason to get up, then what do you have to live for?

Mark Twain said, "The two most important days in your life are the day you are born and the day you find out why." If you don't have a purpose in life, ask God to show it to you. It doesn't have to be a massive vision; start small and God will promote you when the time is right.

Often one hears of highly successful businesspeople who dream of buying a cottage down by the sea where they can retire, slow down, have fun, and enjoy life. However, people like this are used to having a purpose. They retire and keep themselves busy by going fishing or taking long walks on the beach. They do this for a few weeks and then get bored because they miss the sense of purpose their work gave them. But in the Christian life, with the Lord's work, there's no such thing as "retirement." If one is in Christ, life just gets more exciting as one grows older; God gives us more and more insight into why we were put on this earth.

A. W. Tozer, who was a great man of God, said that "God made us for Himself; that is the first and last thing that can be said about human existence and whatever more we add is but commentary." God made us for Himself, for His purpose; and all that's left for us is to find out what it is. Ask God and He will give you a purpose for living.

PRAYER: Lord, please clarify my purpose and make my heart
beat for it, and for the fulfillment of Your will. Amen.

August 10
WASHED IN RIGHTEOUSNESS

YOU DIED, AND YOUR LIFE IS HIDDEN WITH CHRIST IN GOD.
COLOSSIANS 3:3

JESUS, EVEN though He was the Son of God, was obedient in all His Father required of Him. When He came from Galilee to be baptized in the Jordan by John the Baptist, John told Jesus that he wasn't worthy to baptize Him (Matt. 3:14).

Even though this was true, the Lord said, "Permit it to be so now, for thus it is fitting for us to fulfill all righteousness" (Matt. 3:15). Is that not a good enough reason for every believer to be baptized? I'm not talking about the dedication that takes place when a baby is born; I'm talking about full submergence in and through the waters of baptism—a public, adult decision. If Jesus was baptized, we need to be baptized too.

The pull of tradition is strong, but the living Word of God is stronger. Baptism is so much more than a tradition; it's a symbolic act that makes public our acceptance of God's cleansing and rebirth. Quite simply, it confirms to the world and to ourselves what has taken place within us spiritually. You're never too old, and it's never too late; speak with your pastor and see what can be arranged. If you have already been washed in the waters, encourage those you love or mentor in the faith to take that step too.

Serious Christianity is getting back to the Word of God and doing what the Bible says, not what we think it says, or what tradition may interpret the Word of God to say. If Jesus says that we're to go into all the world, preach the gospel, make disciples, and baptize them in the name of the Father, the Son, and the Holy Spirit, let's not leave out a single step!

PRAYER: Lord, thank You for the rebirth You gave us through our baptism.
I pray that all Your children would experience it to the full. Amen.

August 11
CHARITY BEGINS AT HOME

"HONOR YOUR FATHER AND YOUR MOTHER, THAT YOUR DAYS MAY BE
LONG UPON THE LAND WHICH THE LORD YOUR GOD IS GIVING YOU."
EXODUS 20:12

I WAS recently reading through the book of Exodus and came across the commandment in today's verse. Then, in the next chapter we read, "And he who curses his father or his mother shall surely be put to death" (21:17). Anyone who struck his or her father or mother was put to death according to the law of Moses. It was a crime so severe that it warranted the ultimate punishment. God takes honoring parents seriously.

Children, remember that your parents, no matter how they treat you, are still your parents. Honor them according to the Word of God so that you will live long in the land. If we turn to the book of Matthew, Jesus said, "You say, 'Whoever says to his father or mother, "Whatever profit you might have received from me is a gift to God"—then he need not honor his father or mother.' Thus you have made the commandment of God of no effect by your tradition" (Matt. 15:5–6).

You cannot give your money to the church while your parents struggle. You cannot say, "I am serving the Lord; my parents must find a way on their own." I believe this verse in Matthew is saying that charity begins at home. We have a responsibility to start at home first; then we can reach out to others in need. The Lord tells us to get our priorities in order; we must look after those who are our responsibility, and then give any money left over to the church—not the other way around. Let's listen to what God says and obey Him.

PRAYER: Lord, thank You for my parents. Help me show patience,
love, forgiveness, and respect to them at every chance. Amen.

August 12
STILL THE STORM

LET THE PEACE OF GOD RULE IN YOUR HEARTS, TO WHICH
ALSO YOU WERE CALLED IN ONE BODY; AND BE THANKFUL.
COLOSSIANS 3:15

THE LORD Jesus warned us that we would have trouble in this world, but that He would be our peace (John 16:33). True peace can only come from God in us. We need to be the kind of Christians who still the storm rather than fan the fire.

The Lord did not say blessed are the peace lovers, but the peacemakers. Sometimes in order to make peace we need to sacrifice our wants for the good of another. Husbands and wives, it takes two to tango. Bring peace into the home because your children are watching. You don't always have to have your own way in the home. Does it really matter if the new curtains are red or blue, or how the dishes are done, as long as you have house to live in and a family to love?

Remember—peacemaking does not mean compromising our faith just to avoid conflict. Peace comes from a clear conscience, from doing what is right, from calling sin by its name, from having the courage to lead your loved ones on the path of righteousness. We cannot find this peace from our business, money, fame, our family, the government, or even tranquilizers!

Matthew 6:33 reads, "But seek first the kingdom of God and His righteousness, and all these things shall be added to you." May God bless you as you focus on Jesus and spend time with the Prince of Peace.

PRAYER: God, please open my eyes to opportunities to promote peace today, whether at work, in my family, in my community, or on a larger scale. Amen.

August 13
MAKING THE RIGHT CHOICES

"I COMMAND YOU TODAY TO LOVE THE LORD YOUR GOD, TO WALK
IN HIS WAYS, AND TO KEEP HIS COMMANDMENTS, HIS STATUTES,
AND HIS JUDGMENTS, THAT YOU MAY LIVE AND MULTIPLY; AND
THE LORD YOUR GOD WILL BLESS YOU. . . . THEREFORE CHOOSE
LIFE, THAT BOTH YOU AND YOUR DESCENDANTS MAY LIVE."
DEUTERONOMY 30:16, 19

OUR LIVES consist of a series of choices. When we obey the Lord, He blesses us.
When we disobey God, we separate ourselves from Him. God's will is like a big
umbrella: when we are underneath it, we are safe; but when we go out from under
it, the rain falls down and we are on our own.

If you look at your life and see a lot going wrong, consider where you are
disobeying God. The Lord says that if you obey the Word of God you will prosper.
Obey His Word and you will be blessed. Disobey His Word, and it will inevitably
bring strife (Rom. 6:23). Life is not always fair, but God is good. Nourishing rain
falls on the believer and the unbeliever, and so does the hail; but God always gives
His children a way through the storm, because He walks with them through it. So
in your choices, get back to basics: love your fellow man and love the Lord your God
with all your mind and all your might. I promise you that your life will change.

When things aren't going well, fight the instinct to run away or blame God. Go
back to the drawing board. Do what the Word says and turn to Christ, and all of a
sudden you will have an abundance of grace and righteousness (Rom. 5:17).

PRAYER: Lord, please bring my attention to areas in which
my choices have separated me from You. Draw me back
to You, and set me on the right track. Amen.

August 14
FERVENT PRAYER

PRAY WITHOUT CEASING.
1 THESSALONIANS 5:17

IT IS said of Martin Luther that the busier he became, the more time he spent in prayer. The more responsibilities he had to shoulder, the earlier he got up in the morning. But with us it is often the opposite: the busier we become, the less time we spend in prayer. When you think about it, it's completely nonsensical!

Remember how much time you spent in prayer when you first gave your life to Jesus? How much did your faith grow in that time? And why should we not have the same energy now? Prayer is a basic ingredient of our faith for a reason: we need it to survive.

As today's verse says, we have to pray continually. Ever since becoming a believer I have prayed on the hoof, so to speak: on my horse, in the pickup, in the fields—it has become a way of life. Continuous prayer might take discipline at the start, but after a while it becomes a beautiful way to live, and a hallmark of a vital relationship with the Lord.

There are different types of prayer. There is corporate prayer, when we pray together. There is intercessory prayer, when we stand in the gap and pray for a certain situation or person. The prayer I am speaking about, however, is personal prayer—prayer between one believer and God.

God designed prayer to be as natural for a Christian as breathing. If this does not describe your prayer life, take heart and keep at it. Prayer is not just talking; it is also listening, waiting upon God. Remember the saying, "When men work, they work. But when men pray, God works."

PRAYER: Lord, please revitalize my prayer life with You. I long for
our conversation to flow naturally and intimately. Amen.

August 15
A FRIEND OF THE CARPENTER

IN HIM WE HAVE REDEMPTION THROUGH HIS BLOOD, THE
FORGIVENESS OF SINS, ACCORDING TO THE RICHES OF HIS GRACE.
EPHESIANS 1:7

THERE WAS once a circuit preacher who went from town to town, preaching the Word of God. Out on the great prairies one day, he was caught in a dust storm. As he took cover under his saddle blanket, he fell asleep and had a dream.

An angel of the Lord came and said, "You have died, and I have been sent to direct you."

The preacher said, "What's that big book you've got in your hand?"

The angel said, "It's a register of people who are going to heaven."

The preacher asked, "Well, is my name there?" The angel checked the book and said, "Sir, your name is not here." The preacher was devastated. "It must be there. I'm a preacher and I gave my life to Jesus years ago."

So the angel took the preacher to stand before God. Once there the preacher heard a voice like thunder: "Who are you? What do you want here?"

The preacher was terrified. Just then he felt big, strong carpenter's hands lifting him to his feet, and a voice said, "Father, it's all right. He's one of My friends."

God said, "All right, My Son. Let him in."

This dream serves to illustrate the heavenly results of grace. Because Jesus loved us so much and paid the full price for our sins, we can honestly say, like the preacher, that we belong to Him. When we get to heaven, God will not see us, but rather Jesus standing in front of us. His unlimited grace is our only way to heaven.

PRAYER: Jesus, I am forever grateful for Your grace! Amen.

August 16
IT STARTS WITH YOU

BE AN EXAMPLE . . . IN WORD, IN CONDUCT, IN
LOVE, IN SPIRIT, IN FAITH, IN PURITY.
1 TIMOTHY 4:12

I READ a book that quoted a camel herder in Kenya as saying, "When you can put your Church on the back of my camel, then I will think that Christianity is meant for us Somalis." Our faith has to be practical if it's going to be effective, especially among the younger generation.

Church on Christmas Day and Easter and the odd funeral or wedding is just not enough. Our Christian belief has to be simple and straightforward enough for everybody to understand. Don't just tell people that Jesus loves them—show them. People must be able to relate to your faith and see it in action.

Christianity is not something that happens inside a building. It is what happens inside a person's heart and is lived out in day-to-day life—even on the back of a camel. Fancy cathedrals or churches are nice, but the essence of our faith has nothing to do with all that. Jesus is glorified when He lives in the hearts of Christians and enables them to live in a loving and winsome way.

You can't force people to become Christians; they must want to become Christians because they long for the peace, joy, and contentment that you have. If they see those traits in your life, free of hypocrisy or acting, then it's easy to introduce them to Christ.

PRAYER: Dear God, help me to communicate my faith in a
real, practical way to those I meet every day. Amen.

August 17
JESUS CHRIST IS THE WORD

"SO SHALL MY WORD BE THAT GOES FORTH FROM MY MOUTH; IT
SHALL NOT RETURN TO ME VOID, BUT IT SHALL ACCOMPLISH WHAT I
PLEASE, AND IT SHALL PROSPER IN THE THING FOR WHICH I SENT IT."
ISAIAH 55:11

GOD'S HOLY Word is our guide and compass in this turbulent life. Without it we would lose our way completely. We have the ability to choose who and what we listen to; if something anyone says or preaches does not line up with the Word of God, then we know to disregard it completely.

Jesus Himself quoted the Word when He was tempted by the devil in the desert, exposing the devil's lies. He promised, "Heaven and earth will pass away, but My words will by no means pass away" (Matt. 24:35). His words still go on far beyond the "wisdom" of the world.

So let's give thanks for the privilege of having God's Word as our light, and for our ability to weigh everything in our lives against it. Slow down, reflect, and take your time in the Word. We don't have to make rash decisions or hasty plans, allowing ourselves to be pressured into making decisions that could later on cost us dearly. Instead, our heavenly Father desires prayer and earnest seeking before committing to anything. If you are in any doubt, wait!

PRAYER: God, thank You for my compass—Your Word. Show
me how to slow down and follow it today. Amen.

August 18
THE SPOKEN WORD

**THE TONGUE IS A LITTLE MEMBER AND BOASTS GREAT THINGS.
SEE HOW GREAT A FOREST A LITTLE FIRE KINDLES!**
JAMES 3:5

I WAS fascinated to see a group of Jewish men speaking the Word of God in an airplane when I was on my way to Israel some years ago. They put a shawl over their heads, just as Jesus would have done when He walked into the synagogue. Then they opened up the Torah—the first five books of the Old Testament—and started to speak the Word of God aloud. The group walked up and down the aisles as they spoke the Word over the airplane. Just about every terrorist group in the world wants to target El Al Airlines, but I felt so safe that day because of the power of the spoken word.

Words have such impact in our lives; the power of the tongue can build up or break down. For instance, the headmaster of the school I attended told my mother that she should take me out of school because I would never amount to much. Those negative words impacted my life for many years because I believed them, until I met the Lord. He changed everything. When I started to believe His Word, it changed my thinking radically. What an amazing difference His Word has made in my life—it was truth that defeated a lie.

The same can be true for you. Negative spoken words or curses can be broken by the Word of God, which speaks light and life. There is dynamic power in the spoken Word of God. I encourage you to use the gifts that are within you to use the power of words so that you can have a fulfilled life in Christ.

PRAYER: God, guide me in the use of words. May I always
use them to build and never to destroy. Amen.

August 19

NEW LIFE

ACCORDING TO HIS MERCY HE SAVED US, THROUGH THE WASHING
OF REGENERATION AND RENEWING OF THE HOLY SPIRIT.
TITUS 3:5

PEOPLE SOMETIMES pretend that all you have to do to become a Christian is to stop drinking, stop swearing, start paying your income taxes, treat your family properly, hold down a regular job, and change your behavior a little.

But where does it say that in the Scriptures? The Bible says in Romans 10:9, "If you confess with your mouth the Lord Jesus and believe in your heart that God has raised Him from the dead, you will be saved." Faith comes before actions.

It is by faith that we are saved. Remember the night when Paul and Silas were put in jail (see Acts 16:23–34)? The jailer was supposed to look after them, but an earthquake shook the jail, freeing the prisoners.

The jailer was about to commit suicide because he thought he'd lost the prisoners, when Paul said, "Do yourself no harm, for we are all here." The jailer fell to his knees and asked, "Sirs, what must I do to be saved?" Paul said, "Believe on the Lord Jesus Christ, and you will be saved, you and your household" (vv. 28–31).

Faith is belief, but faith has feet. It's a doing word. When you're born again, when you come into a living experience with the Lord Jesus Christ, of course there must be change. After the jailer was saved, the Bible says the jailer took them straight to his house that night. He cleaned their wounds, and he and his whole family were baptized. There must be genuine change once you are born again—so much more than spruced up behavior.

PRAYER: God, I thank You that Your salvation reaches deep within,
far beyond external symptoms, and right to my heart. Amen.

August 20

THE FATHER OF THE FAITH

LET US DRAW NEAR WITH A TRUE HEART IN FULL ASSURANCE
OF FAITH, HAVING OUR HEARTS SPRINKLED FROM AN EVIL
CONSCIENCE AND OUR BODIES WASHED WITH PURE WATER.
HEBREWS 10:22

FAITH IS what God treasures most in His children. James 2:23–24 says, "'Abraham believed God, and it was accounted to him for righteousness' . . . You see then that a man is justified by works, and not by faith only." This and many other similar verses say exactly the same thing—that faith is very important to God.

Abraham is the only man in the Bible who is called a friend of God. How do you think he earned this title? He wasn't a perfect man, because twice he offered up his own wife as his sister in order to save his own neck (Gen. 20:2, 12:13). So why was he called a friend of God? Because Abraham was a man of faith. He was a successful farmer, but when God told him to leave everything and go to an unknown destination, he didn't hesitate (Gen. 12:1–4). He had faith in God's promise to give him a son, and God finally gave him a son by the name of Isaac. When God requested Abraham to give Isaac back, Abraham didn't question the Lord (Gen. 22). That is complete and utter faith. God was so touched that He called Abraham His friend.

When we pray, it's often just one-way traffic: us talking to God. But with Abraham it was a two-way street; he loved and obeyed God, and listened to His voice. He really was the father of faith. I want to encourage you to increase your faith so that God can call you His friend.

PRAYER: Lord, allow me to increase my faith and
obedience to You in every area of life. Amen.

August 21

TILL HE COMES

"SO HE CALLED TEN OF HIS SERVANTS, DELIVERED TO THEM
TEN MINAS, AND SAID TO THEM, 'DO BUSINESS TILL I COME.'"
LUKE 19:13

MAYBE YOU are facing an overwhelming test in your life right now and you feel as if you've come up empty-handed, unable to see a solution. Everywhere you look you see the pressure mounting. It is at such times that you can turn to the wisdom in the parable of the talents. In Luke 19:13, the Lord gave a very simple command: "Do business till I come."

This can serve us in even the most daunting tasks. When Moses stood before God at the burning bush (Ex. 3–4), God said, "I want you to lead My people, Israel, out of Egypt and into the promised land." Moses faltered, asking, "But Lord, what if they don't believe me?" God replied, "What is that in your hand?" Moses answered, "A staff." So God told him to use what he had to persuade the people, and with it he performed wonders.

God is saying to you and me, "What have you got in your hand?" He is not asking what have we *not* got. He says, "Use what you have. Do business till I come." It is by faith that we please God and by faith that God opens up the resources of heaven for our disposal.

It's not by our abilities; otherwise we'd be tempted to steal God's show. As we live each day, taking one day at a time, let us determine to do business God's way, in His power, until He comes.

PRAYER: Lord, I thank You for being gracious enough to work with what I have to give. Alone it's not enough, but with You anything is possible. Amen.

August 22

SALT OF THE EARTH

"YOU ARE THE SALT OF THE EARTH; BUT IF THE SALT
LOSES ITS FLAVOR, HOW SHALL IT BE SEASONED?
IT IS THEN GOOD FOR NOTHING BUT TO BE THROWN
OUT AND TRAMPLED UNDERFOOT BY MEN."
MATTHEW 5:13

SALT IS essential for life; our bodies cannot exist without it. Jesus tells us that we need to become more like salt—more Christlike. "Salty" people have a sense of loyalty, durability, fidelity, usefulness, and, most of all, value. One of the most remarkable features of salt is that when it has been used, it "loses itself," or dissolves. It's no longer visible, although the taste remains and adds flavor. Can you see the similarities and implications? Just as salt makes its contribution and then is gone, so we are expected to do what God has called us to do, then become invisible—drawing people not to ourselves, but to God.

When one thinks of salt, one thinks of purity. As Christians, we are called to be examples to our neighbors, our colleagues, our employers, and especially our children. As we add "flavor" to their lives by loving them with Christ's love, they will come to know that they can depend on us, and on Him. Only when we look to the Source, which is the Lord Jesus Christ, will we be able to be godly, steadfast men and women who have something positive to offer our nation.

PRAYER: Dear Jesus, I want to be salt and light to my family and all I come into contact with. Please help me to be a righteous witness for You, living my life according to Your commands. In Your precious name, I pray. Amen.

August 23
PEARLS OF WISDOM

HAPPY IS THE MAN WHO FINDS WISDOM, AND THE MAN
WHO GAINS UNDERSTANDING; FOR HER PROCEEDS ARE
BETTER THAN THE PROFITS OF SILVER, AND HER GAIN THAN
FINE GOLD. SHE IS MORE PRECIOUS THAN RUBIES.
PROVERBS 3:13–15

TODAY'S VERSE compares wisdom to priceless jewels; to a believer, wisdom brings more than riches. On the other hand, another verse says that "fools hate knowledge" (Prov. 1:22). That's why I appeal to young people to seek knowledge: glean as much as you can from those who are older than you.

On our farm we have trees that are well over thirty-five years old, planted when we bought the farm. I've told my sons to think very carefully before cutting them down. They are beautiful trees that were strategically planted for shade and shelter. It's easy to take a chain saw and cut down a tree. In fact, it would take less than half an hour to cut one down, but many, many years for it to grow back.

We often make spur-of-the-moment decisions without seeking wisdom and perspective; and sometimes these decisions are irreversible. Some other pearls of wisdom to remember: When in doubt, don't! Anything done in haste is not done in wisdom. Don't be afraid to ask your neighbor for advice. Befriend people who are godly and successful, and learn from them. Avoid the foolish.

If we want to take shortcuts, mix with unsavory people, or risk it all on get-rich-quick schemes, then we'll pay a terrible price. Stick to principles that are trustworthy and steadfast and you'll be well on your way to success.

PRAYER: Dear Lord, show me where to find the great treasure of
wisdom. Let all my decisions be informed by it each day. Amen.

August 24

SUMMER IS NEAR

"NOW LEARN THIS PARABLE FROM THE FIG TREE: WHEN ITS
BRANCH HAS ALREADY BECOME TENDER AND PUTS FORTH LEAVES,
YOU KNOW THAT SUMMER IS NEAR. SO YOU ALSO, WHEN YOU SEE
ALL THESE THINGS, KNOW THAT IT IS NEAR—AT THE DOORS!"
MATTHEW 24:32–33

THE SUBJECT of "end times" is often treated with fear and trepidation. But today's verse offers a different, refreshing visual image: it will be like a tender branch in the springtime. The Lord talks about the signs of summer being as obvious as the signs He is coming. I personally believe that we are living in the last days, but I am totally at peace. There is nothing we can do to speed up the end or slow it down. It is totally beyond our control. We can, however, make sure that our own lives are in order.

The Lord says that He is going to come like a thief in the night; we don't know the hour or the day (see Matt. 24:36–44), so we need to be prepared, going about our lives with integrity.

Many of us tie ourselves into knots worrying about things that are completely out of our control (and often never happen). God says, "Call to Me, and I will answer you, and show you great and mighty things, which you do not know" (Jer. 33:3). Being paralyzed by fear will hold us back. Let us rather commit to whatever it is we are led to do, and do it well, giving all the glory and honor to the Lord.

PRAYER: God, You are in control. I praise You that You have everything
in hand as I work out the life You've given me to live. Amen.

August 25

JESUS, THE MIRACLE WORKER

"ASK, AND IT WILL BE GIVEN TO YOU; SEEK, AND YOU WILL
FIND; KNOCK, AND IT WILL BE OPENED TO YOU. FOR EVERYONE
WHO ASKS RECEIVES, AND HE WHO SEEKS FINDS."
LUKE 11:9–10

ONE OF my favorite Bible stories is about the blind man Bartimaeus, who was determined not to give up. He had been blind from birth, and had heard about a carpenter's son from Nazareth who was coming to his village. This Jesus was a miracle worker, and the blind man had a feeling that the day had come for his miracle.

Maybe today is the day for your miracle. To lay hold of it, apply the same principles that Bartimaeus did (Mark 10:46–52). He begged Jesus to heal him, even though the people told him to keep quiet and to leave the Lord alone.

You see, when you are persistent with God, He will always respond to you. If you let others shush you or take away your resolve, you'll get nowhere. Conversely, if you are resolute and remain determined in asking God to intervene for you, you will see an answer.

The people told Bartimaeus to be quiet, but he didn't care, because he knew that this was his last chance. If Jesus of Nazareth got past him, he would never get another opportunity to see Him again; so he shouted even louder. After all, the people telling him to keep quiet couldn't heal him.

Don't worry about what other people say to you or think of you. They cannot help you—only Jesus can—so be persistent. Continue to believe God; continue to ask for your miracle.

PRAYER: God, You are the only one who can help me! I'll come to You day and night, because You're the true source of all miracles. Amen.

248

August 26
THE BREAD OF LIFE

"DO NOT LABOR FOR THE FOOD WHICH PERISHES, BUT
FOR THE FOOD WHICH ENDURES TO EVERLASTING
LIFE, WHICH THE SON OF MAN WILL GIVE YOU."
JOHN 6:27

I WAS born in central Africa, and I have been back many times to preach the gospel. We used to travel in what we called the Seed Sower truck—a huge Mercedes Benz truck rigged with a sound system and platform for preaching the gospel in often inaccessible areas. During these trips, it always amazed me that people would ask for Bibles before anything else. We've gone into many primitive areas where there are unreached people. When we ask them if they need food, clothes, or Bibles, almost without exception they ask for Bibles first. The Word of God is so precious to them that people will actually fight each other for a Bible.

On one trip we took thirty-eight thousand New Testaments into Botswana and came back with nothing. My nephew, Fraser, was almost trampled when people literally knocked him to the ground in their rush to get Bibles. There have been times when I have taken boxes of Bibles and thrown them into the crowds in an attempt to disperse them for fear of the children being hurt.

There is no substitute for the Word of God. You can feed a man and he will be hungry tomorrow. But if he receives the Word of God, he receives hope, direction, and fulfillment that will last a lifetime. Jesus is the hope of the hopeless. We have a God-given obligation to tell people about the King of Glory before we do anything else. I am convinced that as long as we keep preaching, He will supply every need we have and the needs of those who give their lives to the Lord.

PRAYER: God, Your Word is powerful and precious.
Thank You for giving us hope. Amen.

August 27
A GODLY HOME

ABOVE ALL THINGS HAVE FERVENT LOVE FOR ONE ANOTHER,
FOR "LOVE WILL COVER A MULTITUDE OF SINS."
1 PETER 4:8

WHENEVER I am not away preaching, I set every Thursday aside to counsel and pray for people. Many of them come to see me because they have family problems. Divorce is a major issue in today's world, and men and women sit and weep in my office because of their broken homes.

At the end of the day I find that the Word of God contains all the counsel I need. When we get back to basics and people run their families according to godly principles, most problems are solved.

It is very hard for spouses to love or respect each other when one party is not living up to his or her responsibility in the family; each must pull his or her weight. Jesus said husbands are to love their wives, and wives to submit to their husbands. I do not believe for one moment that because a wife submits to her husband, she is the lesser of the two. If you look at any of the patriarchs in the Old Testament—like Abraham, Moses, Isaac, or Jacob—you will find that their wives played very important roles in the formation of the nation of Israel. It is a foolish man who does not take his wife's counsel into consideration.

Parents need to set standards when their children are still young. If you allow them to do what they like, you will have insecure children. Children need boundaries, and they need to know that you love them.

The Bible is the blueprint for any successful family. Jesus created the family, and He is the final authority. Jesus' love is the essence of a godly home.

PRAYER: God, I pray Your blessings in my family, and
wisdom to live by Your principles. Amen.

August 28
LIFE'S PRIORITIES

JESUS ANSWERED AND SAID TO HER, "MARTHA, MARTHA,
YOU ARE WORRIED AND TROUBLED ABOUT MANY THINGS.
BUT ONE THING IS NEEDED, AND MARY HAS CHOSEN THAT
GOOD PART, WHICH WILL NOT BE TAKEN AWAY FROM HER."
LUKE 10:41–42

WHEN I was a young man we had an old crank telephone system. My signal was "two shorts and one long," and my neighbor's was "two longs and one short." I tell you what—we still did business, and we seemed to have more time than we have today. Today our cell phones are in our pockets and we can call anybody at any time, and yet we seem to have less time available to us.

It reminds me of the story of Mary and Martha. When Jesus came to visit them, Martha was running around trying to get everything ready, while Mary left everything and sat at Jesus' feet. Martha got so upset about doing everything on her own that she said, "Lord, do You not care that my sister has left me to serve alone?" (Luke 10:40). Jesus replied, "Mary has chosen that good part, which will not be taken away from her" (v. 42).

Jesus wasn't saying to Martha that she was wrong in working; He was talking about priorities. I encourage you to get your own daily priorities in order. First thing in the morning, sit at the feet of the Master. Visit your friends and family, because you never know what the next day will bring. When your friend is sharing something with you, switch off your phone and really listen. Don't get too busy "living" that you miss the most important part of life.

PRAYER: Jesus, thank You for the blessings in my life. Help me to put
down all distractions today and really show people love. Amen.

August 29

GREAT EXPECTATIONS

MY SOUL, WAIT SILENTLY FOR GOD ALONE,
FOR MY EXPECTATION IS FROM HIM.
PSALM 62:5

DO YOU feel that someone has let you down? Jesus can sympathize. He knew how people can disappoint us. John 2:24–25 says, "But Jesus did not commit Himself to them, because He knew all men, and had no need that anyone should testify of man, for He knew what was in man." In other words, the Lord kept certain things to Himself because He knew people are fallible. Instead, He shared His heart with His Father. I want to encourage you to do the same. That is not to say that we should not trust our fellow man, but we need to understand that everyone has limitations. No one person can carry the weight of your every need, but your Father in heaven can.

Don't put unnecessary pressure on your loved ones, expecting them to perfectly fulfill your needs, because they are only human and can only do so much. And don't forget that you're only human as well—you're not perfect and will disappoint yourself too. So when that happens, ask God for a heart of forgiveness, grace, and resilience. Place your expectations in the Lord; He will never disappoint you.

PRAYER: God, You are ultimately and unshakably dependable.
Thank You for being the one I can always lean on. Amen.

August 30
GOD IS LOVE

IN THIS THE LOVE OF GOD WAS MANIFESTED TOWARD
US, THAT GOD HAS SENT HIS ONLY BEGOTTEN SON INTO
THE WORLD, THAT WE MIGHT LIVE THROUGH HIM.
1 JOHN 4:9

THE OTHER day I was reading the account of Joseph (Gen. 37–47). He was sold by his brothers into slavery and then became prime minister of Egypt. He forgave his brothers and invited them to come out of the drought in Israel to Egypt, where he had food for them. And the Bible says that when Joseph saw his father, he came to him and hugged him, put his head on his father's neck, and wept for a long time (Gen. 46:29).

The love between a father and his son is something to behold. That love is amazing—it overcomes past hurts and even the dramatic separation that Joseph endured. There truly is power in love; and especially the love our Father has for us. It chases us across boundaries and will never fail no matter what we do. Our heavenly Father ultimately gave up His Son for us so that we might have eternal life with Him in heaven. That's how much He wants to be with us.

May we seek to reflect that love in the world. One of the most well-known chapters in the Bible is 1 Corinthians 13, which talks about love: Love is patient. It is kind. It is not proud or arrogant. We need to be quick to forgive. We need to be patient and give people a second chance. That is how God loves us.

PRAYER: God, I thank You for Your great, overwhelming love. Please
expand my heart to accept it and pour it out again. Amen.

August 31
JUST OPEN THE DOOR

"COME TO ME, ALL YOU WHO LABOR AND ARE HEAVY
LADEN, AND I WILL GIVE YOU REST. TAKE MY YOKE UPON
YOU AND LEARN FROM ME, FOR I AM GENTLE AND LOWLY
IN HEART, AND YOU WILL FIND REST FOR YOUR SOULS.
FOR MY YOKE IS EASY AND MY BURDEN IS LIGHT."
MATTHEW 11:28–30

PAUL AND Barnabas had led some Gentiles to Christ. The church in Jerusalem agreed to welcome them into the body of believers on one condition: they must be circumcised, like every Jew. But Peter objected. He pleaded, "Why do you test God by putting a yoke on the neck of the disciples which neither our fathers nor we were able to bear? But we believe that through the grace of the Lord Jesus Christ we shall be saved in the same manner as they" (Acts 15:10–11).

Peter said salvation is about acknowledging Jesus Christ as Lord and Savior, not about external rules.

Sometimes we, as believers, shut the door on unbelievers. We give them a list of laws that they have to obey if they are to become Christians. My dear friend, we don't have to tell them. When an alcoholic comes to know Jesus Christ as Lord and Savior, he will stop drinking because the Holy Spirit will compel him and give him the strength to do so.

Be careful that you don't make it too hard for people to enter the kingdom of God. Open the door and lead people to Christ. Then, when the time is right, they will increasingly obey the Word of God. Let's not force an agenda on new believers. Let's just love them.

PRAYER: Lord, how beautiful is the transformation You bring to the hearts of new believers. Help me to get out of the way and let You do Your work. Amen.

SEPTEMBER

September 1
NO SIN IN TEMPTATION

"THERE IS NOTHING THAT ENTERS A MAN FROM OUTSIDE
WHICH CAN DEFILE HIM; BUT THE THINGS WHICH COME OUT
OF HIM, THOSE ARE THE THINGS THAT DEFILE A MAN."
MARK 7:15

THERE IS no sin in temptation. Jesus Himself was tempted by the devil in the desert, but He did not succumb to it (Matt. 4:1–11). But temptation often gives birth to sin, and that is where the problem comes in.

King David was tempted by a beautiful woman he saw bathing near the palace (2 Sam. 11). She was the wife of Uriah the Hittite, who was one of David's generals. David summoned her and committed adultery with her. Then David had her husband killed in battle so that no one would suspect his involvement. As a result he became a murderer and a liar.

Maybe someone you know has a very nice car and you like to look at it and appreciate it. That is not sin. It is when you covet it and feel as though you must own it at all costs that it turns into sin. Thus, it is not what goes into the mouth that defiles; it is what comes out of the heart.

When you are tempted, simply turn around and walk away. The Holy Spirit, your conscience, will tell you when something isn't from God; and then you must walk away from it. If you don't flee temptation, you will slowly get caught in that spider's web and eventually succumb to it.

Always remember: what we think and how we respond to temptation determine whether we defile ourselves or not. May God bless you as you discipline yourself and follow in Jesus' footsteps.

PRAYER: God, please protect my heart when I face
temptation, and help me to do the right thing. Amen.

September 2

HUMBLE YOURSELF

"WHOEVER EXALTS HIMSELF WILL BE HUMBLED, AND
HE WHO HUMBLES HIMSELF WILL BE EXALTED."
MATTHEW 23:12

HUMILITY IS the mark of a mighty man or woman of God. Proud and arrogant people are on their own mission, with their own agendas, rules, and priorities—with Jesus Christ tagged on at the end. But the Bible says that pride comes before a fall (Prov. 16:18), which we have seen time and again. When any person makes a grasp for God's glory, a crash is inevitable.

One of our greatest examples of humility in the Bible is John the Baptist. Jesus said he was the greatest man ever born (Matt. 11:11), but John said he was not even worthy to tie the Master's sandals (John 1:27). John's only purpose in life was to point men and women to Jesus.

That is exactly what we must do if we are going to live a fulfilled and godly life on this earth. Our sole objective, our main reason for living, is to magnify the name of Jesus Christ. The Lord says that if we lift Him up, He will draw all people to Himself (John 12:32). As we do this, we will experience the abundant life He promised.

The Bible says that if we cast our bread upon the waters, it will return to us in time (Eccl. 11:1). The more we give to Jesus, the more we receive. It is such a pleasure and an honor to be known as an ambassador of Jesus Christ. We do not have to prove anything to ourselves or to anyone else. All He asks is that we be obedient and follow in His footsteps in humility.

PRAYER: God, You are the center of the universe. Keep
me humble—in right relation with You. Amen.

September 3

AVERSION TO SIN

WE HAVE KNOWN AND BELIEVED THE LOVE THAT
GOD HAS FOR US. GOD IS LOVE, AND HE WHO ABIDES
IN LOVE ABIDES IN GOD, AND GOD IN HIM.
1 JOHN 4:16

I'VE ALWAYS been astounded when a man comes up to me and tells me that he is a born-again, Spirit-filled Christian, and yet he cannot reconcile himself to his brother because of some slight that happened years ago.

How could that be? Jesus made it very clear in 1 John 4:20 that "if someone says, 'I love God,' and hates his brother, he is a liar; for he who does not love his brother whom he has seen, how can he love God whom he has not seen?" Hatred is the opposite of love, and God is love. Love for God will automatically produce love for your brother.

The only thing worthy of hate is sin. Psalm 97:10 says, "You who love the LORD, hate evil." It is very easy to hate sin when you become passionate for God. The more one loves God, the more one hates sin. It's like a chasm that continues to grow and grow.

The Lord says that in the last days evil shall become more evil (2 Tim. 3:13). Can't we see it today? Years ago people would engage in sin privately, but now they do it in public, almost challenging the Lord to see what He will do about it.

The righteous are seeking the Lord. Even as we hate sin more, we pray that God would give us an intense love for Him, that we would feel a strong aversion to sin and hate it with a passion.

PRAYER: God, fill me up with such love for You that there
is no room for sin or unforgiveness. Amen.

September 4
CHRISTIAN SERVICE

"WHOEVER DESIRES TO BE FIRST AMONG YOU, LET HIM BE YOUR
SLAVE—JUST AS THE SON OF MAN DID NOT COME TO BE SERVED,
BUT TO SERVE, AND TO GIVE HIS LIFE A RANSOM FOR MANY."
MATTHEW 20:27–28

THE LORD called me to evangelize. He instructed me to book town halls, large tents, and stadiums, and to preach the gospel to the lost. The scripture He impressed upon my heart is found in Acts 18:9: "Do not be afraid, but speak, and do not keep silent." That Bible verse has encouraged me to press on through deep waters and dark nights.

Motivation is very important for any ministry effort. When Jesus walked this earth, His main objective was to be obedient to His Father's will. Saving souls was purely a result of this obedience. In the same way, Christian service in its pure form is always the result of a believer's love for Jesus Christ. If it is for any other reason, it will fade, dry up, and blow away, just like a flower in the field.

Our Christian service to the Lord should never be judged on mere statistics. Whether one or one thousand respond to Christ at a campaign, it doesn't matter; we judge by a different, eternal standard. After all, it is the Holy Spirit who does the work.

Christian service involves far more than going into foreign lands as missionaries, evangelists, pastors, or church planters. We are missionaries wherever God puts us—in the factory, the school, the office, or at home.

Remember, the main objective of Christian service is not what we can do for others, but what we can do for God.

PRAYER: God, thank You for placing me where You have; please help
me to serve there in the way that best pleases You. Amen.

September 5

BECOMING SUCCESSFUL AND WISE

"BEHOLD, THE FEAR OF THE LORD, THAT IS WISDOM,
AND TO DEPART FROM EVIL IS UNDERSTANDING."
JOB 28:28

IT'S SAID there's no fool like an old fool. And as I get older, I have to keep reminding myself I don't know everything. In fact, the older I get, the more I realize how little I do know. *Fear* in today's verse doesn't mean that we should be afraid of God; in this context it means "reverence." When we revere God, He gives us wisdom.

It touches me so deeply when I see people giving God a place in their organizations, and it's wonderful to see an employer humble himself in front of his staff and pray. Humility is a sign of a wise man, a man who has been blessed with incredible favor from God. When you meet such a person, he'll speak mostly about you and very little about himself. That too is a sign of wisdom.

If you depart from evil, forget about yourself, and start living for other people, you'll become both successful and wise. I tend to speak too much and listen too little. We need to listen twice as much as we speak—that's why God gave us two ears and only one mouth!

We must also be prepared to seek counsel from other people, particularly from those who are older and wiser. A foolish man is one who thinks he knows everything. True wisdom comes only from God. Seek His counsel above all else and your plans will succeed, because He will be in them.

PRAYER: God, I pray for Your gentle wisdom and the humility to
acknowledge that I don't know as much as I think I do. Amen.

September 6

MANY ARE CALLED

"SO THE LAST WILL BE FIRST, AND THE FIRST LAST.
FOR MANY ARE CALLED, BUT FEW CHOSEN."
MATTHEW 20:16

AT THE height of Jesus' ministry, He had many followers. At times there were more than five thousand people at a single gathering (Matt. 14:13–21). Multitudes followed and thronged around Him wherever He went. But when Jesus started to preach holiness and righteousness, slowly the people started to dwindle. Toward the end of His ministry, He seemed to be spending most of His time teaching His disciples about the truths of the Word of God.

When the going got even tougher, of the twelve there were only three who stuck really close to Jesus, and eventually only one. John was the only one found at the foot of the cross when the Lord was crucified. This is one of the biggest tragedies of the Christian journey: people just do not seem to be able to finish the race. Many are called, but few are chosen.

As we start to grow older in the Lord, it's almost as if the little path that leads to eternal life gets narrower and harder, because we are continually confronted with difficult issues and disappointed by people we believed would not let us down. Maybe the Holy Spirit even allows this to happen in order for us to put all our faith and hope in the King of Glory.

Christianity is about finishing the race strong. It's about hanging in there when it seems everybody else has had enough. The Lord has never promised us that He would take us out of the fire. Indeed, quite the opposite. There is a fire, but the Lord has promised us that He will walk with us through it!

PRAYER: Lord, help me to press on till the end in faith! Amen.

September 7

GRATITUDE FOR CALVARY

BELOVED, I PRAY THAT YOU MAY PROSPER IN ALL THINGS
AND BE IN HEALTH, JUST AS YOUR SOUL PROSPERS.
3 JOHN 2

THERE'S A difference between a hireling and a son. A hireling keeps his eye on the clock. As soon as it's knock-off time, he can't wait to get home. The son, the one who's going to inherit everything his father has built for him, never looks at the clock. He works until the job is finished. The same thing applies to those who offer themselves up to serve the Lord Jesus Christ.

I think of Charles Colson, who was special counsel to President Richard Nixon. He gave the president of the United States of America advice on how to run the country and was known as a man who would do anything to get ahead. He was not at all a good man, and everyone knew it.

After the Watergate scandal, Colson left the White House and tried to rebuild his career as a lawyer. It was during this time that he had a conversion experience that led him to plead guilty to the criminal charges facing him.

He was sent to jail for several months, and when he came out, he was totally, completely different: formerly one of the "movers and shakers," he became a humble man with a prison ministry.

A church I know has a sign on the wall that reads, "Missionary work is gratitude for Calvary." I think that's so aptly put. When Jesus Christ comes into a person's life, it is changed forever. What can you do to show your gratitude for Calvary?

PRAYER: God, thank You for the miraculous way You've saved us.
Help me to show my thankfulness in my actions. Amen.

September 8
WHEN JEALOUSY LURKS

A SOUND HEART IS LIFE TO THE BODY, BUT
ENVY IS ROTTENNESS TO THE BONES.
PROVERBS 14:30

JOHN BUNYAN wrote that "jealousy never thinks it is strong enough," and that is so true. We might think of jealousy as something small, but it can lead to total destruction—even murder. Jealousy is the reason why Cain murdered his brother Abel (Gen. 4:1–15). He was jealous of his brother because God respected Abel's offering more than his.

Jealousy always covets what other people have. It is telling yourself that you are not beautiful enough or that you are not good enough. It is believing that someone else has it better than you do and that you deserve what they have. How does a person combat jealousy? Be content with what God has given you and the way God made you.

Be content with your life and be happy where He has placed you. In 1 Timothy 6:6, the Bible says, "Godliness with contentment is great gain."

Be careful when jealousy lurks at your door. Concentrate on the Lord and realize that He always gives what is best. Don't compare yourself to those around you. It poisons you, and no good can come from it.

Look at yourself in the mirror every morning and tell yourself that God lives in you. Wherever you go today, God is going with you. If you do this simple exercise, jealousy will fly out the window because you will remember how much God loves you. Trust His plan for you. Keep your eyes on Jesus.

PRAYER: Lord, please root out any jealousy in my heart.
I want to live in the truth instead! Amen.

September 9
PRAYER AND FASTING

"THIS KIND DOES NOT GO OUT EXCEPT BY PRAYER AND FASTING."
MATTHEW 17:21

MATTHEW 17 records an incident when the disciples could not cast out a demon. When they asked the Lord why this was so, He said that it was because of their unbelief (v. 20). That kind of demon only responded to prayer and fasting. When we fast, it brings us into the dimension of the spirit world.

John Wesley wrote in his biography that he fasted twice a week because he wanted to be closer to Jesus. After I met Jesus, I started to fast on a regular basis, and my life was really transformed.

For me, fasting is extremely hard. I am a talkative person by nature. When I go to the mountains to spend a few days on my own with Jesus, the first thing I notice is that I become weak physically, so I talk less and listen more. I spend less time in prayer and more time in meditation and reading the Word. The presence of Jesus becomes very real.

If you are unable to fast due to medical reasons, you can still fast by giving up certain luxuries and spending time in prayer.

Fasting is a tough exercise, but it is an integral part of a Christian's lifestyle. If Jesus found it essential to fast, then so much more for us. Fasting results in a complete cleansing of one's life and ministry. It removes all the cobwebs and skeletons. Your life is highlighted, and you will be able to see how closely you walk with Jesus. Fasting gives you the opportunity to get back to God and enables you to see things with clarity.

PRAYER: God, please guide me as I make fasting part of my regular routine and speak to me in the silence. Amen.

September 10
WALKING BY FAITH

NOW FAITH IS THE SUBSTANCE OF THINGS HOPED
FOR, THE EVIDENCE OF THINGS NOT SEEN.
HEBREWS 11:1

LIVING LIFE based on our emotions is like a roller coaster: a terrifying journey on a closed loop. But living by faith, instead of by sight, is a stable, forward-moving journey. This is what comes of looking at our circumstances through God's eyes.

Take in God's Word and see what God says about you. God does not make junk. God created you in His own image, even though people will push you down. I know because I've been there: you can be popular one minute and deserted the next.

In walking by faith, we believe what God says about us. Remember, the Bible says that we can do all things through Christ who strengthens us (Phil. 4:13). It is God in us that will do the job. It helps to befriend positive people—those who love God. We need to keep away from the negative influences, from people who are always pulling others down. Get in among believers, those who love Jesus and have their eyes focused on heaven rather than the "sight" of the world.

When we get up every morning we've got to say, "Lord, maybe today. Maybe You are coming back today." Perhaps today we are going to meet Jesus; perhaps today the Lord is going to come back. Walking by faith is living with expectancy. We need to be sure that when the Lord comes again, He will recognize us as His children—not because of what we have done, but because of what we believe.

PRAYER: God, when I start to live by sight, please pull me off the roller coaster and set me back on the track of faith. Amen.

September 11
THE DANGERS OF DISILLUSIONMENT

THE HOPE OF THE RIGHTEOUS WILL BE GLADNESS, BUT
THE EXPECTATION OF THE WICKED WILL PERISH.
PROVERBS 10:28

YOU MIGHT be young and newly married. You've dreamed all your life of your big wedding day and perfect spouse. You have expectations of what your marriage will be like. However, after the wedding, your spouse doesn't live up to your expectations and you become disillusioned. With every disappointment your disillusionment builds, until you end up having a big fight.

Perhaps your children disappoint you. They aren't doing as well at school or sports as you would like. You wanted them to make the first team, but they only made the second team. You've become disappointed in them and make them feel horrible because they have let you down. Remember that they are trying their best. It doesn't help them or you to place unnecessary strain on them because your expectations are too high.

Don't put pressure on your loved ones; you will only end up being disappointed and making them feel worthless. Do your best and trust others to do the same. Your relationship with the ones you love will be so much better if you accept them for who they are and encourage them in whatever they do, appreciating their genuine efforts rather than how much they conform to expectations.

God is the only one who will not disappoint you. Let Him be your source of trust for your vision, your dreams, and your goals. Treat others with compassion, knowing that you will disappoint others as well!

PRAYER: Jesus, when I'm disappointed with people and the world around me, please refocus my heart on You so I can be understanding with others. Amen.

September 12
LEARNING TO DANCE IN THE RAIN

THE LORD GOD IS MY STRENGTH; HE WILL MAKE MY FEET LIKE
DEER'S FEET, AND HE WILL MAKE ME WALK ON MY HIGH HILLS.
HABAKKUK 3:19

MY WIFE and I recently went to an annual flower show. Flower arrangements from all over the country demonstrated the beauty of the natural world. Yet again, we realized how privileged we are to live in this corner of God's vineyard.

In one of the smaller stands, a lady was making wooden signs. The one that caught my eye said, "Life is not about waiting for the storm to pass. It's about learning to dance in the rain." I thought this was such an appropriate saying for Christians in the world today.

I have met many businesspeople who say they're waiting to see the outcome of the political or economic situation. I don't believe that's the right attitude at all. There's no such thing as standing still—if you're not going forward, then you're going backward! This applies to most walks of life.

The Lord says we must carry on doing business until He comes (see Luke 19:13). As Winston Churchill once said, "Never give in. Never, never, never!" This is a time to continue planting. There's not much we can do individually about the situation in our country or the world, but there is something we can do in our businesses and in our homes. We can be better husbands, better wives, better parents, better friends, better employers, and better employees. We can learn to dance in the rain—and remember, every storm finishes with the sun coming out from behind the clouds!

PRAYER: God, make my heart joyous no matter
what life's storms may bring. Amen.

September 13

WITH HIM OR AGAINST HIM

"HE WHO IS NOT WITH ME IS AGAINST ME, AND HE WHO
DOES NOT GATHER WITH ME SCATTERS ABROAD."
MATTHEW 12:30

WE ARE currently facing the culmination of the greatest battle that will ever be fought in the history of mankind. The battle of Armageddon is closer than we think, and the Lord wants to know whose side we are on. As today's scripture tells us, we cannot serve two masters.

It is time to nail our colors to the mast. The world needs to know whose side we are on. Either we are serving the Lord or we are serving the devil. We cannot be indifferent. That is a lie from the evil one.

Jesus said very categorically and clearly that He is the only way. There may be many paths to heaven, but there is only one door. There is no other entrance into heaven, except by Him. We are not of this world. I know that only too well, and I cannot wait to go home to be with my blessed Savior. But until such time, we must understand one thing: we are in this world to make a difference. The victory is already ours.

The last great battle is before us. We must be absolutely sure that we are on the right side and that we are clothed with the armor of God. If today you are undecided, let me challenge you to get onto the right side without delay. Enlist in God's army, equip yourself, and get ready for the battle, because it is coming.

PRAYER: God, I am for You! Guide me as I ready
myself to fight Your battles. Amen.

September 14
WE PASS THIS WAY BUT ONCE

AS IT IS APPOINTED FOR MEN TO DIE ONCE, BUT AFTER THIS
THE JUDGMENT, SO CHRIST WAS OFFERED ONCE TO BEAR THE
SINS OF MANY. TO THOSE WHO EAGERLY WAIT FOR HIM HE WILL
APPEAR A SECOND TIME, APART FROM SIN, FOR SALVATION.
HEBREWS 9:27–28

EVERY DAY presents unique opportunities to show kindness to others; and by tomorrow, those opportunities may have passed you by. Therefore, don't hesitate to show Jesus' love to the world at every opportunity you are given. Even in the smallest things, make it as if you have done it for the Lord. Matthew 10:42 says, "Whoever gives one of these little ones only a cup of cold water in the name of a disciple, assuredly, I say to you, he shall by no means lose his reward."

Life is too short to waste time on arguments or bitterness or to put off something important until tomorrow, because you don't know for sure if there will even be a tomorrow.

At the back of my Bible I have written, "Keep short accounts with men and God, for the time is now very short." It is written underneath Revelation 22:20: "He who testifies to these things says, 'Surely I am coming quickly.' Amen. Even so, come, Lord Jesus!"

Give the homeless man something to eat and drink, love the person who is unlovely, and forgive the person who wrongs you, because you pass this way but once.

PRAYER: Dear God, the time You've given me is so limited and precious. Help me to be wise, compassionate, and effective as I walk the path toward You. Amen.

September 15

THE JOY OF GIVING

"FREELY YOU HAVE RECEIVED, FREELY GIVE."
MATTHEW 10:8

IT IS in giving that we receive contentment, peace of mind, fulfillment, and a reason for living. We have a children's home here on our farm, and what an absolute blessing those young children have been. The eldest boy has just finished school. He is going to university to study social science in order to come back and help us run the home. We have other boys and girls who are excelling at sports. We really believe we've got the next Usain Bolt living here with us!

Being able to see what God is doing in the lives of these children is such a blessing and a reward for us. We have no doubt that the Lord will raise up mighty men and women from this humble children's home—not because of us, but because He loves them.

Follow your dream, and make it plain so that others can run with you. Sow into the community in which you live and make a difference. Keep giving, give until it hurts, and watch God work in many different ways (financially probably being the least of them).

God is a giver, a trait you will find in all of His followers. Be a giver, and may God bless you as you make your community and family a brighter and more loving place in which to live.

PRAYER: Lord, You've given me so much. I want to
give it away so I can see Your smile. Amen.

September 16
OUR PROTECTOR AND GUIDE

"THE SPIRIT OF THE LORD GOD IS UPON ME, BECAUSE THE
LORD HAS ANOINTED ME TO PREACH GOOD TIDINGS TO THE
POOR; HE HAS SENT ME TO HEAL THE BROKENHEARTED,
TO PROCLAIM LIBERTY TO THE CAPTIVES, AND THE
OPENING OF THE PRISON TO THOSE WHO ARE BOUND."
ISAIAH 61:1

I ONCE had the privilege of preaching in Leicestershire in the UK. There's a place there called Coalville and, unsurprisingly, it's where they discovered coal. When you are underground, sometimes you encounter a deadly poisonous gas called methane. You can't see it, you can't smell it, and you can't see it coming.

The early miners used to carry a canary; its distress would be the first indication of danger. They also carried a lamp to show them the way and to warn them of danger. When the flame turned from orange to blue, they knew that methane gas was being released in the mine shaft and they had to get out immediately.

In the same way, God is like a protector lamp for you and me—not just to light the way of our path, but to warn us when we get into certain dangerous situations. Our protector lamp is called the Holy Spirit. If you love the Lord and take His lamp with you wherever you go, you will never get into trouble.

When your Protector says, "Don't associate with that person, because you will get into trouble," then you should listen. And when your Protector says, "Don't go into that pub, even for one drink," pay attention.

I want to encourage you not to ignore the flickering of the protector lamp—the Holy Spirit. He will lead you and guide you all your life if you follow Him.

PRAYER: God, I am so grateful You've given me a Protector. Open
my eyes and ears so I don't miss a single warning. Amen.

September 17

FUELING THE FIRE

WHERE THERE IS NO WOOD, THE FIRE GOES OUT; AND
WHERE THERE IS NO TALEBEARER, STRIFE CEASES.
PROVERBS 26:20

SOME PEOPLE love drama and are experts at pouring fuel onto fires. As you know, when you do that, the fire literally explodes in your face. This is what the verse from Proverbs implies. If we set a fire of negative words and gossip, it eventually will blow up in our faces.

Changing our mind-sets and being positive starts with watching our mouths. Gossiping fuels fires of negativity. One thing I have learned in my life is that there are always two sides to every story. Don't believe everything you hear or read in the newspapers.

In the third chapter of James, the Bible tells us that we put a bit in a horse's mouth so that the horse obeys us and we can turn its whole body. Verse 5 tells us that though the tongue is one of the smallest parts of our body, it can achieve many things.

It only takes a small spark and drip of gasoline to light a huge forest fire, and so it is with the tongue: a word said without thinking can cause strife in an entire community. A word said in a moment of anger can destroy a marriage or a family. If we haven't got anything good to say about something, let's rather not say anything. Instead, let's speak life, hope, peace, and joy.

**PRAYER: God, You've given enormous power to words. Help
me to cause life and not destruction with mine. Amen.**

September 18
HURRY UP AND WAIT

FOR THE VISION IS YET FOR AN APPOINTED TIME; BUT AT
THE END IT WILL SPEAK, AND IT WILL NOT LIE. THOUGH IT
TARRIES, WAIT FOR IT; BECAUSE IT WILL SURELY COME.
HABAKKUK 2:3

SOMETIMES WAITING is the hardest thing for a Christian to do, and it can make a Christian feel extremely vulnerable. At one point in my life the Lord called me to get back to my first love—to put all my preaching appointments on hold and spend time with Him. When you give the Holy Spirit the opportunity, He will reveal areas that are not pleasing to the Lord. This is what He did with me during that waiting period.

These days everything is instant, and that makes waiting even more difficult. However, it is sad to see what all this rushing is doing to families. Very rarely do I meet families who sit down together for a meal and a good chat about the day's affairs. But the grab-and-go, fast-food industry is growing rapidly. How much strife and how many emotional problems would be solved if people had more quality contact with each other—if they were forced to wait together?

One thing about waiting is that it teaches us patience, and it opens our eyes to what's around us. Waiting is good for us, and I think that is why the Lord often makes us wait before He uses us. God is never in a hurry. I have read of many people who have had to go through a time of waiting on God before He was able to use them in the capacity to which He had called them. When Jesus Christ is the King of your life, you will be prepared to wait, and wait, for as long as it takes.

PRAYER: God, I'll wait as long as You want me to. Keep my spirit calm
and focused as I put aside distractions and wait on Your call. Amen.

September 19
BE SINGLE-MINDED

YOU WILL KEEP HIM IN PERFECT PEACE, WHOSE MIND
IS STAYED ON YOU, BECAUSE HE TRUSTS IN YOU.
ISAIAH 26:3

DURING ONE of our Mighty Men Conferences, I was lying in my bed in the middle of the night listening to the rain, which is twice as loud as normal because we have a tin roof and no ceiling. Multitudes had come from all over the world to camp on our farm, and we still had the whole day of Saturday, Saturday night, and Sunday morning to get through. I will never forget lying there, literally breaking down, and saying, "Lord, this cannot be. We can't manage with all this rain."

When I walked outside early the next morning, it was absolutely quiet. I looked up and saw one star. That meant there was a break in the clouds, and we would have a clear day. I felt so guilty. I said, "Lord, please forgive me." There I was, stressing about the rain, and it turned into a beautiful weekend. After everyone packed up and left at the end of the conference, we had a mighty thunderstorm with hailstones. Isn't God amazing?

If you are resolute, if you know where you are going and what you have to do, you know you can leave the rest to God. It doesn't pay to obsess about the signs of the times or the negative news stories swirling around us, when He has so much more in mind.

Being single-minded, we place our lives in God's hands; it doesn't matter what happens because He will protect us. Your standing with the Lord is the only peace you need in this world. Be unwavering, and rest assured that God will raise you up to be a mighty warrior for Him.

PRAYER: God, I thank You that I can rely on You to work out
the details that I so easily stress out over. Amen.

September 20

A GOOD IDEA VERSUS A "GOD IDEA"

MAY THE GOD OF PEACE . . . MAKE YOU COMPLETE IN
EVERY GOOD WORK TO DO HIS WILL, WORKING IN YOU
WHAT IS WELL PLEASING IN HIS SIGHT, THROUGH JESUS
CHRIST, TO WHOM BE GLORY FOREVER AND EVER.
HEBREWS 13:20−21

THE NATURAL inclination is to act on every good idea, but as I always like to say, a good idea is not always a "God idea." In fact, it sometimes gets in the way of God's plans. For instance, the work I am busy with—sharing the good news with others through preaching—is not something that I always felt was a good idea or even something that I myself decided to embark upon. I was a farmer, and my dream had always been to farm. In my eyes, working hard to become a successful farmer was a good idea. Preaching the Word of God was not part of my plan. Rather, it was a mandate that I received from almighty God.

We try to do something good that in most cases won't hurt anyone, then we ask God to bless our idea. When He doesn't, we feel despondent, thinking God doesn't care. But it might not be part of His plan.

It is so hard to abandon our good idea, fall on our faces before God, and wait for Him to show us His plan for our lives and what He wants us to do. God has it all in hand. We must first pray, and only then will God reveal His plan to us. Prayer removes the impulse of a good idea. We need to pray, then plan.

PRAYER: Jesus, give me discernment to know the difference
between my own ideas and Yours. Amen.

September 21

LIONS IN YOUR LIFE

BE SOBER, BE VIGILANT; BECAUSE YOUR ADVERSARY THE
DEVIL WALKS ABOUT LIKE A ROARING LION, SEEKING
WHOM HE MAY DEVOUR. RESIST HIM, STEADFAST IN
THE FAITH, KNOWING THAT THE SAME SUFFERINGS ARE
EXPERIENCED BY YOUR BROTHERHOOD IN THE WORLD.
1 PETER 5:8—9

THE AFRICAN lion is one of the most intimidating animals in the wild. Those eyes hold no fear, and when he looks at you, he looks straight through you. Today's verse casts Satan as a prowling lion: he does not play clean; he is vicious; and he always comes from behind. However, the Lord does not give you a spirit of fear, but of love and of power and a sound mind (2 Tim. 1:7).

The Bible is called the sword of the Spirit, and that is how we protect ourselves from the devil who stalks us like a lion. To sharpen the sword, memorize Scripture and believe what the Lord says about you so that you can kill the enemy.

The opposite is also true: if you don't sharpen the sword or you don't know how to use it, the lion will devour you. Abraham Lincoln once said that if given six hours to chop down a tree, he would spend the first four hours sharpening his ax. Preparation is so important.

I want to encourage you not to allow any lions into your life. Draw the line, and deal with them once and for all. The best way to do that is not to compromise on God's Word.

PRAYER: God, thank You for the weapons You give us to
fight the devil. Help me to wield them well. Amen.

September 22
BE ZEALOUS AND REPENT

FOR WHOM THE LORD LOVES HE CORRECTS, JUST AS
A FATHER THE SON IN WHOM HE DELIGHTS.
PROVERBS 3:12

DISCIPLINE IS not always fun, but it's essential if we want to reach great heights for God.

Revelation 3:19 says, "As many as I love, I rebuke and chasten. Therefore be zealous and repent." We have to be eager to say we are sorry. We are going to make mistakes, but we must be willing to ask Him for forgiveness.

Saul was on his way to Damascus to capture some of Jesus' followers when a bright light shone on him (Acts 9:1–19). It was Jesus, wanting to know why Saul was persecuting Him. Suddenly Saul could not see. He obeyed God's command to go to Damascus, and Jesus sent Ananias, one of His disciples, to restore Saul's sight. Saul received the Holy Spirit that day, and he became one of Jesus' most passionate and dedicated disciples.

So what happened? Saul was not at all a good man, and Jesus chastened him by taking away his sight. Jesus did this because He knew that Saul, as soon as his eyes were opened to the truth, would be sorry for what he had done and turn to Jesus.

Sometimes we too need to be chastened by God in order to be saved from eternal damnation. It is better for God to discipline us now so that we may become responsible citizens of heaven. Don't look down on discipline; it is painful at the time, but can result in eternal life.

PRAYER: God, I accept Your discipline. You are wise,
and know how I should correct my path. Amen.

September 23
PRAY WITHOUT CEASING

THE EYES OF THE LORD ARE ON THE RIGHTEOUS,
AND HIS EARS ARE OPEN TO THEIR PRAYERS.
1 PETER 3:12

PRAYER IS simply communication with God. Oswald Chambers wrote, "To say that 'prayer changes things' is not as close to the truth as saying, 'Prayer changes me and then I change things.'"

When you're speaking to God, you don't need any set format. You could be driving home from work or to the grocery store, and you can talk to Him. First Thessalonians 5:17 tells us, "Pray without ceasing." If you're going through a rough time at the moment, I would encourage you to pray and to come before the Lord in a childlike attitude and tell Him about your needs.

I talk to the Lord, and I sing, cry, and argue with the Lord. I think He would prefer you to be angry rather than not to speak to Him at all. Think of your own children—when they don't speak to you, that's when you get concerned. So speak to God about your financial, work-related, and domestic needs, and you'll be surprised how God answers.

I have seen Him change the wind, bring the rain, and put out the fire. Remember, however, that prayer is not a proverbial grocery list that you take to God; He wants you to be His friend. He'll talk back to you, not necessarily audibly, but in your heart and through nature, through godly neighbors or circumstances.

When you go out today, speak to Him. Tell Him about your joys, expectations, anxieties, and fears, and you'll feel a lot better that the Lord of the universe is looking out for you.

PRAYER: Jesus, remind me today to bring all the little
things to You. Thank You for listening! Amen.

September 24
YOUR LIFE IS NOT YOUR OWN

NONE OF US LIVES TO HIMSELF, AND NO ONE DIES
TO HIMSELF. FOR IF WE LIVE, WE LIVE TO THE
LORD; AND IF WE DIE, WE DIE TO THE LORD.
ROMANS 14:7–8

I'VE OFTEN heard young people say, "It's my life, and I can do what I want with it!" But as we get older, we realize such an attitude is extremely selfish, and also far from the truth.

Being placed into a family—whether a church family, a work family, or a natural family—makes us accountable to them for our actions, our way of life, and the decisions we make. When we make mistakes or act inappropriately, it doesn't only affect us—it has repercussions on a wide range of people.

Many times business owners can be completely oblivious to the mood of their workers. Then, out of the blue, a strike occurs and the owner never saw it coming. If he had been spending time with his workers and building strong communication channels with them, he wouldn't have been caught off guard.

I have seen through Mighty Men Conferences our ministry organizes in South Africa and other countries, that when men go home and start praying with their families, employees, and colleagues, it sets the tone for the rest of the day's work. It's impossible to pray with somebody if you aren't in good standing with them. Deal with offenses and pray together.

The best example is our Lord Jesus Christ. In John 15:13, He said, "Greater love has no one than this, than to lay down one's life for his friends." When we start living for each other, life becomes more pleasant, fruitful, and rewarding.

PRAYER: God, help me remember that my life is not my
own. Show me how to live for others today. Amen.

279

September 25
THE PENALTY FOR PRIDE

SURELY HE SCORNS THE SCORNFUL, BUT
GIVES GRACE TO THE HUMBLE.
PROVERBS 3:34

KING UZZIAH, who was a wonderful man of God, lost everything to pride. Second Chronicles 26:5 reads, "He sought God in the days of Zechariah, who had understanding in the visions of God; and as long as he sought the LORD, God made him prosper." Then verse 15 tells us, "His fame spread far and wide, for he was marvelously helped till he became strong." We work hard our whole lives to become successful, but success can be very dangerous. When you become a success, pride can move in.

Then Uzziah became presumptuous; he decided he was qualified to enter the temple of the Lord and burn incense. In the Old Testament only the high priest could go into the Holy of Holies in the temple—not the king. When Uzziah became successful, he became proud.

The Lord does not like pride; He turns away from those who are proud. In this story, the priests told Uzziah to leave (2 Chron. 26:17–23). He became so angry that leprosy broke out on his forehead while he was still standing in the temple. He was a leper until the day he died, and because he was a leper, he lived in isolation while his son managed the kingdom.

Success can be a dangerous place. God may prosper us, but He does not like pride. So let us be careful, because none of us are exempt from falling. We need to stay humble and give God all the glory.

PRAYER: Dear God, please protect my heart from pride at
all costs. Humble me and keep me close. Amen.

September 26
TAKING IT SLOW

WHO TEACHES US MORE THAN THE BEASTS OF THE EARTH,
AND MAKES US WISER THAN THE BIRDS OF HEAVEN?
JOB 35:11

NOT LONG ago, my wife and I had a few days' break in the Kruger National Park in South Africa. In a game reserve the maximum speed is usually about twenty miles per hour. I chuckled to myself when I saw big cars coming past at a great speed, driven by younger people obviously used to living in the "fast lane." They didn't really get to see the animals God has created for us to enjoy, and they missed many wonderful sightings.

At the camp where we stayed, I was able to sit on the verandah and look over a nearby river. I watched herds of elephants, noticing how slowly they moved and yet how efficient they were. I went inside to get a cup of tea, and when I came out about three minutes later, there wasn't an elephant to be seen! They had blended into the bush and disappeared. Experts say they can cover up to thirty miles in an evening at a steady walk.

Driving the next day, we came around a bend to find a bull buffalo standing in the middle of the road—chewing the cud, totally unperturbed by all the people in their fancy cars gingerly trying to get around him. He was totally relaxed, enjoying life and taking it slowly, not moving for anyone. God was showing me very clearly that's how we're supposed to live.

To be like the elephant and the buffalo, do everything you can manage and leave the rest in God's capable hands. You'll find your life will become a lot more enjoyable and you'll be a lot less stressed.

PRAYER: Lord, Your creation is so beautiful. Help me to
be part of it, fulfilling my role with peace. Amen.

September 27
THE IMPORTANCE OF ROOTS

SING TO GOD, SING PRAISES TO HIS NAME; EXTOL HIM
WHO RIDES ON THE CLOUDS. . . . A FATHER OF THE
FATHERLESS, A DEFENDER OF WIDOWS, IS GOD IN HIS HOLY
HABITATION. GOD SETS THE SOLITARY IN FAMILIES.
PSALM 68:4—6

A VERY dear brother in Christ once came to visit me when my sons were younger, and we started talking about the ministry we have here at Shalom. He stressed that what impressed him most was the family atmosphere he sensed on our farm.

Some of our older boys from the children's home play sports in the area. At that stage one of them played polocrosse with my son. With tears in his eyes, my friend told me that he had been at a practice the previous week and overheard some boys teasing my son. They asked, "Is this your brother?" Without batting an eyelid, my son hugged him and said, "Of course he is." That touched my friend more than any sermon he had ever heard.

Family is close to God's heart. That is one area the devil likes to pull down. We live together as a community at Shalom. I can assure you it is not always easy, but God molds us and teaches us to give and take. We have to work together.

It is important to have roots; a family provides that, and it prevents identity crisis. It is vital for the family of God to nurture their children and not disregard humble beginnings. We need to nurture the children and foster Christian values in order for the church of the Lord to mature and grow into what God meant it to be.

PRAYER: God, thank You for my roots; help me to grow new
ones and nurture the ones You've given me. Amen.

September 28
NO REASON FOR DESPAIR

"DO NOT FEAR ANY OF THOSE THINGS WHICH YOU ARE ABOUT
TO SUFFER. INDEED, THE DEVIL IS ABOUT TO THROW SOME OF
YOU INTO PRISON, THAT YOU MAY BE TESTED. . . . BE FAITHFUL
UNTIL DEATH, AND I WILL GIVE YOU THE CROWN OF LIFE."
REVELATION 2:10

POLYCARP—THE BISHOP of Smyrna in Asia Minor (in modern-day Turkey)—was one of the first recorded martyrs after New Testament history, at a critical time when the gospel was being established in the second generation of believers.

Days prior to his death, Polycarp had a vision in which he was burned alive. When he was arrested, he simply stated, "God's will be done." He went calmly with those who came to arrest him, appeared before the local proconsul, Statius Quadratus, and was interrogated. He endured it all calmly and with dignity.

Quadratus threatened Polycarp, saying he'd be thrown to wild beasts, that he'd be burnt alive, and so on. Polycarp replied by saying that while the proconsul's fire might last for a short time, the fires of judgment could not be quenched. "Eighty-six years have I have served Him," Polycarp declared, "and He has done me no wrong. How can I blaspheme my King and my Savior?"

The soldiers took him away and were about to nail him to a stake when Polycarp stopped them, assuring them that he would stand in the fire. He knew that the Lord would give him the strength to endure. When the fire was lit, Polycarp was not burned up. Instead, an arch formed around him. Eventually a solider reached in and stabbed him. Polycarp died a martyr for Jesus Christ. He suffered, but did not despair. His suffering had meaning.

PRAYER: God, when I suffer, help me to remember the meaning behind
it, and like Polycarp, endure to the end without despair. Amen.

September 29
THE CHRISTIAN WALK

TEACH US TO NUMBER OUR DAYS, THAT WE
MAY GAIN A HEART OF WISDOM.
PSALM 90:12

THE DISCIPLES were living every day for Jesus. On one occasion they were in a boat going across to the other side of the lake. Along came the Master walking on the stormy water—an astounding miracle! Jesus said, "'Be of good cheer! It is I; do not be afraid.' Then He went up into the boat to them, and the wind ceased. And they were greatly amazed in themselves beyond measure, and marveled" (Mark 6:50–51). Imagine how awestruck they must have been. Jesus did this miracle as they were going about their usual business. He wanted to open their eyes to His presence and teach them to trust Him. There are miracles happening around you every day if you only have eyes to see them.

The Christian walk is a process, not a one-off event. God is training us right now, in the present, and it is this process of learning that brings glory to God. We should start living for the present and not keep looking behind us, or even too far into the future. Don't live for tomorrow, since we don't know if we have tomorrow. Yesterday is gone, so the present moment is what we have. Don't waste your life yearning for a future event. Instead, live for the moment. Who knows? Maybe Jesus will come back tomorrow. Or He could come back many years from now. People are watching, and your greatest witness is your day-to-day living.

PRAYER: God, in the small things I do each day, please
make me conscious of Your visitation. Amen.

September 30
PUT YOUR HOPE IN GOD

"THIS BOOK OF THE LAW SHALL NOT DEPART FROM YOUR
MOUTH, BUT YOU SHALL MEDITATE IN IT DAY AND NIGHT,
THAT YOU MAY OBSERVE TO DO ACCORDING TO ALL THAT
IS WRITTEN IN IT. FOR THEN YOU WILL MAKE YOUR WAY
PROSPEROUS, AND THEN YOU WILL HAVE GOOD SUCCESS."
JOSHUA 1:8

THE WORD *expectation* in the dictionary means "a strong belief that something will happen." Is your expectation—your hope—in your business? The degree you are going to get at the end of the year? Your marriage? The medal you are hoping to win?

I have walked this road a long time, and every time I put my hope and expectation in man I have been disappointed. Put your expectation and hope in the Lord and you will not be disappointed.

Psalm 62:5–7 tells us, "My soul, wait silently for God alone, for my expectation is from Him. He only is my rock and my salvation; He is my defense; I shall not be moved. In God is my salvation and my glory; the rock of my strength, and my refuge, is in God."

When we put our expectation and hope in our family, our company, or our sporting abilities, we get disappointed and put tremendous pressure on our loved ones. Expecting our spouse or our children to excel where we didn't is putting an unnecessary burden on them. Your spouse is not your provider: God is. He may use your spouse to provide for your family, but ultimately it is God who cares for you. Let's prevent frustration and disappointment by placing our hope and our trust in God alone.

PRAYER: Dear God, You are the only one I can trust with my hopes and dreams. Help me to put my expectations in the right place. Amen.

285

OCTOBER

October 1

MY REDEEMER LIVES

LET US THEREFORE COME BOLDLY TO THE THRONE OF GRACE, THAT
WE MAY OBTAIN MERCY AND FIND GRACE TO HELP IN TIME OF NEED.
HEBREWS 4:16

I KNOW that my Redeemer lives. He is the same yesterday, today, and forever. Heaven and earth will pass away, but His Word will never pass away. I am not concerned when I turn on the radio or the TV, because we are promised, "For whatever is born of God overcomes the world. And this is the victory that has overcome the world—our faith" (1 John 5:4).

If God is for us, there is no one who can ever stand against us. That is why I love the Word of God. We hear negative news, but the Word of God combats it. The Lord has made a promise to never leave us.

Jesus loves you with a passion. He loves you so much that He died for you (1 Cor. 15:3–8). I am confident of this very thing: that He who has begun a good thing in you and me will carry it out till Jesus returns. That promise should keep us happy, buoyant, and feeling so alive that it gets us up in the morning with a spring in our step.

We can speak to Jesus when we are feeling down. Go to the Lord and He will undertake for you. You've got problems in your home? Go to the Lord. Problems in your business? Go to the Lord. Health problems? Go to the Lord. He will hear you and answer the prayer of faith every single time. He says, "Call unto Me," and so we must.

PRAYER: God, thank You for Your promises and the gift of Your Word. Amen.

October 2
CHOOSE LIFE

ELIJAH CAME TO ALL THE PEOPLE, AND SAID, "HOW
LONG WILL YOU FALTER BETWEEN TWO OPINIONS? IF THE
LORD IS GOD, FOLLOW HIM; BUT IF BAAL, FOLLOW HIM."
BUT THE PEOPLE ANSWERED HIM NOT A WORD.
1 KINGS 18:21

LIFE IS full of choices. Elijah, the great prophet of God, challenged the people of his day to make a choice as to whether they would follow Baal or the living God, but the people didn't answer him. They were not prepared to openly confess that there is no other God than Jehovah, the God of Israel.

The Lord says, "I am the First and I am the Last; besides Me there is no God" (Isa. 44:6). We may respect people of other faiths, but we cannot agree with them. How can we agree with something that keeps people away from the truth? If we have a heart for lost souls and know they are destined for hell unless they acknowledge Jesus Christ, how can we agree that anything else is the answer?

The reason Elijah had such a powerful ministry was because he chose to follow God. As a result, when he called down fire from heaven, the Lord honored his word and consumed the sacrifice. Choices are a part of life. When you are a follower of Jesus and He is enough in your life, choices are easier to make; we just have to ask what He would do.

Will we choose Jesus, or listen to man's counsel and do things our own way? We need to make a choice today and say, "I'm going to put Jesus Christ first in my life." Never let your decisions be determined by your circumstances, but always by the Word of the living God.

PRAYER: Lord, help me to never be shy about openly
confessing that You are the one true God. Amen.

October 3

THE GOD OF ALL COMFORT

GOD WILL WIPE AWAY EVERY TEAR FROM THEIR EYES; THERE SHALL
BE NO MORE DEATH, NOR SORROW, NOR CRYING. THERE SHALL BE
NO MORE PAIN, FOR THE FORMER THINGS HAVE PASSED AWAY.
REVELATION 21:4

I LOST my little nephew, Alistair, when he was just four years old. I never knew on that fateful afternoon that it would be the last time I would see him on this earth. I'll never forget walking up the path to the tractor, his little hand holding mine, icing sugar on his hand from baking a cake in the kitchen.

The good news is that I will see little Alistair again. Jesus has promised me that because He lives, we can face tomorrow. Death for us is not something to fear, because it actually means the start of eternal life.

A Christian nursing sister once shared with Jill and me about tending unbelievers who are in the last throes of death. As patients die, they often grind their teeth, and there is an atmosphere of absolute fear in the room. The dying person thrashes about in their bed, sometimes screaming, cursing God, and using profane language as they go to a lost eternity.

The complete opposite for her is going into the room of a believer who is about to meet Jesus. There is serenity, a sense of peace, a fragrance in that room. It is almost like a perfume as the Lord comes to take that person home to be with Him in glory. The person rejoices, totally at peace.

I trust that you too know beyond any shadow of a doubt where your eternal home will be.

PRAYER: God, I so look forward to meeting You. I
thank You that death is not the end! Amen.

October 4

AS FOR ME AND MY HOUSE . . .

CHOOSE FOR YOURSELVES THIS DAY WHOM YOU WILL SERVE. . . .
BUT AS FOR ME AND MY HOUSE, WE WILL SERVE THE LORD.
JOSHUA 24:15

A FEW years ago I spoke to a group of farmers. Afterward, a big, strong man came up to me with his two sons. He said to me, "You can't be a farmer with hands like that!"

Since my sons took over the farming, I often joke that when I preach to farmers, I have to speak with my hands in my pockets so they don't see how soft my hands have become. I was a little dumbfounded, not knowing at the time what to say. I said to him, "Let me see your hands." His hands were gnarled and full of calluses, just like mine used to be when I was actively farming. (Now I have calluses on my knees!)

I pointed to the young men beside him. "Are these your sons?" He replied that they were. I asked, "When are you going to hand the farm over to them? Then you'll also have hands like mine." A big smile cracked the faces of both boys. They really appreciated that. The old farmer didn't know what to say.

We need to respect our young people. They are the future. If you put no time or effort into your children when they are growing up, then they will never be ready to take over because they won't have sufficient knowledge. The sooner we get our young people involved, the sooner we can hand over our responsibilities to them.

The same applies to teaching them about the Word of God. If we instill a love for God in our children, they will have a solid foundation on which to stand later in life.

PRAYER: God, help me to encourage adult responsibility
in the young people in my life. Amen.

October 5

ANSWER ONLY TO GOD

LET MY VINDICATION COME FROM YOUR PRESENCE; LET
YOUR EYES LOOK ON THE THINGS THAT ARE UPRIGHT.
PSALM 17:2

TO VINDICATE is to try and explain your side of a story. I myself am always trying to explain things to someone, sometimes feeling as though I must defend the Lord. But there's no need to wear ourselves out giving an account to everyone about everything. The gospel doesn't need a defense because it speaks for itself.

We serve such a mighty, awesome, sovereign God that we don't have to vindicate Him in any way, for anything. Neither do we need to defend ourselves and our past mistakes. The only person to whom we need to give an account is the Lord Jesus Christ.

The devil can fill your mind with terrible accusations. He can speak into your heart, if you allow him to, and make you feel so guilty that you feel you have to apologize to everyone. But 1 John 1:9 says that if we confess our sins, God will forgive us and cleanse us from all unrighteousness.

Jesus died for sinners like you and me. Sometimes the hardest thing for believers to accept is the fact that their sins have been washed away by the blood Jesus shed on the cross of Calvary. Once we can accept that, we don't have to justify our past actions. The only person we have to account to at the end of the day is the Lord Jesus Christ, because He alone is qualified to ask us what we did with what He gave us.

PRAYER: Dear God, help me to remember that justification is Your job.
Thank You for the gospel and for wiping my slate clean. Amen.

October 6

CREATION SPEAKS HIS NAME

THE EARTH IS THE LORD'S, AND ALL ITS FULLNESS, THE WORLD
AND THOSE WHO DWELL THEREIN. FOR HE HAS FOUNDED IT
UPON THE SEAS, AND ESTABLISHED IT UPON THE WATERS.
PSALM 24:1–2

PSALM 121:1–2 reassures us, "I will lift up my eyes to the hills—from whence comes my help? My help comes from the LORD, who made heaven and earth." When I lift up my eyes to the hills, there is such peace and strength in them. To think that they have stood there from the very beginning of time and will still be there when you and I are no longer! And yet with all the beauty, majesty, and strength the hills display, that is not where our hope lies. No, our hope lies completely in their Creator—in the saving, protecting grace of Jesus Christ.

If we read on, the psalmist says in verse 3 that "He will not allow your foot to be moved; He who keeps you will not slumber." God is our Protector. When the heat is hard to bear, Jesus is our shade. Our Master has promised us that as long as we keep our eyes fixed on Him, He will ensure that we are able to persevere and finish this race. He will preserve us from all evil.

Let us enjoy God's creation and be rejuvenated, for it is truly magnificent. It gives us just a glimpse of the incredibly artistic and creative God we serve. However, let us be careful to worship the Creator, and never creation itself. We must never forget that our help comes from Christ alone. Let's praise God for the work of His hand: experience the colors, fragrances, and sounds. And may our experience of creation remind us of God's power and protection.

PRAYER: God, thank You for Your handiwork, and for always
being my Protector. I am safe in Your hands. Amen.

October 7
LIBERTY AND FREEDOM

NOW THE LORD IS THE SPIRIT; AND WHERE THE
SPIRIT OF THE LORD IS, THERE IS LIBERTY.
2 CORINTHIANS 3:17

JOHN NEWTON was the captain of a slave ship, but after he found salvation and received freedom from God, he wrote these words: "I once was lost but now am found, was blind, but now I see." God is able to save anyone who is willing to believe in Him, no matter what they have done in the past.

Do you feel oppressed today? Perhaps you are chained by guilt. Maybe you feel like a failure. Your life doesn't have to be like this. Jesus came to set the captives free, to heal the brokenhearted. John 8:36 says, "Therefore if the Son makes you free, you shall be free indeed." And 2 Corinthians 3:6 adds, "The letter kills, but the Spirit gives life."

People often cannot forgive themselves for the things they've done in the past, but the Word of God says, "There is therefore now no condemnation to those who are in Christ Jesus, who do not walk according to the flesh, but according to the Spirit. For the law of the Spirit of life in Christ Jesus has made me free from the law of sin and death" (Rom. 8:1–2). When people hear these words, I can literally see the shackles of guilt falling off. They find freedom in God through His Spirit.

The Lord can and will do this for you. He died for you and me on the cross of Calvary. He took all our sin upon His shoulders. Believe that the Lord will forgive you, then choose to let your life be governed by His Spirit.

PRAYER: God, what You've done for me on the cross is unfathomable.
Help me to accept it into my soul and to live in freedom. Amen.

October 8
WHAT'S YOUR HERITAGE?

PUT ON THE NEW MAN WHICH WAS CREATED ACCORDING
TO GOD, IN TRUE RIGHTEOUSNESS AND HOLINESS.
EPHESIANS 4:24

MY PARENTS both originate from northeast Scotland, and we have our own tartan. I have a national Scottish kilt that was given to me many years ago, which I wore at the wedding of my youngest daughter, Jilly.

Some time after the wedding, a big strong young Zulu man came up to me and said that he enjoyed seeing me wearing my family tartan, displaying my culture unashamedly. He said that most young men are too embarrassed to wear their kilts.

I told him that as long as our cultural roots do not in any way clash with the teachings of our Lord Jesus Christ, I don't have a problem. However, the minute there are differences between our culture and the Word of God, that's when our cultural legacy must take second place.

When people get serious with God they must understand that they are new people in Christ. They have a new culture when they become believers. The culture we have been born into through Jesus Christ is one that has never changed in more than two thousand years. It's a culture that goes back to the very beginning, to Adam and Eve—a heritage in which the Lord Himself, our heavenly Father, meant us to live and prosper.

Jesus said that He came so that we might have abundant life, but we have to live it according to God's culture and not our own. Our cultural heritage should never take precedence over our faith in Jesus Christ.

∞

PRAYER: God, I praise You for my roots; let me
honor them, but honor You first. Amen.

October 9

IN EVERYTHING GIVE THANKS

THE LORD IS MY STRENGTH AND MY SHIELD; MY HEART
TRUSTED IN HIM, AND I AM HELPED; THEREFORE MY HEART
GREATLY REJOICES, AND WITH MY SONG I WILL PRAISE HIM.
PSALM 28:7

WHILE I was out jogging one morning, the sun broke through the clouds, turning them deep crimson. As I continued along the farm road, I began to think of all the good things God has given me. It made my heart glad, and I realized that when we begin to think of what we have, we truly understand how much it is. I was thankful for eyes to see the beautiful morning; ears to hear the birdsong; and a family at home—my wife, children, and grandchildren. My wife loves me and is faithful to me. My children love the Lord and have a relationship with Him.

My heart was so grateful for all these things; and then I also remembered that my name is written in the Lamb's Book of Life, that Jesus is my Savior, and that eternity awaits me. I have such peace in my heart—something money can't buy— and I sang to the Lord all the way home.

Later, as I sat at my desk, I thought of those who didn't see the sunrise, whose thoughts are dark and negative, and whose health is affected by their unhappy outlook on life. This often results in physical manifestations such as ulcers, migraines, and high blood pressure. Why should they suffer so, when relief comes from a simple change of heart?

Cultivating a positive, thankful heart affects yourself and others. God smiles at our endeavors when we enjoy His world, the work of our hands, and a real relationship with Jesus.

PRAYER: Lord, unleash a flood of thankfulness in my life. I
cannot count the ways You've blessed me. Amen.

October 10

NO SUCH THING AS COINCIDENCE

"BUT SEEK FIRST THE KINGDOM OF GOD AND HIS RIGHTEOUSNESS,
AND ALL THESE THINGS SHALL BE ADDED TO YOU."
MATTHEW 6:33

NOTHING THAT happens to a Christian is by accident—all things work together for good. No matter what we've experienced, no matter what suffering or what calamity we're going through, it's not an accident; it's part of God's universal plan.

Every patriarch that I've read about in the Bible—from Adam to Paul—went through testing and character building. Our circumstances at the time may seem traumatic and unnecessary as we cry out, "Lord, how can You as a God of love allow this to happen to me?" But the Lord says, "I have My reasons." If you're going through a tough time in your life, stand fast. Allow the Lord to work out His plan for your life, knowing that "all things work together for good."

William Walford sums up the thought beautifully in the following stanza from "Sweet Hour of Prayer."

> *Sweet hour of prayer! sweet hour of prayer! / That calls me from a world of care, / And bids me at my Father's throne / Make all my wants and wishes known.*
> *In seasons of distress and grief, / My soul has often found relief / And oft escaped the tempter's snare / By thy return, sweet hour of prayer!*

It is in times of trial that we find comfort and solace in God and trust His workings in our lives.

PRAYER: God, in times of grief I hold on to the promise that You're
working for my good. Lord, have mercy on me. Amen.

October 11

POWER IN THE WORD

HAVE RESPECT TO THE COVENANT; FOR THE DARK PLACES
OF THE EARTH ARE FULL OF THE HAUNTS OF CRUELTY.
OH, DO NOT LET THE OPPRESSED RETURN ASHAMED!
LET THE POOR AND NEEDY PRAISE YOUR NAME.
PSALM 74:20—21

IN THE early 1500s only scholars could read God's Word. In fact, it was illegal to own an English Bible or even to memorize scriptures! In Coventry, England, seven Christians were burnt at the stake in 1519 for teaching their children the Lord's Prayer and the Ten Commandments in English. The Bible was believed to be "vulgar" if it was written in any language other than Latin, and its use was believed to be heresy.

William Tyndale was a highly educated man, fluent in several languages including Greek and Hebrew, and he committed to translating the Bible into English. One doctor of divinity said to him that English was suitable only for plowmen and shopkeepers, but not for the Bible.

William Tyndale's eyes blazed. He knew he could—and should—write an accurate translation for those whose mother tongue was English, so that the poor and uneducated could see the plain Word of God for themselves.

We praise God for William Tyndale, who was steadfast and resolute in bringing the Word of God to the masses.

The Word of God is the temperature gauge, the compass, the direction finder—everything that you could think of and more. It's life itself. William Tyndale knew this—he knew that if he could translate the Bible into English, people would be set free. There is indeed power in the Word of almighty God.

PRAYER: God, Your Word is life. Let me never take it for granted. Amen.

October 12

ONLY GOD'S OPINION COUNTS

THE LORD, HE IS THE ONE WHO GOES BEFORE YOU.
HE WILL BE WITH YOU, HE WILL NOT LEAVE YOU NOR
FORSAKE YOU; DO NOT FEAR NOR BE DISMAYED.
DEUTERONOMY 31:8

"KEEPING UP with the Joneses" is a dangerous practice. If your neighbor has bought a new car, that does not mean you have to do the same. I can assure you that when it comes to paying the bill for that expensive car, the people we try to impress will be nowhere to be seen. We must live and work according to the standards that the Lord, and no one else, has set for us.

Since becoming a believer, one of the things that the Lord has set me free from is trying to find favor with men. We can see it among young and old: our fear of others causes us to do things that we would not ordinarily do in order to find favor from our peers. We place undue weight on their opinions. This often gets us into trouble.

Christianity gives us freedom, which can be defined as the power or right to act, speak, or think freely. You might ask, "Where we can find examples and advice from, if not from others?" This comes from spending time with God. When we have fear of God, we have no more fear of man, and we can start operating according to what God wants us to do. If you spend enough time with God, your fear of man will diminish automatically, and your reverence for God will increase.

PRAYER: Jesus, You're the only one I need to keep up with.
Let me love my fellow man, but never fear him. Amen.

October 13
LET GO AND LET GOD

TRUST IN THE LORD WITH ALL YOUR HEART, AND LEAN
NOT ON YOUR OWN UNDERSTANDING; IN ALL YOUR WAYS
ACKNOWLEDGE HIM, AND HE SHALL DIRECT YOUR PATHS.
PROVERBS 3:5–6

LEGALISM IS a disease that affects more mature Christians. When we first come to Jesus, we are so conscious of the fact that we are sinners that we rely totally on God's forgiving nature, on God's grace—His loving-kindness. We're conscious that we do not deserve it. We are freshly, painfully aware that if it weren't for Him, we would be lost.

But then we face a terrible danger as Christians who have been walking with the Lord for many years. Slowly but surely we start thinking that we're pretty good after all, that we don't really need God's grace because we have already been forgiven.

Nothing could be further from the truth. After walking for nearly forty years with the Lord, I have been brought to the realization that there's nothing good in me, save the Lord Jesus Christ. At the end of the day, if it weren't for God's divine love and forgiveness, I would slide right back into that miry pit from whence I came.

As long as we are trying to sort things out ourselves, the Lord Jesus Christ cannot move. We effectively tie His hands. However, when we hand the matter over to the Lord and say, "Lord, I can't anymore," that's when He kicks in and things start to happen. Just trust the Lord with all your heart and don't rely on your own strength. Then you will see that He has a perfect plan for you.

PRAYER: God, no matter how long I walk with You, I pray that I always
will hold on to You as tightly as I did when I first met You. Amen.

October 14
FIND YOUR IDENTITY

BLESS THE LORD, O MY SOUL, AND FORGET NOT ALL HIS BENEFITS:
WHO FORGIVES ALL YOUR INIQUITIES, WHO HEALS ALL YOUR
DISEASES, WHO REDEEMS YOUR LIFE FROM DESTRUCTION, WHO
CROWNS YOU WITH LOVINGKINDNESS AND TENDER MERCIES.
PSALM 103:2–4

A HIGH-PROFILE businessman goes to the airport to catch his flight. He's running a bit late, but because he's well-known, he thinks there won't be any problem. But the young lady behind the counter says, "I'm so sorry, sir, but that flight is now closed."

He is absolutely indignant and won't take no for an answer. "Do you know who I am?" he demands. She replies, "No, sir, I don't, but just hang on a moment." She gets on the intercom and says, "Attention, ladies and gentlemen. I have a man here who does not know who he is. Could somebody please come and identify him?"

Do you know who you are in Christ? It is absolutely essential to know who you are, because if you don't, the devil will try to tell you. Satan will say that you are a waste of time, that you've made mistakes in your life, and that you'll never come right again—but that is a lie. The Bible says in Romans 3:23, "All have sinned and fall short of the glory of God." Having been born again, our sins are forgiven; but that does not mean that we never sin again. We need to know who we are in Christ—forgiven sinners.

Remember, it's Christ in you that is the hope of glory. When we know who we are in Christ, nothing can hold us back.

PRAYER: Lord Jesus, I treasure my identity in You and
thank You for Your miraculous forgiveness. Amen.

October 15

GENUINE WEALTH

RICHES DO NOT PROFIT IN THE DAY OF WRATH, BUT
RIGHTEOUSNESS DELIVERS FROM DEATH.
PROVERBS 11:4

THE OTHER morning I went for a ride on my mountain bike, just before the sun came up. As I cycled along the road, a large and expensive car passed me. The occupants hardly noticed the lone cyclist pedaling along for all he was worth. There is a small airport nearby, and I watched as the car drove up to an airplane parked on the runway. The sweat was pouring off my face as I pedaled strenuously up the hill while the plane took off effortlessly into the air.

"Who is the truly rich man?" I asked the Lord quietly. Later that morning, I sat in my office and counted my blessings. "You have truly blessed me, Lord," I said gratefully. "No money can buy what You have given me." Why not sit down right now and count your blessings? You may find that the things that seem so important are worth little at the end of the day.

It's a lesson we would do well to learn. If those people in the jet did not know Jesus Christ as their Lord and Savior, they had no future. If they were to become terminally ill, all the money in the world would not be able to help them. If they and their families were not serving God, their loss would be incalculable.

There is so much unhappiness in the world because the very things that we think will bring us peace, contentment, and fulfillment only bring us true poverty. Fame and wealth will not bring us life, peace, and joy—only the Lord our God can give us true wealth.

PRAYER: God, thank You for my many blessings. Help me keep
a right perspective of what true wealth really is. Amen.

October 16

WHERE IS YOUR HEART?

I WAIT FOR THE LORD, MY SOUL WAITS, AND IN HIS WORD I DO HOPE.
PSALM 130:5

WHAT DO you daydream of? Many of us may sit at work, but our minds are somewhere else. Matthew 6:21 says, "For where your treasure is, there your heart will be also." Many of us go to church on Sunday, but we sit there thinking about something totally different: sports or a relationship or work. Our minds are racing all the time, and we don't know how to slow down. Ultimately this can lead to things such as addiction, depression, anxiety, and fear.

When you have a quiet time in the morning, turn off your mobile phone and anything else that might distract you from spending quality time with God. If you focus on the Lord, the rest of your day will go so much better. When you spend time with God and give Him the firstfruits of your day, you will think more clearly and not be so easily tempted or distracted.

If I have heaven on my mind, that's where my heart will be. If I have the things of the world on my mind, then *that's* where my heart will be. This is the reason why some of us feel such despair—because we think from a carnal point of view, where there is just no hope. When we look at the political situation, the economic situation, or the moral situation, things seem hopeless. However, when we look to God without distraction, we know that all of these other things will come right.

PRAYER: God, please teach me to watch my drifting thoughts and
bring them back to valuable things that bring life. Amen.

October 17

NO GREATER LOVE

"GREATER LOVE HAS NO ONE THAN THIS, THAN TO
LAY DOWN ONE'S LIFE FOR HIS FRIENDS."
JOHN 15:13

I REMEMBER reading about a story that took place during the Second World War, in a Japanese prisoner of war labor camp. In fact, the story was made into a movie called *To End All Wars*. In this camp, the prisoners of war were treated savagely by the Japanese. The prisoners were half-starved and brutalized, and worked extremely hard to build the Burma Railway.

At the end of one particular day, they returned to camp and were made to stand at attention, as usual. A soldier took their tools and counted them as he put them away in a shed. He came back and told the sergeant that they were one spade short.

The men were shattered. They were sure that no one would have betrayed their comrades. The sergeant started screaming at the prisoners, claiming that if the spade was not returned immediately, every prisoner would be shot.

By this time the soldiers were lined up with their rifles, ready to shoot the prisoners one by one. The sergeant said one last time, "Who took the spade?" One American, a self-interested man whose allegiance was often unclear, stepped forward just in time to save his friends. The sergeant was so angry that he took a rifle and beat the man to within an inch of his life. Moments later, the soldier who had done the count came running back, saying he'd made a mistake. All the spades *were* accounted for.

That is love—the most powerful force on earth.

∞

PRAYER: Jesus, thank You for standing in my place
and for saving me with Your love. Amen.

October 18

TWO ARE BETTER THAN ONE

CHARM IS DECEITFUL AND BEAUTY IS PASSING, BUT A
WOMAN WHO FEARS THE LORD, SHE SHALL BE PRAISED.
PROVERBS 31:30

I HAVE spoken to so many heartbroken wives who come to seek prayer and encouragement. They are trusting God to change the hearts of their husbands who have turned their backs on God. Often a change of heart occurs because of the prayers of a faithful wife who refuses to give up on her husband.

God created us to be in close relationship with one another. In the book of Ecclesiastes, the writer says two people are better off than one because they can help each other succeed (4:9). If one person falls, the other can reach out and help him. But someone who falls alone is in real trouble. Likewise, two people lying close together can keep each other warm. But how can one be warm alone? Three are even better, for a triple-braided cord is not easily broken (4:12). Of course, the Lord Jesus is the one who makes up the third cord.

If a woman stands in her husband's corner, backing him all the way, that man—irrespective of size or stature—will knock out the heavyweight boxing champion of the world with no problem at all. We need to affirm and pray for those we love on a continual basis. Let's do everything in our power to strengthen our closest relationships, and in so doing, honor the Lord.

PRAYER: Jesus, please be the third cord as we hold each other up. Amen.

October 19

TIMING IS OF THE ESSENCE

TO EVERYTHING THERE IS A SEASON, A TIME
FOR EVERY PURPOSE UNDER HEAVEN.
ECCLESIASTES 3:1

TIMING CAN be tricky, but it is so important. For instance, a good Christian woman might be so desperate to see her husband come to Christ that she leaves Christian magazines all over the house, hoping her husband will come in, pick up the magazine, read it, and be saved. Unfortunately, it doesn't work like that; in fact, if anything, it may chase him further from God. Timing is of the essence.

I pray that God would give us all a perception and an understanding of the right time to make a move. What we must do for our loved ones, especially those who do not love Jesus, is to live a life of love—showing them the peace, joy, and tranquility in our lives.

I received a phone call this morning from a young lady who was so excited because she had just led her husband to Christ. His timing is perfect, so don't give up!

There is a time to sow and a time to reap. We prepare the land, we nurture the crop, we fertilize it, we make sure it is well watered, and then when it's ready for harvest, we get that sickle and we sharpen it. Only then can the field be reaped. Timing is of the essence. Prepare the soil, pray the prayer of faith, and get ready for the harvest.

PRAYER: God, I trust in Your perfect timing. Help me
to track with You in my daily moves. Amen.

October 20

SPIRITUAL SEPARATION

THEREFORE WITH JOY YOU WILL DRAW WATER
FROM THE WELLS OF SALVATION.
ISAIAH 12:3

ONE WINTER'S day, my wife, Jill, and I went to visit my mother. My mother was always a gentle soul. We had a good relationship, and we chatted for a while.

Then, without warning, she burst into tears. "Mom, what's wrong?" I asked.

She retained her strong Scottish accent her whole life, even though she'd come to Africa as a young girl. "Laddie, it's no' the same anymore," she said. "Something is different." I thought for a moment, then realized what it was: the Holy Spirit had come into my life, and my mother felt separated from me. I got on my knees and said to her, "Mom, don't you want the Lord to be your Lord and Savior as well?"

She replied, "Aye, laddie, that would be fine." With that, Jill and I led my mother to Christ. Another family member had come home!

My father was a different kettle of fish. He refused to talk about politics and religion. After my mom passed away, Dad's health went downhill, and I decided to talk to him again about Jesus. With my whole family praying, I drove to the hospital where he had been admitted. When I got there, all I could do was hug him and tell him I loved him. He broke down and started weeping. I asked him if he would like to invite Jesus into his heart, and he agreed. When I looked up, everyone was weeping. A nurse said through her tears, "Mr. Buchan, welcome to the family of God!" Six weeks later, my dad went to be with the Lord.

To anyone who might have a loved one who is unsaved: do some fasting and praying, and trust that God will move their hearts.

PRAYER: Jesus, thank You for my loved ones. Let me not
weary of praying for their salvation. Amen.

October 21

THOSE WHO SUFFER

GIVING ALL DILIGENCE, ADD TO YOUR FAITH VIRTUE, TO VIRTUE
KNOWLEDGE, TO KNOWLEDGE SELF-CONTROL, TO SELF-CONTROL
PERSEVERANCE, TO PERSEVERANCE GODLINESS, TO GODLINESS
BROTHERLY KINDNESS, AND TO BROTHERLY KINDNESS LOVE.
2 PETER 1:5–7

EARLY THIS morning, while having my quiet time, the Lord reminded me again that just because we are believers, we are not exempt from experiencing hardship, sorrow, or suffering.

Jesus was without sin, yet He had to endure suffering because He took our sins upon Himself. He paid the price for our redemption so that if we are born again of His Spirit, and by faith believe and follow Him, we would receive eternal life.

History tells us that very few of Jesus' disciples died a natural death. All but one died a martyr's death. John, the one who was not martyred, still suffered greatly: he was boiled in oil, beaten, arrested, and starved on many occasions. We must remember that we are also fighting the fight of our lives. Yes, we have victory in Jesus Christ our Lord, but we still need to run our race, and by God's grace, finish strong.

In these times in which we live, we must be prepared to face hardships, sorrow, suffering, and persecution for our faith in Jesus. Yet the Lord has said in the Word that He will not allow us to be tempted above what we are able to bear (1 Cor. 10:13). He will always make a way for us, and He promises that He will never leave us nor forsake us (Heb. 13:5).

PRAYER: Dear God, I know that suffering is inevitable. Please guard my heart and fill me with peace as I endure to the end with You. Amen.

October 22

THE MAN IN THE MIRROR

"JUDGE NOT, THAT YOU BE NOT JUDGED. FOR WITH WHAT
JUDGMENT YOU JUDGE, YOU WILL BE JUDGED; AND WITH THE
MEASURE YOU USE, IT WILL BE MEASURED BACK TO YOU. AND
WHY DO YOU LOOK AT THE SPECK IN YOUR BROTHER'S EYE,
BUT DO NOT CONSIDER THE PLANK IN YOUR OWN EYE?"
MATTHEW 7:1–3

PEOPLE ARE not as interested in what we believers say as they are in what we do. They want to see a change in our lives. When they see that there is no longer a plank in our eye, then they will come and ask us to remove the speck from their eye.

If a man is continually unfaithful to his wife, how can he possibly counsel people who are going through separation? Go home, get your house in order, and then come and help other people sort out their problems. Charity begins at home. The Lord says clearly in His Word that a man who cannot take care of his own family is worse than an unbeliever (1 Tim. 5:8).

I exhort you to come before the Lord, get on your knees, and confess your failings and shortcomings before telling others how to live their lives. The worst kind of Christian is one who is a hypocrite, and we don't want the secular world believing that all believers are like this.

Let your words have merit: be transparent so that people can see who you are. Remember, if you really want to see a positive change in this world, it needs to start with you.

PRAYER: Lord, above all else, make me truehearted. I pray that You will
stamp out hypocrisy in the Christian faith, so that all may know You. Amen.

October 23

LIVE LIFE TO THE FULL

HE WILL FULFILL THE DESIRE OF THOSE WHO FEAR HIM;
HE ALSO WILL HEAR THEIR CRY AND SAVE THEM.
PSALM 145:19

I HAVE good news for people who make mistakes (which should cover all of us): the only way of learning *is* by making mistakes. If you never try, you'll never know. I've met many men coming to the end of their lives who are filled with regret because they passed on opportunities that frightened them. But the Lord gives us the courage to attempt the impossible.

Live life to the full! Go for it, because you have nothing to lose and everything to gain. One of our favorite verses at Shalom is Psalm 37:4: "Delight yourself also in the LORD, and He shall give you the desires of your heart."

It's not the length of life that makes a difference, but the quality of life. What an opportunity for us in this day and age to do all that we can, and to do it for God: to climb the highest mountain, to run the longest race, to be different for Jesus, and to keep that light burning brightly.

Jesus said He came that we might live life abundantly, and that's what we've got to do. We must do what we can with the time we have left, knowing we have a glorious future waiting for us in heaven.

PRAYER: Jesus, I thank You that You use my mistakes for
growth. Use me without reservation! Amen.

October 24

THE POWER OF THE MIND

YOU HAVE MADE THE HEAVENS AND THE EARTH
BY YOUR GREAT POWER AND OUTSTRETCHED ARM.
THERE IS NOTHING TOO HARD FOR YOU.
JEREMIAH 32:17

GOD SPECIALIZES in using nobodies and making them somebodies—like taking donkeys and making them into racehorses. He took a man by the name of Saul who was out to kill Christians, changed his life, and made him into a mighty apostle. God took Moses—a man who lost his temper, killed a slave, and then ran for his life like a coward—and used him to lead an entire nation. God uses people like you and me.

I read a book recently, written by a South African scientist who has been studying sports science for more than forty years. The author claims that success is 90 percent about what happens in your mind and only 10 percent about what happens in your body.

It's not about being the best; neither is it about being the most qualified. No, it's about knowing who you are and believing in what God can do. Christ in us gives us the strength and ability to achieve the impossible.

I don't know where you are at the moment, but if you feel there is no hope, I want to challenge you to rededicate your life to Jesus. Christ has promised that we can do all things though Him (Phil. 4:13). You *are* a winner, and you *can* do it, because God designed you to be a victor.

PRAYER: God, I believe—help me to believe! You are the designer
and approver of my life and abilities, and I trust You. Amen.

October 25

LOVE ONE ANOTHER

[THE LORD] WILL TURN THE HEARTS OF THE FATHERS TO THE
CHILDREN, AND THE HEARTS OF THE CHILDREN TO THEIR FATHERS.
MALACHI 4:6

LIKE NEVER before, I have seen fathers turning back to their children and children turning back to their fathers. What a blessed time on our journey toward the climax of the age. This is a time for fathers to reconcile with their children, and children with their fathers; a time for seeking forgiveness and restoration, so that the Lord can come in His glory.

Dear friend, I want to stress the importance of putting our personal differences aside. There are consequences for every decision we make. The Bible says, "There is no fear in love; but perfect love casts out fear" (1 John 4:18). I've seen so many feuds that destroy families. Let us not make the same mistake!

I'm so grateful that I personally have Jesus Christ as my Lord and Savior. If it weren't for Him, I don't know where I'd be today or, more to the point, where my family would be. Because I've met Him, and because He showed me my faults, my shortcomings, and my failures, I have been able to rectify many of them. I can now speak honestly to my children. I can be transparent. They know I'm not perfect—far from it—but they also know that God is not finished with me yet.

Spend lots of time with your loved ones. Time is passing by. Redeem the time. Ask for forgiveness, even if it's not entirely your fault. Respect one another, and God will heal those wounds and those misunderstandings.

PRAYER: God, I pray for reconciliation in my family and with
my loved ones as we get closer to Your coming. Amen.

October 26
RESPECT AND GRATITUDE

"THE KING WILL ANSWER AND SAY TO THEM, 'ASSUREDLY,
I SAY TO YOU, INASMUCH AS YOU DID IT TO ONE OF THE
LEAST OF THESE MY BRETHREN, YOU DID IT TO ME.'"
MATTHEW 25:40

THE BEST way of saying thank you to God is taking care of the least of the Lord's brethren by helping those in need: the widows, the orphans, those who are sick, prisoners, or people who are without food or clothing. What does it cost to say thank you to the shop attendant? What does it cost to say thank you to the waitress who just served you a tasty meal?

What about your spouse who has been so faithful to you for many years? Show your appreciation by giving them something you know they'll love. You can't take money with you to heaven. And be just as generous with words of affirmation. My younger son bought some cattle recently, and he asked me to have a look at them and say what I thought of them. I responded that I could not have done better, and saw his face light up when he said, "Thanks, Dad." Affirmation is so important in a world that is so negative. So don't leave for tomorrow what you can do today. Be gracious to one another, because it costs absolutely nothing.

Be kind and considerate to your colleagues, your friends, and strangers too. Offer to carry a bag for the elderly woman at the airport or offer her your seat on the bus. Respect your elders, remembering that you too will one day get old. Do all you can to sow into the kingdom of God, bearing in mind that what you do for someone on earth is the same as ministering to Jesus Himself.

PRAYER: Jesus, I pray for a supply of kindness that flows
straight from You into the ones You set in my path. Show
me how to be generous and loving today. Amen.

October 27

SEEK HIS FORGIVENESS

"IF MY PEOPLE WHO ARE CALLED BY MY NAME WILL HUMBLE
THEMSELVES, AND PRAY AND SEEK MY FACE, AND TURN FROM
THEIR WICKED WAYS, THEN I WILL HEAR FROM HEAVEN,
AND WILL FORGIVE THEIR SIN AND HEAL THEIR LAND."
2 CHRONICLES 7:14

I RECENTLY returned from spending some time on a game farm. As part of my quiet time with the Lord, I went for long walks on my own in the mornings, just taking in God's glory. As I walked, I saw symptoms of mistreatment of the land. Many times an unthinking, desperate farmer will overwork the land because of financial needs, or overgraze the land with too many livestock per acre. This can lead to soil erosion. But if that land is left alone for a number of years it will miraculously recover. I thought of how we humans thoughtlessly plunder this amazing creation all around the world, taking what we want for profit. However, if given the time, the land does heal. This is truly a miracle from God, who can be so forgiving. And so it is with us as people.

Take Peter, for example. He denied Jesus three times, and yet Jesus forgave him and told him to carry on and lead the church (John 21:15–17). It doesn't matter what we've been through, as long as we turn to God. Like no one else can, He will heal us and make us even stronger. God uses ordinary people like you and me, who have made so many mistakes, to do His work and help others start again.

As you go about your week, ask God to open your spiritual eyes to view His creation in a new way. You'll see there's plenty of hope left if you continue to follow His way.

PRAYER: God, thank You for healing us. Please help me to see
regeneration in my own life, as well as in the world around me. Amen.

October 28

A JUST AND HOLY MAN

HEROD FEARED JOHN, KNOWING THAT HE WAS A JUST AND
HOLY MAN, AND HE PROTECTED HIM. AND WHEN HE HEARD
HIM, HE DID MANY THINGS, AND HEARD HIM GLADLY.
MARK 6:20

DO YOU know what I love about John the Baptist? He was a no-nonsense man. There was no gray area with John; it was either right or wrong, sinful or godly, but there was no in-between.

I have been to the Judean Desert, and I don't know how a human can exist there. There's no water, no grass, no food, and the temperature goes up to 109 degrees. Yet John lived there, eating wild honey and locusts. If he walked into a city today, the citizens would probably lock him up and call him insane.

When John spoke, people came from all over to hear him. They wanted to know the truth. John the Baptist had a call from God, so he did what God wanted him to do. He was set aside for God and was different from the world. Herod eventually had him beheaded, but the Bible says that Herod secretly admired John because he was a man of substance who did not fear other men. He told the truth.

I struggled for a long time with fear of man. As a little boy I couldn't speak to more than two people at the same time, and if I saw a girl I'd run a mile. So what happened? I met the Man from Galilee. I met Jesus Christ, and He became my Lord and Savior. He took me out of a miry pit and gave me a second chance.

I no longer have a fear of man—God took it away and replaced it with fear of Him. And when I say, "I fear God," I am talking about respect and love.

PRAYER: God, thank You for the example of John the Baptist.
Help me to listen for my own call from You. Amen.

October 29
THE PARABLE OF THE LOST SON

"HE AROSE AND CAME TO HIS FATHER. BUT WHEN HE WAS STILL
A GREAT WAY OFF, HIS FATHER SAW HIM AND HAD COMPASSION,
AND RAN AND FELL ON HIS NECK AND KISSED HIM."
LUKE 15:20

IN THIS parable, we have a farmer who has worked hard all his life. The younger son comes to his father and says, "I'm tired of working here. I'm tired of planting crops. I'm tired of getting up early in the morning. I want some fun in my life."

The father is brokenhearted. He says, "But son, half of this is going to be yours one day."

The boy replies, "I don't care! I want my inheritance now!"

The son takes his inheritance, goes to the big city, and squanders his money. Eventually he ends up with no money, no friends, and no job. He becomes a beggar on the streets. One day he comes to his senses and thinks, *Even the workers on my father's farm are doing better than I am. I'll go back and ask for a job.*

Can you imagine the father every afternoon, scanning the horizon as the sun goes down, hoping to see his son? Can you imagine the joy in the father's heart when he looks up and sees a bedraggled figure at the bottom of the road?

The father leaves the house and takes a few steps toward the figure. Hope swells in his heart and he breaks into a run. "Is that you, son?" Hesitantly, the son raises a hand. "It's me, Dad." The father runs toward his son, arms open wide. Tears fall from his cheeks as he gathers his son into a great big hug. "Son! It's so good to see you. Once you were lost, but now you're home!"

PRAYER: Heavenly Father, thank You for welcoming me home. Amen.

October 30
THE BEAUTY OF THE BIBLE

IN THE BEGINNING WAS THE WORD, AND THE WORD WAS WITH
GOD, AND THE WORD WAS GOD. HE WAS IN THE BEGINNING
WITH GOD. ALL THINGS WERE MADE THROUGH HIM, AND
WITHOUT HIM NOTHING WAS MADE THAT WAS MADE.
JOHN 1:1–3

MY BIBLE is old and tattered. It has a leather cover and looks as though it has been carried around in a farm vehicle for years, which is precisely what has happened to it. It is falling apart. I call it my "agricultural manual": it tells me when to plant, when to buy, and when to sell. It instructs me not to muzzle the ox that treads out the corn; to love my wife and not to antagonize my children; to respect my elders; and to walk by faith and not by sight.

The Bible is called the Living Word because it has life-giving power. It is the only book in the world that is always in season, topical, and totally up-to-date. No wonder it is the world's best seller. It is a wonderful friend to have, especially during dark nights.

When I have to make decisions, I always turn to the Word and trust the Lord to give me direction. The Bible promises to be "a lamp to my feet and a light to my path" (Ps. 119:105); but the onus is on us to read it, meditate on it, and believe it. Then we are sure to receive guidance for our lives.

There is power in the Word of God. When a preacher declares, "The Word of God says . . . ," incredible power is released.

PRAYER: Jesus, thank You for the gift of Your Word, and for inspiring its writers throughout the ages. Guide me as I delve in every day. Amen.

October 31

A PLACE OF REFUGE

"GOD DID NOT SEND HIS SON INTO THE WORLD TO CONDEMN THE
WORLD, BUT THAT THE WORLD THROUGH HIM MIGHT BE SAVED."
JOHN 3:17

A PLACE of refuge is a place where you can go and be safe from the storms of life. In Numbers 35, Moses was instructed by God that when the children of Israel came into the promised land, they were to keep certain places separate to serve as places of refuge.

Jesus Christ is a place of refuge for you and me. Perhaps you have a shady past, or did something you're not proud of, and you are finding it very hard to forgive yourself. At the end of the day you must learn to live with yourself and your circumstances. Maybe you've injured someone in an accident or been through an ugly divorce, and you don't know how to come to terms with it.

Go to the place of refuge. Jesus says that if you confess your sins, He is faithful and just and will forgive your sins and cleanse you of all unrighteousness (1 John 1:9). That's why I love Him so much. He is the friend of sinners, of those who have made mistakes.

My place of refuge is my quiet-time room. Early in the morning I come before the Lord; I spend time with Him, and I pray and refresh myself. I confess my sins, and then I move on.

Remember, there is a place of refuge for you, and it doesn't matter what you've done or what you've been through. Jesus is there, where you can go and hide and be with Him so that He can restore you. He is loving and forgiving, and He is waiting for you.

PRAYER: Jesus, it is such a relief to have refuge in You. Lead
me to You when I become overwhelmed. Amen.

NOVEMBER

November 1

A TIME OF PRUNING

MANY ARE THE AFFLICTIONS OF THE RIGHTEOUS, BUT
THE LORD DELIVERS HIM OUT OF THEM ALL.
PSALM 34:19

WHEN DO you prune a tree? In the middle of summer? No, because you will cut off all the new buds, all the new fruit. You do it in a dormant time, in the winter. Why do you prune a tree? So that it will produce more fruit.

The Lord doesn't worry about trees that don't bear fruit. Those trees He cuts down and uses for firewood. But the Lord prunes a good tree that produces good fruit so that it will produce even more good fruit. The Lord uses our wintertime, our time of difficulty, to prune us so that we can produce more fruit.

The pruning process is very difficult for us and is not pleasant at the time. But it must be done. This is the bottom line: life's purpose is to bring glory to God, and the only way to do that is by bearing fruit. The fruit that the Lord wants us to produce is "love, joy, peace, longsuffering, kindness, goodness, faithfulness, gentleness, self-control" (Gal. 5:22–23).

Whenever you experience a winter in your life, remember that spring is coming and that the Lord will give you the strength to get through it. All you have to do is rest in Him.

PRAYER: God, I trust that You are a wise and careful pruner. Please remove
from me all the things that are keeping me from bearing fruit. Amen.

November 2

THE TRUE HANDICAP

"THEREFORE IF THE SON MAKES YOU FREE,
YOU SHALL BE FREE INDEED."
JOHN 8:36

SELF-CENTEREDNESS IS an inescapable part of man's fallen nature. I believe that only Jesus can free us from being selfish, self-centered people. As long as we are focused on ourselves, we cannot see the plight of those who live around us.

Freedom from self is the greatest freedom we will ever know. It enables us to live in peace, with joy and love in our hearts. It enables us to be unconcerned about what people think of us or say about us because we are more concerned for others than we are for ourselves. It enables us also to live as givers and not takers, and to value things such as love, family, honor, integrity, and true friendship—things that money can't buy.

Nick Vujicic came to visit me here in the ministry office on our farm, accompanied by two or three friends who travel with him and help him. As you may know, Nick was born with no arms and no legs. The assistants lifted him onto the boardroom table, and we spoke for some time.

I felt very humbled in his presence because he so easily reaches out to others. He was interested in me, in our work here, and in our children's home. He was full of God's love and grace, and so unconcerned about himself. He is now married to a lovely woman and is proud to be called a father. He lives life to the full, despite circumstances that can't always be easy for him.

Jesus said that unless we deny ourselves, take up our crosses daily, and follow after Him, we cannot be His disciples. Let's die to self and live for Jesus and others.

PRAYER: God, I pray for freedom from self-centeredness.
Fill my heart with love for others instead. Amen.

November 3

THE POWER OF THE SPIRIT

WHEN THE DAY OF PENTECOST HAD FULLY COME, THEY WERE ALL
WITH ONE ACCORD IN ONE PLACE. AND SUDDENLY THERE CAME
A SOUND FROM HEAVEN, AS OF A RUSHING MIGHTY WIND, AND
IT FILLED THE WHOLE HOUSE WHERE THEY WERE SITTING.
ACTS 2:1–2

A DEFINITION of the word *power* is the capacity to influence the behavior of others, their emotions, or the course of events. The main evidence of the visitation of the Holy Spirit was the power that the disciples experienced in today's verse.

Charles H. Spurgeon said, "There is no telling how much power God can put into a man." We all have the power available to us; the only question is, how much are we prepared to believe God for? He gives us power through the Spirit. "If the Spirit of Him who raised Jesus from the dead dwells in you, He who raised Christ from the dead will also give life to your mortal bodies through His Spirit who dwells in you" (Rom. 8:11).

The Holy Spirit is the One who is known as the Comforter, the Helper, and the Friend who sticks closer than any brother. He is also known as the Advocate. In Greek, He is called the *Parakletos*. God wants to impart a fresh hunger for His presence and for the supernatural move of His Spirit in our hearts. In many places around the world the church has lost its hope. The answer is revival. Nobody and nothing can stop the work of the Holy Spirit.

Put aside any doubt, skepticism, and judgment, and allow the Holy Spirit to take full control of every aspect of your life. He will direct your path all the way home, so you have nothing to fear.

PRAYER: God, Your Spirit is synonymous with power. Please
flow through me and change the world. Amen.

November 4

PROTECTED BY PRAYER

NOW WE KNOW THAT GOD DOES NOT HEAR SINNERS; BUT IF ANYONE
IS A WORSHIPER OF GOD AND DOES HIS WILL, HE HEARS HIM.
JOHN 9:31

IT IS our habit on our farm to begin the day by singing Zulu hymns, reading God's Holy Scripture, and praying. One day, after we did exactly that, my son sent some of the staff off in a truck to fetch some building poles from a nearby plantation.

The driver, two teenage girls, and one helper were in the truck going down a steep hill when they lost control of the truck. It careered off the mountain and rolled.

One of our young herdsmen came riding down on his bike weeping uncontrollably, just half an hour after the prayer meeting had concluded. He said, "There's been a terrible accident. The truck has rolled." He wasn't sure if anyone had survived.

Fearing for the lives of the occupants, my son and I jumped into another vehicle and drove straight to the scene. As we came down the hill, I started to pray to God, "Please, Lord." The truck was at the bottom of the mountain, an absolute wreck.

Miraculously, no one was killed. One of the young girls broke her arm, and the passenger sitting next to the driver had a slight back injury, from which he has completely recovered. The driver had a neck injury, from which he has also recovered. The second young girl didn't have a scratch on her.

The young herdsman who had reported the accident reminded me how earlier that morning we had spent time in prayer. He firmly believed that the Lord Jesus Christ protected all four of those people in the vehicle. Yes, indeed, we can never underestimate the power of prayer.

PRAYER: Jesus, make prayer my first line of defense. Amen.

November 5

THE EMPTY TOMB

JESUS OF NAZARETH, A MAN ATTESTED BY GOD TO YOU BY
MIRACLES, WONDERS, AND SIGNS . . . WHOM GOD RAISED
UP, HAVING LOOSED THE PAINS OF DEATH, BECAUSE IT
WAS NOT POSSIBLE THAT HE SHOULD BE HELD BY IT.
ACTS 2:22, 24

MATTHEW HENRY once said, "Our duty as Christians is always to keep heaven in our eye and earth under our feet." We live on earth, but we are citizens of heaven. We are mere sojourners, travelers in a foreign land, and yet to see the way some of us stress and worry about things, you would think we are going to be here forever. No, our allegiance belongs to another land.

Things we do on earth have eternal value. Jesus only lived on this earth for thirty-three years and His ministry only lasted for three years, yet there is no one who has ever lived who has impacted the world more than Jesus Christ of Nazareth.

The Spirit of God that raised this carpenter's Son from the grave also dwells in us. Second Timothy 1:7 says, "For God has not given us a spirit of fear, but of power and of love and of a sound mind." So cast off those graveclothes you've been wearing. You are made alive, eternally, in the Spirit.

If we concentrate on Him and give Him first place in our lives, we will see change in our lives and in our outlook toward the future. Let us trust God, going out to attempt great things for Him.

PRAYER: Jesus, how amazing that Your life-giving Spirit dwells in
me. Please keep me focused on my heavenly home. Amen.

BOLDNESS, COURAGE, AND COMPASSION

I AM NOT ASHAMED OF THE GOSPEL OF CHRIST, FOR IT IS
THE POWER OF GOD TO SALVATION FOR EVERYONE WHO
BELIEVES, FOR THE JEW FIRST AND ALSO FOR THE GREEK.
ROMANS 1:16

THE FIRST campaign I ever held was in Ladysmith, South Africa, in 1989. God asked me three questions as I drove into that town: "Are you prepared to be a fool for Me? Are you prepared for people to say all manner of evil about you for My name's sake?" And the hardest one: "Are you prepared to see less of your family for My name's sake?" And I said, "Lord, only by Your grace, I'll drink of the cup." I don't sleep in my own bed very often anymore, but it's a small price to pay when I think of what Jesus did for me.

It's a privilege and an honor to be known as an ambassador of Jesus Christ, and you can be one too. You don't have to wait till you think you are holy and perfect to start sharing the gospel. So go out and preach the good news. Neither do you have to call a pastor to pray over people; you can pray for them yourself wherever you are. If somebody says they are feeling sick or have a problem, pray for them. Do you know that I have never had a man refuse prayer? I am talking about Hindus, Muslims, atheists, backsliders. There is great power in prayer.

God is calling you somewhere; your life is a mission field. You may have to overcome fear, you may have to sacrifice, but all this is more than made up for by the love you'll experience through the Spirit. I am praying for you to have boldness, courage, and compassion for the lost.

PRAYER: Jesus, prepare me to give what it takes to
speak Your Word effectively, with love. Amen.

November 7
FACE YOUR FEARS

THE RIGHTEOUS CRY OUT, AND THE LORD HEARS, AND
DELIVERS THEM OUT OF ALL THEIR TROUBLES.
PSALM 34:17

DID YOU know that if you put on the armor of God, the only part of the body that is vulnerable is your back? The Bible says to put on the belt of truth, the breastplate of righteousness, the shoes of the gospel of peace, the shield of faith, the helmet of salvation, and the sword of the Spirit (Eph. 6:14–17). It does not say anything about the back. You are not supposed to turn your back on your problems, just as you should not turn your back on an opponent, because your back is unprotected. Instead, face your problems head-on with the full armor of God.

In a storm, sailors will turn their boat to face the storm, pull in all the sails, and ride it out. If you don't turn the boat to face the storm, the wind will tear it apart. The same thing applies to everyday life: we have to face our problems and the storms of life, or we will not make it safely through them. Let's face them with God at our side.

If you don't run away from your problem, you may be surprised to find out how small it really is. It is often the "little foxes that spoil the vines" (Song 2:15). If you face your problems—no matter the size—God will go before you and make a way for you (Isa. 45:2).

Take your problems to Jesus. He will give you a game plan, and when you follow it, you will be set free. All you have to do is to trust God to get you through your storm.

PRAYER: God, please show me how to take the first step
toward facing my problem—trusting in You. Amen.

November 8
WHAT IS SALVATION?

FOR ALL HAVE SINNED AND FALL SHORT OF THE GLORY OF
GOD, BEING JUSTIFIED FREELY BY HIS GRACE THROUGH
THE REDEMPTION THAT IS IN CHRIST JESUS.
ROMANS 3:23–24

THE DAY after I gave my life to Jesus I was walking through my beautiful, green cornfield that was fully pregnant with a heavy crop of maize—and also extremely vunerable to hail and storm damage. Normally I would have been very worried, but I can honestly say I was only happy, because I knew my newly found Savior had forgiven my sin and taken my life in His hands. He was more than capable of protecting that crop.

God loves you and created you to be in a relationship with Him too. God is good, loving, and holy—and that means He is without sin. We humans, on the other hand, are born with a sinful nature and sin continually. When we choose to do wrong and to turn our backs on God, we separate ourselves from Him because He is holy and cannot look upon sin. God does not want anyone to be separated from Him—He wants us to be washed clean—but sin has caused our relationship with Him to be broken.

Jesus is God's only provision for man's sin. Only through Him can we know God personally and be forgiven. Some people try to bridge the gap between themselves and God by doing good works or getting involved in religious activities. But this is all in vain because it is impossible to earn salvation. Salvation is a free gift we receive through Jesus' sacrifice on the cross. When we're saved, we can be confident that Jesus' work has wiped out our sin so He can walk with us and take care of us in a loving, close relationship.

PRAYER: Dear God, thank You for sending Jesus to reconcile us to You! Amen.

November 9

THE PRINCE OF PEACE

"THESE THINGS I HAVE SPOKEN TO YOU, THAT IN ME YOU MAY
HAVE PEACE. IN THE WORLD YOU WILL HAVE TRIBULATION;
BUT BE OF GOOD CHEER, I HAVE OVERCOME THE WORLD."
JOHN 16:33

JEWISH PEOPLE say "Shalom" to one another, which means *peace*. If you speak
Afrikaans, I would say to you, "*Vrede*." If you speak isiZulu, I would say, "*Ukuthula*."

Jesus is the Prince of Peace. I don't know where you are at this moment: Maybe
you are trying to make as much money as you can in order to find peace for your
soul. You will not find peace there. I have tried it; it does not work. Or you may
think that if you do good works and help the poor and take care of the needy, you
will find peace. You won't find peace there.

Maybe you think that if you become a great athlete, or if you do well at university,
you will find peace. But you won't find peace there either. Peace comes only from
one place: the Prince of Peace.

An anxious spirit is contagious. The peace of God we're talking about here
comes from within. Spend time with God, and that peace can be transferred from
you to your loved ones.

Thomas à Kempis, that great man of God, said, "All men desire peace, but all do
not care for the things which belong unto true peace." Those things are the things
of God. When you find the peace of God, there will be no more fear in your heart.
There is nothing that can compare to it. You cannot buy peace. You can't earn it,
and you can't create it. You will find this peace when Jesus comes to live in your
heart. I pray that the peace of God will be a significant part of your life.

PRAYER: God, I look to You to show me real peace. Amen.

November 10

EVIL SCHEMES

NOW A GREAT MANY OF THE JEWS KNEW THAT HE WAS THERE; AND
THEY CAME, NOT FOR JESUS' SAKE ONLY, BUT THAT THEY MIGHT ALSO
SEE LAZARUS, WHOM HE HAD RAISED FROM THE DEAD. BUT THE CHIEF
PRIESTS PLOTTED TO PUT LAZARUS TO DEATH ALSO, BECAUSE ON ACCOUNT
OF HIM MANY OF THE JEWS WENT AWAY AND BELIEVED IN JESUS.
JOHN 12:9–11

AFTER COMING back to life, Lazarus was visited by many people because they knew him; he was part of their community. They had watched him die, be buried in a tomb, and come back to life because of Jesus. One can imagine that he probably became an overnight celebrity!

Lazarus was dead, and then God raised him up through Jesus. When people saw him alive and well, they believed that Jesus Christ was the Son of God. The sad part is that even as more and more people were coming to the faith, the high priests wanted to kill Lazarus. They were jealous because the people were more interested in Jesus than the priests. This kind of jealousy—the perceived stealing of "our" spotlight—is one of the most insidious things mankind can face.

The high priests refused to see what was right in front of them; they thought Jesus was taking people away from the faith, when in fact He was building the church. As Christians, we are called to make people hearers from heaven rather than hearers of our own personal message or agenda. Encouraging individuals toward good deeds or even belonging to a church will not get people into heaven. It is only when we acknowledge Jesus Christ as Lord and Savior that He forgives our sins and gives us eternal life.

PRAYER: God, You bring eternal life. Help me to align with Your
plan and power, rather than cherishing my own. Amen.

November 11

A REASON TO REJOICE

BEHOLD, THIS IS OUR GOD; WE HAVE WAITED FOR HIM, AND
HE WILL SAVE US. THIS IS THE LORD; WE HAVE WAITED FOR
HIM; WE WILL BE GLAD AND REJOICE IN HIS SALVATION.
ISAIAH 25:9

ARE YOU dejected because you did something terrible that you are ashamed of? If so, take it to Jesus. We all make mistakes, but we need to remember that there is no more condemnation for those who are in Christ (Rom. 8:1).

Don't beat yourself up every time you do something wrong. Rather, focus on Jesus Christ. The Bible says in 1 John 1:9 that "if we confess our sins, He is faithful and just to forgive us our sins and to cleanse us from all unrighteousness." The devil wants to keep you down—he does not want you to get up again. Don't give him the satisfaction.

When we make restitution, we break free from the evil one—the "accuser of our brethren" (Rev. 12:10). When we apologize and put the relationship right, then a strange and beautiful freedom takes place. The devil can no longer trouble us with his accusations. That's when true freedom comes into a person's life. If you've hurt someone, go to that person and ask them to forgive you. If they don't want to accept your apology, all you can do is pray for them and know that you did your best to put things right. Confess your sins, say you are sorry, and move on.

Take your sins to the Lord, repent, and ask Him to forgive you. And when He does, you need to forgive yourself too and move on. Once you realize this, you will have every reason to rejoice.

PRAYER: Lord, thank You for forgiving me and freeing me from the
past. Please give me the strength to move forward. Amen.

November 12
LIFE IN ABUNDANCE

IF YOU CONFESS WITH YOUR MOUTH THE LORD JESUS
AND BELIEVE IN YOUR HEART THAT GOD HAS RAISED
HIM FROM THE DEAD, YOU WILL BE SAVED.
ROMANS 10:9

THE MOMENT you receive Jesus Christ by faith, many things happen, including:

- Jesus Christ comes into your life: "To them God willed to make known what are the riches of the glory of this mystery among the Gentiles: which is Christ in you, the hope of glory" (Col. 1:27).
- Your sins are forgiven: "He has delivered us from the power of darkness and conveyed us into the kingdom of the Son of His love" (Col. 1:13–14).
- You become a child of God: "But as many as received Him, to them He gave the right to become children of God" (John 1:12–13).
- You receive eternal life: "He who hears My word and believes in Him who sent Me has everlasting life, and shall not come into judgment" (John 5:24).
- You begin the adventure for which God created you: "I have come that they may have life, and that they may have it more abundantly" (John 10:10).

You might think that you don't feel any different now that you are saved. As a Christian, it is important not to be led by feelings that come and go, but by faith in God and the truth of His Word. We can rest in the absolute certainty of it.

PRAYER: God, thank You for the wonderful gift of salvation; I
rejoice in the changes You've wrought in me! Amen.

November 13

FOLLOW THE SHEPHERD

"I AM THE GOOD SHEPHERD. THE GOOD SHEPHERD GIVES
HIS LIFE FOR THE SHEEP. BUT A HIRELING, HE WHO IS NOT
THE SHEPHERD, ONE WHO DOES NOT OWN THE SHEEP, SEES
THE WOLF COMING AND LEAVES THE SHEEP AND FLEES; AND
THE WOLF CATCHES THE SHEEP AND SCATTERS THEM."
JOHN 10:11–12

THE DIFFERENCE between a shepherd and a hireling is very simple: the shepherd is working for his inheritance, while a hireling is working for a wage. A shepherd makes sure his sheep are well fed and comfortable. If those sheep decide to lamb in the middle of the night, the shepherd will be there to help them.

A hireling has no dedication to the flock. He doesn't really care whether or not the flock is doing well, because as long as he is doing his job he will get his wage. A good shepherd, however, will give his life for his sheep.

There may be some people who care for us, but as soon as we need help, they are nowhere to be found. But Jesus is the Good Shepherd. He will walk with us right through to the other side.

In the Middle East, the shepherd used to lie down in the doorway of the fold because there was no gate. If there were any predators who wanted to devour the sheep, they would have to cross over him first.

Jesus does that for us. If you've been hurt, Jesus will restore you. If you've taken the wrong road and you're lost, He'll find you and bring you back. Jesus laid down His life for you. Put your hope and trust in Him, and He will see you through.

PRAYER: Jesus, thank You for Your overwhelming sacrifice.
I know I can count on You above all others. Amen.

November 14

HEALING RAIN

"BEHOLD, I WILL BRING [THE CITY] HEALTH AND
HEALING; I WILL HEAL THEM AND REVEAL TO THEM
THE ABUNDANCE OF PEACE AND TRUTH."
JEREMIAH 33:6

I RECENTLY returned from a sports arena where about three thousand people had gathered to pray for rain. The farmers in the area couldn't take the drought any longer, and someone had phoned and asked our team to come along and join in the prayer rally.

We started by asking God to forgive us for being so stubborn, for being so disbelieving, for having racial issues in our hearts, and for being unforgiving in marital situations. Then we asked God to bring rain. When the meeting ended, I could feel the heaviness lift off the crowd. When I walked outside, there was no sign of rain, not even a cloud.

The first message came from a farmer who hadn't even left the auditorium. Someone had called to tell him that nearly two inches of rain had already fallen on his farm. Two days later, I received phone calls from every part of the region where gentle, soaking rain was falling. One farmer sent me an e-mail and said that as he was driving home, the rain got heavier and heavier. It was the first time in months that he'd had mud on his truck.

We gave God all the praise, honor, and glory. It's got nothing to do with man; it has everything to do with God. We asked God to send rain and we prayed, believing in Him, and He answered our prayers. In the same way, all believers can lift up their heads to call on the Lord in their time of need.

PRAYER: Lord Jesus, I believe You answer when I pray.
Please bring Your healing rain in my life. Amen.

November 15
DON'T HATE—COMMUNICATE!

LET ALL BITTERNESS, WRATH, ANGER, CLAMOR, AND EVIL
SPEAKING BE PUT AWAY FROM YOU, WITH ALL MALICE.
EPHESIANS 4:31

CONFLICT IS part of life. Misunderstandings will occur. This is why boundaries are so important—without them, law and order break down. This is true in the family unit, in business, on the farm, and even in politics.

There are authorities in place for a reason. We might not respect a certain person in authority, but we should respect the office he or she represents. In a family, where there is mutual respect for the roles we carry out there is harmony. But chaos evolves from of a lack of respect.

This brings me back to something I often speak about, a subject close to my heart: prayer. The family that prays together, stays together. I believe prayer in the morning before work and school is essential for harmony in the family, and to learn to be sensitive and respectful to one another's needs. In my family we pray and read the Scriptures every day, and this creates a healthy attitude among us.

The Bible says, "Do not let the sun go down on your wrath" (Eph. 4:26). There should be no long faces before a family goes to bed at night. Life is short, and you don't know if you are to have another day on this earth, so don't waste time!

Conflict is always resolved by confrontation, unpleasant as it might be. So address problems and talk about them. Communicate—speak to your spouse, child, or colleague, and get to the bottom of the problem. Don't let things simmer and boil over. Once you've talked it through, you'll see there's no problem too big for God.

PRAYER: God, I pray for wisdom in conflicts. Help me to bring potential bad feeling out in the open, and to solve things with gentleness and grace. Amen.

November 16

THE KEY TO ABUNDANT LIVING

"HEAR, O ISRAEL, THE STATUTES AND JUDGMENTS
WHICH I SPEAK IN YOUR HEARING TODAY, THAT YOU MAY
LEARN THEM AND BE CAREFUL TO OBSERVE THEM."
DEUTERONOMY 5:1

IF YOU make a decision today that you are not going to compromise with the world, God will give you the key to abundant life. So many people are bending the rules these days. Many people are telling white lies, compromising their stand for God, and expecting the Lord to bless them. The Lord says that you cannot serve two masters.

Matthew 12:30 tell us, "He who is not with Me is against Me, and he who does not gather with Me scatters abroad." You cannot serve God and the world. It's either God's way or no way at all.

Now, if you do things God's way, He will bless you and you will have an abundant life. That's a fact. But when you start to bend the rules and allow other gods into your life, the anointing will depart from you.

It's what happened to Saul, the first king of Israel, when he departed from God's ways, and it's what happened to David when he committed adultery: the anointing of God left them. You can't fool God. You might fool everybody else, but God lives in your heart and understands the reason behind everything you do. If we get back to God and live a holy life, we will have a fulfilled life. Let's obey God's commandments. God put them in place for you and me so that we might live joyful lives of abundance.

PRAYER: God, please help me to be honest, obedient, and always
open with You, my Creator and lover of my soul. Amen.

November 17

WORKING FOR THE LORD

NOW GODLINESS WITH CONTENTMENT IS GREAT GAIN.
1 TIMOTHY 6:6

IF WE'RE going to be effective in our work—for our family, for other people who might be counting on us, and most of all, for God—we need to be doing the work He's called us to.

As you read this you might be thinking, *But I have no option but to do the job I'm doing!* I was in the same situation when I left school. My options were limited, but I had a vision, and my dream was to be a farmer. That vision has since multiplied, and now I'm farming people for the Lord. I'm more fulfilled than I've ever been in my life. I can't wait to get to work in the morning, can't wait to go the extra mile. I feel at peace with what I've been called to do by the Lord.

Making the change is worth it, and it *is* possible in your life. If you're called to a specific type of employment, you'll do it successfully and it will work for you. If you're merely doing it to put bread on the table, it may be time to start looking for a change.

Being satisfied and content in your employment will contribute to making you physically, mentally, and spiritually healthy. The Bible tells us in Colossians 3:23–24: "Whatever you do, do it heartily, as to the Lord and not to men, knowing that from the Lord you will receive the reward of the inheritance; for you serve the Lord Christ."

Pray that God will lead you to the right job. Focusing on God will set us free from performance-oriented work anxiety, and when we work with diligence and reverence for God, Jesus Himself will take care of promotion.

PRAYER: Jesus, please help me to work diligently in
the field where I can glorify You most. Amen.

November 18

GOD OF THE IMPOSSIBLE

WITHOUT FAITH IT IS IMPOSSIBLE TO PLEASE HIM, FOR HE
WHO COMES TO GOD MUST BELIEVE THAT HE IS, AND THAT
HE IS A REWARDER OF THOSE WHO DILIGENTLY SEEK HIM.
HEBREWS 11:6

THERE ARE many people who refuse to believe something until they see it with their own eyes. Thomas was one of them (John 20:24–29). It wasn't that Thomas was not sincere or that he did not love the Lord; he just could not bring himself to believe that Jesus had been raised from the dead without seeing Him in the flesh.

And Jesus gave him what he asked for: the disciples were locked inside a room when Jesus suddenly stood among them. He then told Thomas to put his finger in the holes in His hands and to put his hand in His side where the spear had pierced Him. Thomas did as he was told, finally believing that Jesus had risen from the dead. Jesus said to him, "Thomas, because you have seen Me, you have believed. Blessed are those who have not seen and yet have believed" (John 20:29).

You might be going through a particularly difficult time in your life and really need a miracle to help you through. Exodus 14:13–14 says, "Do not be afraid. Stand still, and see the salvation of the LORD, which He will accomplish for you today. . . . The LORD will fight for you, and you shall hold your peace."

Have faith—you are blessed if you have not seen but yet believe. Believe that God is at work.

PRAYER: Jesus, even though it would have been amazing to know You in Thomas's time, I'm thankful that You allow me the blessings of believing without seeing. Help me to have faith when I have nowhere to turn. Amen.

November 19

THE ART OF COURTSHIP

LET LOVE BE WITHOUT HYPOCRISY. ABHOR WHAT IS EVIL. CLING TO
WHAT IS GOOD. BE KINDLY AFFECTIONATE TO ONE ANOTHER WITH
BROTHERLY LOVE, IN HONOR GIVING PREFERENCE TO ONE ANOTHER.
ROMANS 12:9–10

THE WORLD of courtship and dating is a quickly evolving, often confusing place. Whether you are in that world yourself, or are supporting a friend or loved one who is, these simple principles will help bring forth strong, godly relationships. Really, it's not all that complicated. The best way to start is a polite introduction, followed by an invitation for an evening out. It is best to mix with other people and not be entirely alone. This provides both a social buffer and will prevent temptation.

The first priority is to befriend each other. A strong friendship is an essential ingredient for a successful marriage. In courtship, visit each other regularly—get to know each other and discuss the important things in life. You'll know in a very short time whether the two of you are compatible. Falling in love is not just tingles and flashes of light; it's a deep knowing.

The next step is engagement. I'm in favor of a short engagement. Once God has told you and you are both in agreement that you're to be married, set the wedding date and don't beat about the bush. So often couples want to do things their way and move in together before getting married, or they end up having a baby before the bonds of marriage are in place. So much pain is caused in this world because people want to cut corners. Rather, wait and do things the way God intended; then He will bless your union and your life together.

PRAYER: God, I pray for wisdom in relationships. May You be the guide! Amen.

November 20

LOOK OUT FOR OTHERS

LET EACH OF YOU LOOK OUT NOT ONLY FOR HIS OWN
INTERESTS, BUT ALSO FOR THE INTERESTS OF OTHERS.
PHILIPPIANS 2:4

WHEN GOD asked Cain where his brother was, Cain replied, "I do not know. Am I my brother's keeper?" (Gen. 4:9). This challenges us to ask each other, are you your brother's keeper? The answer is yes, you are.

The Lord often sends people our way, but we just send them away again. We don't have time, or place, or food to spare for those who need it. But we have a responsibility for them.

It would be tragic to stand before the Lord and hear Him say, "I sent two angels to your house, but you didn't recognize them and you chased them away." Hebrews 13:2 reminds us, "Do not forget to entertain strangers, for by so doing some have unwittingly entertained angels."

When God sends somebody down your path, make sure that you treat that person with compassion, because it is only by the grace of God that you and I stand. It is our job to look out for the interests of others.

It is one thing to tell people to love one another, but it is quite another to actually love others—the beggar in the street, the abused child, the neglected animal, the drunkard. Don't turn away those who come to you and need your help.

Remember what Mother Teresa said: "Christ prays in me, Christ works in me, Christ thinks in me, Christ looks through my eyes, Christ speaks through my words, Christ works with my hands, Christ walks with my feet, Christ loves with my heart." He wants to do the same with you.

**PRAYER: God, please open my heart to the "angels" You put
in my path, and make me my neighbor's keeper. Amen.**

November 21

LEADING BY EXAMPLE

BE DILIGENT TO PRESENT YOURSELF APPROVED TO
GOD, A WORKER WHO DOES NOT NEED TO BE ASHAMED,
RIGHTLY DIVIDING THE WORD OF TRUTH.
2 TIMOTHY 2:15

THE ATTITUDE of your heart is contagious to those around you—especially in a work situation. Those around us can tell from our hearts what our feeling is toward them. If we have a bad attitude, they will know about it. In other words, if you don't enjoy working with your staff and colleagues and you don't encourage them, it will be tough to move on together as a team. Instead, love and respect each other.

In my travels preaching all over the world, I have had the privilege of staying in castles and being fed six-course meals. I have slept in luxury hotels, but it has been cold and miserable in those places because the employees were just robotically doing their jobs.

On the other hand, I have been to Central Africa, where I have stayed among the poorest of the poor, with a man who had only bread and water to offer, but he gave it to me with his whole heart. You can do all the right things, but if the love of Christ is not in you, those with whom you work will soon pick it up.

I experienced this again when I was working as a cowboy in New South Wales in Australia many years ago. I stayed with one of the poorest families in town. I could have stayed in a local hotel, but it would have been very lonely. Despite the circumstances, those were some of the happiest days of my life.

It's not about material rewards; get your heart right first, before you expect miracles from your staff and colleagues. Don't just tell them what to do; lead by example, as Christ did.

PRAYER: Lord, purify my heart so I can provide a loving example. Amen.

November 22
AN ETERNAL INVESTMENT

SET YOUR MIND ON THINGS ABOVE, NOT ON THINGS ON THE EARTH.
COLOSSIANS 3:2

WHAT ARE you investing in? Are you investing in stocks and bonds? The stock exchange can crash. Are you investing in real estate? There is no guaranteed stability in that either. Instead, let's start investing in eternal things—in people's lives.

I recently had breakfast with one of my adopted children, a young Zulu man who is twenty years old now and studying to become a chef. He showed me his grades—which are very good—and his success reminded me of how happy we are that we invested in the lives of the young people in our children's home more than twenty years ago. What joy it has brought.

Luke 21:5–6 talks about the temple in Israel: "These [beautiful stones] which you see—the days will come in which not one stone shall be left upon another that shall not be thrown down.'" I have been to Israel a number of times and have seen the foundations of the temple, built with stones bigger than my entire house! All that is left is the foundations. Jesus prophesied that it would be destroyed, and it was. How magnificent it must have been. But even that did not last.

So let us keep from trusting in material things, and instead trust in God alone. Invest in the hearts of people, in love of the downtrodden, in the mission of the church, and in the truths of the Bible. Jesus said that heaven and earth will pass away, but the Word of God will remain forever (Luke 21:33).

PRAYER: Jesus, please keep my eyes from things that will pass away, and help me give my life to Your eternal mission. Amen.

November 23

FAMILY TIES

IF ANYONE DOES NOT PROVIDE FOR HIS OWN, AND
ESPECIALLY FOR THOSE OF HIS HOUSEHOLD, HE HAS DENIED
THE FAITH AND IS WORSE THAN AN UNBELIEVER.
1 TIMOTHY 5:8

WHERE IS the hardest place to be a Christian? I think the answer is in your own family. I know; I am a family man. I have five children and many grandchildren. They say you can choose your friends but not your family, and that is true, isn't it?

When I go overseas, people don't ask me about my qualifications. Instead, they ask me how my wife and children are; how things are on our farm; and how it's going at our children's homes. Those are my credentials; only then do they say, "Please, tell us what the Lord has laid on your heart for us today."

Now if I had to tell them that my wife had left me because I'm such a terrible person to live with, my children never heard me talk about Jesus, and my employees are constantly on strike because I am so unreasonable, would they really want to hear what I have to say? No, of course not.

I read an article in a Christian magazine the other day and the writer, a Messianic Jew, said that the word *family* comes from a Hebrew word meaning "belonging to." That is exactly what a family is. A family is a group of people who stick together. The problem is that many of us don't give our families enough time and attention. Go back home, do your homework, gather your family, and start working on your relationship with each person. "Bear one another's burdens, and so fulfill the law of Christ" (Gal. 6:2).

PRAYER: God, You've placed me in my family for a reason. Please bring harmony and love where there once was separation. Amen.

November 24

FELLOWSHIP WITH GOD

THE SPIRIT ALSO HELPS IN OUR WEAKNESSES. FOR WE DO
NOT KNOW WHAT WE SHOULD PRAY FOR AS WE OUGHT,
BUT THE SPIRIT HIMSELF MAKES INTERCESSION FOR US
WITH GROANINGS WHICH CANNOT BE UTTERED.
ROMANS 8:26

AN INTIMATE fellowship with God is crucial to every believer, because if you get this right, then everything else will fall into place. Think of the relationship between a mother and her baby. As long as the mom is present, her baby will feel safe. Let the mother leave the room and have a stranger walk in, and the baby will almost immediately start crying.

A similar thing occurs with couples who have been married a long time, and this happens with my wife and me: sometimes I will just look at her and she will know exactly what I'm thinking. She is a calm and safe refuge.

That is the intimacy that you and I need to develop with God. As we've learned from today's scripture, the Holy Spirit is the one who facilitates intimacy between you and your heavenly Father.

I really want to encourage you to spend time with the Lord—to develop this kind of intimacy. After He departed, the Lord sent the Holy Spirit to us. He is the link between us and our heavenly Father. The need to develop a vibrant relationship with the Holy Spirit cannot be underestimated. It takes time, prayer, and peaceful rest in the presence of God. It's only as you spend time with someone that you get to know them.

PRAYER: Jesus, thank You for the gift of Your comforting,
loving Spirit. You are my greatest ally. Amen.

November 25

THE PATH AHEAD

FOR TO ME, TO LIVE IS CHRIST, AND TO DIE IS GAIN. . . . FOR
I AM HARD-PRESSED BETWEEN THE TWO, HAVING A DESIRE
TO DEPART AND BE WITH CHRIST, WHICH IS FAR BETTER.
PHILIPPIANS 1:21, 23

I HEARD a lovely illustration once of a man of God who said, "When I die and you read in the newspaper that I've died, don't believe a word of it. I haven't died; I've just changed my address." Isn't that beautiful? The Lord is not finished with us and is going to keep on helping us, right until our last breath.

So don't keep looking back with regret—only look forward. The Lord will not only see you through those dark times, but He will see you all the way through to the end of this life and the beginning of the next. That is why it's so wonderful to be a Christian: you can't frighten a Christian with heaven! If I live, I live for God; and if I die, I go home to Jesus. We are mere sojourners in this life, and so should hold lightly to the world.

You know already that trials are unavoidable. It's a refining process. I've never met a person worth their salt who hadn't been through their share of trails. God will bring you through, but even if the storm still rages while you're on your deathbed, that is not the end. God brings us peace during trials in this life, and assured victory in the next.

Focus on your heavenly destination and walk purposefully on the path ahead of you.

PRAYER: Jesus, my heart lives with You in heaven. Help me to walk
faithfully through this life until I meet You there. Amen.

November 26

AN ABUNDANCE FOR EVERY GOOD WORK

DO NOT BE DECEIVED, GOD IS NOT MOCKED; FOR
WHATEVER A MAN SOWS, THAT HE WILL ALSO REAP.
GALATIANS 6:7

WHEN I gave my life to the Lord many years ago, I was quite prepared to give our farm to the poor, go to Bible college, and become the preacher God called me to be. However, through Scripture, the Lord told my wife and me to remain where we were. He used 2 Corinthians 9:8, which reads, "And God is able to make all grace abound toward you, that you, always having all sufficiency in all things, may have an abundance for every good work."

The Lord told us that He wanted to use our farm as a platform for the Holy Spirit, and that is exactly what has happened. If we sow where God tells us to sow, then we will reap our reward.

It's not just *where* you sow—it's *what* you sow. If you sow adversity, anger, pain, condemnation, and judgment into your situation, that is exactly what you are going to get back. Rather, sow mercy, grace, and undeserved kindness. See people as God's creation; love them and show them respect, regardless of their station in life. Treat every person as though you are ministering to Jesus Himself.

What you sow is what you will reap, so start sowing love. If you do this consistently, your whole life will change for the better. Ella Wheeler Wilcox said, "With every deed you are sowing a seed, though the harvest you may not see." Remember, good seed costs less than it pays, even though the results may only be evident after you've gone home to heaven.

PRAYER: Jesus, please help me remember the natural laws You've
put in place. I want to sow love in every situation. Amen.

November 27

CHOOSING HOW TO LIVE

I DISCIPLINE MY BODY AND BRING IT INTO SUBJECTION,
LEST, WHEN I HAVE PREACHED TO OTHERS, I
MYSELF SHOULD BECOME DISQUALIFIED.
1 CORINTHIANS 9:27

THE WORLD is a messy place. Things break down and wear out, people fly off the handle, and conflicts get out of hand. It's just the way things are on this broken, fallen planet. But I've got good news for you. Jesus said in John 16:33, "Be of good cheer, I have overcome the world."

I want to encourage you today to concentrate on what Jesus says, not only about you, but about the world. You can live in this world in two ways: either in strength with Jesus, or swimming along in the worldly mess that surrounds us. God gives us tools to combat the mess, and discipline is chief among them. We cannot expect to have a good day if we are constantly late, oversleeping, procrastinating, and living in chaotic, disorganized homes. Instead, take the bull by the horns and bring that mess "into subjection." God will give us strength to be an example to the world. Of course we cannot be perfect by any means, but we do not have an excuse to wallow in messiness: messy in our appearance, messy in our vocabulary, or messy in the way we act. Because we are believers, we should be an example to those who are in darkness by seeking first the kingdom of God and showing them the way.

Make a new start today by getting up early, spending time with God, and getting your directions from Him.

PRAYER: God, I always have a mess to deal with. Grant me Your supernatural strength and holy order so I can wrestle it into a state that glorifies You. Amen.

November 28

A GODLY STANDARD

THE CARNAL MIND IS ENMITY AGAINST GOD; FOR IT IS NOT
SUBJECT TO THE LAW OF GOD, NOR INDEED CAN BE. SO THEN,
THOSE WHO ARE IN THE FLESH CANNOT PLEASE GOD.
ROMANS 8:7—8

AS BELIEVERS, we should set the bar when it comes to the moral standard. The world looks to the church for examples of holiness, righteousness, and morality. Yet there are people out there who are not believers, who live a much godlier life than some Christians do. How can we lead when we neglect respect, honor, hard work, and love for our fellow man? The gospel is not only spread by words; it is spread by our day-to-day living. Aside from telling people you love them, show them you love them by your actions. We have to live by a higher standard.

For the believer, our standard can be found in the Bible. It is meant to be followed—not just read, sung about, and discussed on Sundays. Let us look at our families, at our churches, and at our Christian communities and sort out instances of the "carnal mind" at work. It is a constant battle, but worth the fight to regain our standing as beacons in the night. It is our responsibility to regain our standards, because if we don't, our communities will crumble.

The well-being of our society does not depend on the government; it relies on the church. That is why we need to start modeling our churches and families according to the Word of God and the standards it sets.

PRAYER: God, give me strength to model Your
standards to the world around me. Amen.

November 29
EMPIRE BUILDERS VERSUS KINGDOM BUILDERS

WATCH, STAND FAST IN THE FAITH, BE BRAVE, BE STRONG.
LET ALL THAT YOU DO BE DONE WITH LOVE.
1 CORINTHIANS 16:13–14

ARE WE empire builders or kingdom builders? Empire builders are people who only have one thing on their minds: "What's in it for me, and how does it further my goals?" Their motives are not pure, and they're not doing what they're doing for Jesus. An empire builder also tends to be very controlling; they will direct every single aspect of that empire, from the smallest to the biggest. They never delegate because they feel intimidated and threatened by others. Such an endeavor or ministry is incapable of growing. There is no love in it.

The character of a kingdom builder is the complete opposite. A kingdom-building pastor, for instance, is more than happy when an outside minister comes to preach if it is for the good of all. Kingdom builders will stick to godly principles and will never compromise in holiness. They do not place importance on little things like the color of the new church hall. Their primary concern is to see people saved. Kingdom builders will be the first people to put up their hands and say, "How can we help?" Their endeavor is governed by love.

A kingdom person is always ready for new ideas and innovative change. This is the type of person who is careful never to touch God's glory and is aware that their achievements are only by His grace. Rather than leading people toward themselves, they direct people toward Jesus.

Your work, whatever it may be, is a ministry. And the ministry of the person with kingdom vision multiplies and prospers for the glory of God.

PRAYER: Jesus, make my number one desire the building of Your kingdom. Amen.

November 30

NO LOOKING BACK

THERE IS THEREFORE NOW NO CONDEMNATION
TO THOSE WHO ARE IN CHRIST JESUS.
ROMANS 8:1

EARLY THE other morning I went for a run just as the sun was coming up. A small antelope came diving across the road, through the barbed wire fence, and right up to the edge of the maize field, where he stopped and looked back. He thought he was safe, but he wasn't. If he had carried on running, nothing would have been able to get him. But an experienced hunter saw the moment when the antelope stopped to take a look back—and he took his shot. What the Lord showed me through this was that as soon as you stop and look over your shoulder, the devil climbs in.

Perhaps you have been delivered from heartache or bondage. Maybe you had a drinking problem in the past, but you've given your life to the Lord and He has set you free. However, your friends are tempting you to have just one beer, and it would be your undoing. Don't do it. Don't look back.

If God has redeemed your marriage, keep working on your relationship. Don't speak about the past—it's forgiven and forgotten, so move on.

Keep going forward. If you do, you will grow stronger in Jesus. As long as you keep looking back, you can't run forward. Continue moving ahead, keeping your eyes on Jesus.

PRAYER: God, when I feel hesitation and am tempted to look back at
things You've already struck from my record, please turn me back
around. I accept Your healing and walk forward in victory. Amen.

DECEMBER

December 1

A BRAND-NEW MAN

WE ALL, WITH UNVEILED FACE, BEHOLDING AS IN A MIRROR THE
GLORY OF THE LORD, ARE BEING TRANSFORMED INTO THE SAME
IMAGE FROM GLORY TO GLORY, JUST AS BY THE SPIRIT OF THE LORD.
2 CORINTHIANS 3:18

ONE YEAR the theme of our Mighty Men Conference was "Dying to Live." We have to die to self and let Christ live in us so that we can live life to the full. The Bible includes many illustrations of those who have been transformed through the power of God in their lives. I think of Moses, who was a murderer and a coward; yet when he met with God at the burning bush, his life was transformed. He became not only the head of his family, but also God's spokesman and the head of the whole nation of Israel—which is believed to have been between two and three million people.

What happened? Here's a man who was a deserter, who ran for his life, now single-handedly confronting the most powerful man in the world.

Jesus Christ is indeed a miracle-working God. He transforms people from being fearful and incompetent—full of anger, lust, hatred, and fear—into people of stature, of love, of power, and of a sound mind (2 Tim. 1:7). This is our inheritance; this is what we need to take hold of. Then we will become better in all our relationships.

We don't have to carry the stigma of failure anymore, because Jesus Christ blots it all out. He gives us a new start, a new inheritance, a new beginning, a new opportunity to love Him and serve Him.

PRAYER: Jesus, thank You for transforming us into people
who can act in power for Your purposes. Amen.

December 2

A PERSONAL CHOICE

"KING AGRIPPA, DO YOU BELIEVE THE PROPHETS? I KNOW
THAT YOU DO BELIEVE." THEN AGRIPPA SAID TO PAUL, "YOU
ALMOST PERSUADE ME TO BECOME A CHRISTIAN."
ACTS 26:27–28

DO YOU have friend at the office, at work, at your university, or at your school who seems to gravitate toward the Lord but is not ready to make a commitment? King Agrippa, featured in today's verse, was convinced by Paul's arguments, but he did not take the critical step of giving his life to Jesus. As such, we must conclude that King Agrippa is not in heaven. That's the problem with being a "nominal Christian": it's just not enough.

Either you know Him or you don't know Him. There is no value in saying, "Well, you know, my dad was a great Christian, and my grandfather started this church." The Lord has no grandchildren. Each person has to find Jesus for him- or herself.

Just because a mother is a believer doesn't automatically mean her family members are believers too. A father's or mother's faith does not save their children. But what a saved family member can do is pray for their family and trust that the Holy Spirit will convict them—and He will, because the Bible says in James 5:16, "Pray for one another, that you may be healed. The effective, fervent prayer of a righteous man avails much."

So if you or someone you know is standing on the line, saying, "You almost persuade me to become a Christian," know that a step must be taken. "Almost" is not enough. The only way to be saved is to ask Jesus Christ to be your Lord and Savior, repent of your sin, and follow Him.

PRAYER: God, point out the "almosts" in my life and in others',
and give me the bravery to take definitive steps. Amen.

December 3

THE RIGHT ATTITUDE

"GIVE, AND IT WILL BE GIVEN TO YOU: GOOD MEASURE,
PRESSED DOWN, SHAKEN TOGETHER, AND RUNNING OVER
WILL BE PUT INTO YOUR BOSOM. FOR WITH THE SAME MEASURE
THAT YOU USE, IT WILL BE MEASURED BACK TO YOU."
LUKE 6:38

TRANSFORMATION COMES through a trusting attitude. The thing I love the most is telling people there's a better way to approach this life on earth. We *do* have the answer for reconciliation; our marriages, homes, businesses, and lives *can* be different, if we would only put our trust in God.

Transformation comes from a willing attitude. God is no respecter of persons. He will use any man, any woman, any boy, or any girl who is prepared to put their hand up for Him. You may think you're not a worthy vessel, or suffer from the common afflictions of low self-esteem, an inferiority complex, or a case of "woe is me." Put your hand up anyway. Ask God to change your attitude. Each and every one of us has the opportunity to pursue a God-given vision if we trust God.

Transformation comes from a loving attitude. Remember, too, Jesus said to love your neighbor as yourself. If we truly start to do this, we'll see a change, not only in our personal lives, but in business, in our community, and in the church. God blesses us to bless others.

Transformation comes from a hopeful attitude. Many people feel they've messed up too badly and there's no hope for them. This is a fallacy. If we look in the Bible, God continually used people who had transgressed. However, the requirement is that we repent, which means to stop doing what we have been doing, turn away from sin, and start again.

PRAYER: God, please transform my attitude today. Amen.

December 4

A FRIENDSHIP THAT LASTS

LOVE SUFFERS LONG AND IS KIND; LOVE DOES NOT ENVY; LOVE
DOES NOT PARADE ITSELF, IS NOT PUFFED UP; DOES NOT BEHAVE
RUDELY, DOES NOT SEEK ITS OWN, IS NOT PROVOKED, THINKS
NO EVIL; DOES NOT REJOICE IN INIQUITY, BUT REJOICES IN
THE TRUTH; BEARS ALL THINGS, BELIEVES ALL THINGS, HOPES
ALL THINGS, ENDURES ALL THINGS. LOVE NEVER FAILS.
1 CORINTHIANS 13:4–8

THERE IS no such thing as a perfect marriage, and anybody who tells you otherwise is lying! It is a friendship like none other, but it thrives on the same general principles. Often two people will fall head-over-heels in love with each other, but they are from completely diverse backgrounds. Couples need to be willing to work on their relationship and settle their differences.

As with any relationship, issues need to be addressed without delay, always in love and in gentle honesty. The close proximity of the marriage relationship means we really need to work things out, preferably before the sun goes down, as the Bible says (Eph. 4:26). "Pushing things under the carpet" never helps in the long run: only if we deal with issues as they present themselves can we respect one another and grow to love each other more intimately.

It takes time to build a lasting friendship of any kind, whether it is with Jesus, an acquaintance, or your children. Couples need to work diligently on marriage just like anything else in life. It is not a fifty/fifty deal, but more like a one hundred/one hundred deal if the relationship is to succeed.

PRAYER: Jesus, in Your perfect friendship, please show me
how to grow my most important relationships. Amen.

December 5

FRUITFUL ABUNDANCE

"BY THIS MY FATHER IS GLORIFIED, THAT YOU BEAR
MUCH FRUIT; SO YOU WILL BE MY DISCIPLES."
JOHN 15:8

IN THE Bible, Jesus is called the vine. Whoever is grafted into Him becomes a little branch of His, drawing from the fullness of His strength and sharing in His fruitfulness.

A branch cannot bear fruit if it is not abiding in the vine; likewise we cannot bear fruit if we do not abide in our Savior (John 15:4). There will be no fruit borne from our lives if we cease to pray, read the Word of God, and live by faith. We live as Christians only when Christ lives in us. It is Christ in us that is our hope of glory (Col. 1:27).

Merely stating that you are a believer will not suffice; it is living the life of faith that counts—being "crucified with Christ" (Gal. 2:20). And you cannot live according to God's will for just a season. If you want to bear fruit as a believer, you must constantly strive to live the life of faith.

The fruit we as believers should bear does not just lie in doing good works; it is the fruit of the Spirit: love, joy, peace, long-suffering, kindness, goodness, faithfulness, gentleness, and self-control (Gal. 5:22–23).

Jesus' purpose is not just to make workers of us, but rather to make us Christlike—to make us bloom. No fruit tree consumes its own fruit; we are called to share the fruit of the Spirit with all those around us. If we do this, God will bless us abundantly.

PRAYER: Jesus, thank You for grafting me to Yourself, the
source of all life. Help me bear good fruit for You. Amen.

December 6
CHILDREN OF PROMISE

IF YOU ARE CHRIST'S, THEN YOU ARE ABRAHAM'S
SEED, AND HEIRS ACCORDING TO THE PROMISE.
GALATIANS 3:29

GALATIANS 4:28 says that we have the same inheritance as Isaac, the son of Abraham: "Now we, brethren, as Isaac was, are children of promise."

Abraham was a man of real faith who gave up everything he had. He was a prosperous farmer, and I can only imagine what it must have taken for Abraham to leave it all and go with his flocks of sheep, herds of cattle, camels, donkeys, and his family to an unknown destination, simply because God told him to (Gen. 12).

The Bible tells us that without faith we cannot please God. Abraham made a decision—a covenant—to believe God, irrespective of what might happen. After praying for many years and waiting, the Lord finally gave Abraham a son: Isaac.

Only a few years later God basically said to Abraham, "Now I want him back" (Gen. 22). Abraham faithfully took Isaac up to the mountain, fully prepared to sacrifice him. As we know, God intervened and told him to sacrifice a young ram instead. God keeps His promises.

We who believe are children of the promise. That means that if we believe that Jesus Christ died for our sins on the cross, and if we believe that Jesus is no longer in the grave, then we shall be saved (Rom. 10:9). What a beautiful promise!

PRAYER: Jesus, thank You for making me an heir with
Abraham to Your promise of life. Amen.

December 7

ORDINARY PEOPLE

NOW WHEN THEY SAW THE BOLDNESS OF PETER AND
JOHN, AND PERCEIVED THAT THEY WERE UNEDUCATED
AND UNTRAINED MEN, THEY MARVELED. AND THEY
REALIZED THAT THEY HAD BEEN WITH JESUS.
ACTS 4:13

THE LORD often uses ordinary people to do His work. The word *ministry* means "servant." All the church fathers were ordinary people: Abraham and David were farmers, Moses was a shepherd, Mary the mother of God was a housewife, and Peter was a humble fisherman, as were James and John. Paul, who wrote two-thirds of the New Testament, was a tentmaker.

Recently two young men arrived on our farm to speak to my younger son about raising cattle, yet my son was able to steer the conversation to the things of the Lord. They assured him they would return because they wanted more answers. People are turning more and more to "ordinary people" like you and me—people who have yielded their lives to God—for guidance, leadership, and help.

There's a place for ministers of the Word of God and for educational colleges, but life, the "school of hard knocks," is also a source of education. Don't despise your position in life!

Jesus Christ, God's Son, started out with what seemed an ordinary life. He came down to earth as a defenseless child. He was a carpenter who served a thirty-year apprenticeship before starting to serve people. His entire ministry lasted a mere three years, yet there is not a man who has ever lived who has impacted the world like Christ. Let us "ordinary people" go out into the world and change lives for Jesus.

PRAYER: God, thank You for placing me where I am so You
can reach the people You want me to reach. Amen.

December 8
VENGEANCE IS THE LORD'S

HOW LONG, O LORD, HOLY AND TRUE, UNTIL YOU JUDGE AND
AVENGE OUR BLOOD ON THOSE WHO DWELL ON THE EARTH?
REVELATION 6:10

WHERE IS the justice in the world? We see blatant murder, theft, immorality—and no one takes responsibility. Where will it stop? I want to tell you that justice and revenge belong to the Lord. Today's scripture is the cry of the martyrs—those who have died for their faith. They are asking the Lord just how long they still have to wait. In verse 11, God replies and says they must wait just a little while longer.

People sometimes come and ask me, "What about somebody like Adolf Hitler or one of these dictators? When will they get their justice from God?" God wants us to pray for those who persecute us (Matt. 5:44). They are going to meet their justice, because God is a holy and fair God.

For those who curse God and murder God's people in cold blood, justice is still coming.

You and I must stand on the Word of God, which says very clearly in Revelation 12:11, "They overcame him [the devil] by the blood of the Lamb and by the word of their testimony, and they did not love their lives to the death." So keep on going. Pray for those who hurt you, and leave vengeance to God.

PRAYER: God, justice is in Your hands. Help me to do right until You come. Amen.

December 9

CHOOSE TO BELIEVE

JESUS SAID TO HIM, "IF YOU CAN BELIEVE, ALL
THINGS ARE POSSIBLE TO HIM WHO BELIEVES."
MARK 9:23

GOD IS a God of wonder, and He is all-powerful. But what if I told you that there is one thing that Jesus Christ cannot do in your life and in mine?

The truth is that God can do anything and everything except make us believe in the Father, the Son, and the Holy Spirit. It is up to us to choose to believe in Him or not.

The Bible says that when Jesus was in Nazareth, He performed very few miracles because people did not believe that He was the Messiah (Mark 6:1–6). He grew up in Nazareth, so they knew Him only as the carpenter Joseph's son. Jesus healed only a few people there. However, in Capernaum, not far from Nazareth, Jesus performed mighty signs, wonders, and miracles. Why? Because the people there believed that He was the Messiah (see Luke 4:31–37).

One day Jesus asked His disciples who people thought He was. They replied that some believed He was John the Baptist, others that He was Elijah, and yet others that He was Jeremiah or one of the prophets. So He asked them who they thought He was. Simon Peter answered, "You are the Christ, the Son of the living God" (Matt. 16:16). Jesus said to him, "Blessed are you, Simon Bar-Jonah, for flesh and blood has not revealed this to you, but My Father who is in heaven" (v. 17).

No one made those people believe in Jesus. They had to respond themselves. In the same way, you must choose to believe the good news and reject all other ways. Walk by faith and not by sight (2 Cor. 5:7).

PRAYER: God, help me make the daily choice to believe in You. Amen.

December 10
CALLED TO LIBERTY

FOR YOU, BRETHREN, HAVE BEEN CALLED TO LIBERTY;
ONLY DO NOT USE LIBERTY AS AN OPPORTUNITY FOR THE
FLESH, BUT THROUGH LOVE SERVE ONE ANOTHER.
GALATIANS 5:13

JESUS PAID for your freedom and mine on the cross of Calvary when He said, "It is finished" (John 19:30). And He really meant it! Don't trade your inheritance for a temporary bowl of stew as Esau did when he lost his legacy to his brother, Jacob. For a moment of pleasing the flesh, he lost everything. When we dabble in sin—that immoral relationship, that white lie, bending the rules ever so slightly—we forfeit our freedom.

Once the devil gets his foot in the door, he does not stop there. Things have a way of snowballing and becoming worse than you ever thought they would. When you start breaking the rules, where do you stop?

If you are caught in the snare of the devil and you feel completely trapped, take heart. There is a way out. Quite simply, stop what you're doing, confess your sin to God, and then move on into victory! You might say, "I can't. I'm in too deep," but God says you must; otherwise there is no way He can help you.

There is nothing on this earth that is not worth giving up for your God-given freedom. My prayer for you today is that Jesus would give you the courage to confront the sin that is holding you back from freedom and help you deal with it once and for all through the blood of Jesus. Let us stop simply existing and start living the abundant life God wants for each one of us.

PRAYER: God, please help me in my weakness, and give me
the strength to shake off sin and return to You. Amen.

December 11

THINK TWICE

EVEN A FOOL IS COUNTED WISE WHEN HE HOLDS HIS PEACE;
WHEN HE SHUTS HIS LIPS, HE IS CONSIDERED PERCEPTIVE.
PROVERBS 17:28

THE BIBLE says that those who restrain their lips are wise (Prov. 10:19). Jesus Himself knew that sometimes fewer words are better. Mark 14:60–61 reads, "The high priest stood up in the midst and asked Jesus, saying, 'Do You answer nothing? What is it these men testify against You?' But He kept silent and answered nothing."

Likewise, we need to be careful about the things we say. Don't share intimate things with people who don't understand the context or circumstances. The Lord Himself said, "Do not give what is holy to the dogs; nor cast your pearls before swine, lest they trample them under their feet, and turn and tear you in pieces" (Matt. 7:6).

I have had to learn this lesson the hard way many times. I tend to talk too much, while my wife, Jill, is the opposite. She is quiet and reserved and thinks twice before she speaks. That is why she does not get herself into as much trouble as I do!

The more you grow in God and the more your faith matures, the fewer words you'll need. The words of a person who rarely speaks are like precious jewels. My wife can say something in one sentence that would take me half an hour to say. Why? Because she thinks before she speaks. Think before you speak, and when you speak, speak under the direction of almighty God. Do this and people will pay attention.

PRAYER: God, help me to be wise and selective with
the words that come out of my mouth. Amen.

December 12

THE ART OF CHIVALRY

HUSBANDS, LOVE YOUR WIVES, JUST AS CHRIST ALSO
LOVED THE CHURCH AND GAVE HIMSELF FOR HER.
EPHESIANS 5:25

WHERE HAVE all the knights in shining armor gone? The word *chivalry* comes from the religious, moral, and social codes of the medieval knightly system. The *Oxford Dictionary* definition mentions the "combination of qualities expected of an ideal knight, especially courage, honor, courtesy, justice, and a readiness to help the weak." The definition goes on to include courteous behavior, especially that of a man toward a woman, standing up for the weak and the poor, and the protection of the widow and the orphan.

It is so important for a wife to know that she and her family are completely safe, that her man will take care of them no matter what happens, and that he will literally lay down his life for them, unconditionally. It is no good for a husband to be an amazing staff member in the workplace if, when he goes home, he neglects his duties to his wife and children. The Word of God is very clear that a wife is to submit to her husband and a husband is to love his wife (Eph. 5:22–25). Men are to be knights in shining armor to their damsels. When men take that role seriously and deny themselves, favoring their wives and children, then it is very easy for the wife to respect her man. Women should expect a high standard of chivalry from the men in their lives.

There is a saying that "a man's home is his castle"; if that is the case, then men have the responsibility to bring chivalry to life again.

PRAYER: Lord, give Your strength to all men of God today,
and revive chivalry in their hearts. Amen.

December 13

THE SOURCE

*IT IS VAIN FOR YOU TO RISE UP EARLY, TO SIT UP LATE, TO EAT
THE BREAD OF SORROWS; FOR SO HE GIVES HIS BELOVED SLEEP.*
PSALM 127:2

IN 2 KINGS 2:19–22, the prophet Elisha was called to a city where there was sickness, death, and barrenness. Upon his arrival, he asked the city elders to bring him a new bowl with salt in it. Elisha then took the bowl to the source of the city's water supply and cast the salt into the water.

He announced, "Thus says the LORD: 'I have healed this water; from it there shall be no more death or barrenness'" (v. 21). Like the people in this story, we need to seek out the source of our problems. If we don't do this, we will only ever treat the symptoms. The problem won't go away.

For example, you may find that your children are not doing well at school, or are perhaps showing signs of anxiety or disobedience. Your first step should be to ask the Lord to show you where the source of the problem lies. It could be that there are unresolved issues between you and your spouse, which leads to repeated arguments. Once you sort out your marriage, you may well find your children improving.

Have you been ill a lot in the past few months? Perhaps you are not eating correctly, or are working too hard and not getting enough sleep. Remember what Jesus said: "Come aside by yourselves to a deserted place and rest a while" (Mark 6:31).

Go straight to the source of the problem. Spend time every morning in prayer, putting your day into God's hands. When we give God the first place in our day, He undertakes for us.

PRAYER: God, give me wisdom to see the source of my problems. Amen.

December 14

BE STRONG IN THE LORD

BE STRONG IN THE LORD . . . PUT ON THE WHOLE
ARMOR OF GOD, THAT YOU MAY BE ABLE TO STAND
AGAINST THE WILES OF THE DEVIL.
EPHESIANS 6:10—11

GOD LOVES you so much that He's not prepared to leave you the way you are. He wants you to grow in strength. Farming is a wonderful way of life, but it definitely hones one's character; I know it has mine. It deals harshly with impatience, arrogance, and a know-it-all nature. Maybe that's why God chased Moses into the desert to farm with Jethro for so many years before using him to take the Jews out of slavery.

Isn't that what you're looking for—to have character in your life? Every day when you wake up, be sure to put on the whole armor of God. The devil is out to ruin your character and your good intentions. We have to be a strong, holy people of character. Strength also comes through prayer, and God hears every single one. Live by faith and in the power of the Holy Spirit. Keep speaking to Jesus and don't look behind you.

I'm sure you realize that we are living in the end days. Strength comes in hard work; do whatever your hand finds to do, because the time is nearly up.

I want to encourage you today. There is something you can do for God, no matter how insignificant it might seem. Even the smallest acts of mercy build godly strength. How about donating food or clothes to your local homeless shelter? Showing genuine care for your colleagues? Picking up that stray animal and giving it a home instead of driving past? All these things we do for the Lord. Do something good with what God has given you, and God will build you up.

PRAYER: God, show me new ways to grow in strength for You. Amen.

December 15
A POSITIVE OUTLOOK

COMFORT THE FAINTHEARTED, UPHOLD THE WEAK,
BE PATIENT WITH ALL. SEE THAT NO ONE RENDERS
EVIL FOR EVIL TO ANYONE, BUT ALWAYS PURSUE WHAT
IS GOOD BOTH FOR YOURSELVES AND FOR ALL.
1 THESSALONIANS 5:14–15

AT CERTAIN times of the year, such as holidays, people are often tired, and in many cases quite impatient. In these times it is wonderful to be able to show our true colors in the busy shopping malls, on the roads where traffic is hectic, and waiting in long queues to purchase goods. This is a time when we as followers of Jesus need to be extremely patient and gentle and need to extend grace to one another.

Just like anyone else, we fight the impulse to say rude or counterproductive things in times of pressure. But we're called to take the high road and count to ten before we make that mistake. More often not, by refraining from saying that critical or nasty thing, we prevent an ugly or hurtful situation.

Jesus said we should be more careful about what comes out of our mouths than about what goes in (Matt. 15:11). The food we eat does not affect others, but the words we speak can affect their whole lives. Careless and negative words can hurt, causing people to become downhearted.

On the other hand, encouraging words can give people hope and confidence to face the challenges of life. A kind word can literally change someone's life. The Bible says that life and death are found in the tongue (Prov. 18:21). Both negative and positive words are infectious, so it is good to spend time with people who have an optimistic outlook on life. Perhaps their positivity will infect us.

PRAYER: God, in stressful days, please give me an extra measure of patience and gentleness as I act as Your ambassador in the world. Amen.

December 16
GOD'S LIGHT SHINES THROUGH

HE ENTERED A HOUSE AND WANTED NO ONE TO
KNOW IT, BUT HE COULD NOT BE HIDDEN.
MARK 7:24

JESUS CANNOT be hidden. He is the most popular Man who ever walked this earth. He has more followers today than He had during His ministry two thousand years ago, and He cannot be ignored or explained away. Jesus shines wherever He goes, touching people's lives and bringing hope to the hopeless.

When Jesus comes into our hearts the same thing happens—we too cannot be hidden. The light of God shines through us for all to see, which will make people want to know what it is that has changed in our lives. The answer is, of course, meeting Jesus the Peacemaker, who loves us so much that He died for each and every person on earth.

In the early 1800s, John Williams and another missionary who were trying to spread the good news in the South Sea Islands were killed and eaten by cannibals. Although they were killed, the work Williams had done in the preceding years to bring islanders to God bore great fruit. The tribe eventually stopped their cannibalism, and as they adopted Christian principles they became more stable in their society, embracing love and tolerance rather than aggression and fear. The love of God could not be hidden—it shone clearly. Now, years later, those same islands that used to be filled with cannibals are filled with God-fearing people.

Allow people to see this same love of Christ in your heart. If you do, you will not even have to say anything. People will receive the gospel, not because of what you say, but because they can see God's love in you. When you are filled with the Holy Spirit, the joy, love, and forgiveness of Christ will shine through.

PRAYER: Jesus, shine through me! Amen.

December 17
GIVE YOUR WORRY AWAY

MAY THE LORD OF PEACE HIMSELF GIVE YOU PEACE
ALWAYS IN EVERY WAY. THE LORD BE WITH YOU ALL.
2 THESSALONIANS 3:16

YOU MIGHT have an attitude that is making you sick mentally and spiritually. I am talking about worry. Listen to what Jesus said about worrying in Matthew 6:27–29, 33–34:

> Which of you by worrying can add one cubit to his stature? So why do you worry about clothing? Consider the lilies of the field, how they grow: they neither toil nor spin; and yet I say to you that even Solomon in all his glory was not arrayed like one of these . . . But seek first the kingdom of God and His righteousness, and all these things shall be added to you. Therefore do not worry about tomorrow, for tomorrow will worry about its own things.

Worrying does make a person sick. As you may well know, many illnesses are psychosomatic and come from our thoughts. When you get your mind right, your body follows. They say that laughter is good medicine, but when was the last time you had a really good laugh? Doesn't it feel wonderful to have happy tears rolling down your face?

The opposite of worry is faith, and believing God for miracles. When we worry, we actually make the Lord sad, because He sees that we don't believe Him. Worrying won't help you. Get on your knees and ask the Lord to fill you with faith and to give you a hunger for His Word, the medicine of life.

PRAYER: God, please help me to root out worry in my life
and cast those toxic burdens on You. Amen.

December 18

FAMILY TIME

TRAIN UP A CHILD IN THE WAY HE SHOULD GO, AND
WHEN HE IS OLD HE WILL NOT DEPART FROM IT.
PROVERBS 22:6

THERE'S SOMETHING sacred about sharing a meal together.

If the whole family is running around doing their own thing, and the dining room table seems to be there purely for show, something is missing. That is where the family is supposed to meet, where we need to sit down and talk about the day.

I believe that it is vital that families sit down together regularly—including church families and friends. Sharing a meal with those we love provides an opportunity to tell everyone how God has undertaken for you and how your day has been. Then, later on, when things get tough, your family may well recall God's faithfulness to you. This in turn may help them to keep going.

Let's say, for instance, that a young man finds himself in trouble. He may draw comfort from remembering his father telling him about a difficult situation he himself went through. His father called out to God and God heard him. If God can do that for the son's father, He will surely help the son too.

Sitting down together and sharing a meal also provides an opportunity for family members to share what may be troubling them. Research has shown that children who have an opportunity to do this on a regular basis have a much lower chance of exhibiting risky behavior such as alcohol or drug abuse.

This busy season, don't neglect spending time with each other. We need to remind each other of the blessings of God. We need to impress upon our loved ones that God is with us through the rough times, and make Jesus a part of everyday life.

PRAYER: God, please season our meals together
with good, holy conversation. Amen.

December 19
GOD'S PERSPECTIVE

[JESUS] REBUKED PETER, SAYING, "GET BEHIND
ME, SATAN! FOR YOU ARE NOT MINDFUL OF THE
THINGS OF GOD, BUT THE THINGS OF MEN."
MARK 8:33

TODAY'S VERSE sounds harsh. Why did Jesus talk this way to Peter? Peter was looking at the situation through carnal eyes, while Jesus was talking to him about godly things that he did not understand.

God's point of view is very different from the human point of view. If we look at the world around us from a human perspective, we may be fearful and lose heart. If we walk this road on earth from a human point of view, it equals disaster.

If you value man's opinion, you will be like the waves of the sea: today you will be pushed this way, tomorrow that way. It doesn't matter what people think about you; it is what God thinks about you that counts. Remember, people don't have to like you, but if you obey God, they will respect you. You must be known as someone who keeps his or her word.

In the scripture above, the Lord got very upset with Peter because he was getting in the way of God's plans. If God says He's going to do it, He's going to do it. Don't stand in His way and be an obstacle.

If God has promised you that He will see you through a particular venture, you better believe it. You might say, "But everything is collapsing around me." It doesn't matter—God will see you through to the end because whatever He says, He does. Just keep trusting in Him.

PRAYER: God, take my mind off things of men and
open it to the things of God. Amen.

December 20

A HOLY CALLING

[GOD] HAS SAVED US AND CALLED US WITH A HOLY
CALLING, NOT ACCORDING TO OUR WORKS, BUT ACCORDING
TO HIS OWN PURPOSE AND GRACE WHICH WAS GIVEN
TO US IN CHRIST JESUS BEFORE TIME BEGAN.
2 TIMOTHY 1:9

GEORGE MÜLLER, who is one of my heroes, was sent by his father to school to become a preacher in the Lutheran Church, for no other reason than it was a respectable profession that paid relatively well.

Müller lived up to his father's expectations, but then began living the "high life": he would often be found in the taverns—enjoying women, wine, and song. He became adept at lying, cheating, and stealing.

What is the point of a theology student who does not know Christ? If there's no passion or purpose in his life, he can put on a priest's collar, but it won't make him a Christian any more than going to McDonald's will make him a hamburger. The Lord, however, had His hand on Müller. He never gave up on him.

Müller started with a few pennies in his back pocket and built the biggest orphanage in the world. (I think it has been unsurpassed even to this day.) During his lifetime he cared for thousands of orphans and provided Christian education to countless children. What happened? The prodigal came home.

Don't write off people who may look like a loss. Instead, pray that they would find their purpose and their passion for God in this life.

PRAYER: God, thank You for redeeming human messiness in such spectacular ways. I pray for miracles like this in the lives of my loved ones. Amen.

December 21

SHARE THE LOVE

"A NEW COMMANDMENT I GIVE TO YOU, THAT
YOU LOVE ONE ANOTHER; AS I HAVE LOVED YOU,
THAT YOU ALSO LOVE ONE ANOTHER."
JOHN 13:34

WE AS Christians should be known by our love. People expect us to live lives of good works, to be noble men and women of God. Jesus has set very high standards for us, and we must do our best to keep them.

Following the example of Jesus, we love the unlovable. We stand up against waves of oppression by simply loving those around us, whether they are believers or not. We must trust the Lord to give us the strength to love even those who are against us and seek to bring us down. That's what Jesus did when He was on earth: shine God's love into a world of darkness (John 8:12). In doing this, we will become a sweet-smelling aroma, just like Jesus, wherever we go.

God is love (1 John 4:8). He is the very essence of unconditional love. We stand against the darkness by sharing that love with those around us.

God loved us so much that He gave His only Son in order to save us from our sins (John 3:16). In fact, His love for us is so great that nothing on earth or in heaven can separate us from it (Rom. 8:38–39). How wonderful is that? Jesus died for us, and He asks in return that we serve Him with thankful hearts and share His unconditional love with others.

PRAYER: God, I cannot fathom Your unending love. Help
me to be a reflection of it in this world. Amen.

December 22
THE HOLIDAY OF THE MIND

AND [JESUS] SAID TO THEM, "COME ASIDE BY YOURSELVES TO A
DESERTED PLACE AND REST A WHILE." FOR THERE WERE MANY
COMING AND GOING, AND THEY DID NOT EVEN HAVE TIME TO EAT.
MARK 6:31

WHEN WAS the last time you walked outside as the sun was setting and just meditated on the things of God? When was the last time you took time to rest and watch the world go by? A cow will eat early in the morning when it is still cool. As it gets hot, she will go and sit under a tree and regurgitate the grass she ate, chewing it for the second time in a safe location—that's what makes milk.

When was the last time you "chewed the cud" and just marveled at God's creation? When you take time out to meditate, you will find that God speaks to your soul. God wants to show you what He has created. It is more profitable spending time waiting on God than running around aimlessly.

Quiet meditation is becoming a lost art. It is spending time sitting, waiting, listening, looking, observing, and resting. It is the holiday of the mind.

Jesus told the disciples to "come aside and rest a while." This holiday season, take some time off from the busyness to spend some time resting and recuperating. Fishermen know that you cannot be successful if you haven't repaired your equipment or mended your broken nets. You might catch some fish, but they will just swim through the holes. Spend time mending your nets, and when you go out again, you will bring in a mighty catch for Jesus.

PRAYER: God, show me how to rest fully, even in the busiest of times. Amen.

December 23

MARY, THE MOTHER OF OUR LORD

MY SOUL MAGNIFIES THE LORD, AND MY SPIRIT HAS REJOICED
IN GOD MY SAVIOR. . . . FOR HE WHO IS MIGHTY HAS DONE
GREAT THINGS FOR ME, AND HOLY IS HIS NAME.
LUKE 1:46, 49

WE HAVE Mighty Men Conferences all over the world where we speak about the role of men, and how God has raised up the man to be the prophet, priest, and king in the home. But what about the woman?

In my home my wife is the corner post. The corner post is the "straining post" when you put up a fence. It must be the strongest post—if that post moves, the fence is useless. The husband might be the head of the home, but the woman is the heart.

In today's scripture we read about Mary, the mother of Jesus. She was not divine; she was an ordinary woman. God visited her because she was righteous, and she had the privilege to raise up the Son of God. Can you think of any job on earth more important?

She never defaulted once. When the Lord died on the cross, she was still there. And when the Lord was raised from the dead, she went to the tomb and saw that it was empty. I can't wait to meet Mary one day in heaven.

Don't underestimate the role of the woman in our society. Women are responsible for some of the most important tasks on earth.

PRAYER: Lord, thank You for the strong women in my life.
Please give them strength and endurance. Amen.

December 24

GOD WITH US

"BEHOLD, THE VIRGIN SHALL BE WITH CHILD, AND BEAR
A SON, AND THEY SHALL CALL HIS NAME IMMANUEL,"
WHICH IS TRANSLATED, "GOD WITH US."
MATTHEW 1:23

CHRISTMAS FOR us is family time, and Christmas on the farm is fantastic. Family comes from near and far just to spend time together. It is a very special time, but it can also be a difficult time for some because of broken relationships and sad memories.

Some time ago, our family had organized a surprise luncheon for my dear dad. He was going to be seventy years old, and my brother and sister were all arriving from Johannesburg to celebrate with him. The day dawned, but Dad said, "I am not coming to lunch." And that was that. The family was obliged to attend—we had booked the venue and the food had been prepared—but Dad stayed at home. There were all sorts of emotions, from frustration to anger to disappointment. But looking back now, I realize what his reasons were. Dad was from the old school where "cowboys don't cry," and Dad didn't want to see Mom's place empty at the table (she had passed away not so long before). He could not trust himself not to break down in tears because he would miss her terribly.

We do not always understand the ways people struggle at Christmastime, but let us be gracious to each other. It's easy to get caught up in plans and festivities, but we must not forget the real meaning of Christmas. Though loved ones may not be with us, God is "with us" in Jesus. As His children, may we share His love with special tenderness and sensitivity, celebrating the healing God who never leaves us.

PRAYER: God, thank You for Immanuel, "God with us." I pray You will be among us as we gather together, bringing comfort and hope through Your Son. Amen.

December 25

THE GREATEST GIFT

"GLORY TO GOD IN THE HIGHEST, AND ON EARTH
PEACE, GOODWILL TOWARD MEN!"
LUKE 2:14

IN MY prayer room, I have a beautiful painting of the holy nativity picturing Joseph, a carpenter, who was an earthly father to the Son of God, and the young mother, Mary, a virgin, watching over the baby who is peacefully sleeping in a manger. What a miracle. Faith reveals the wonder of Jesus' birth that night—the greatest gift ever given to mankind. This painting reminds me that Christmas is also about giving of ourselves.

The young man, a carpenter, gave up his reputation in obedience to God in order to take Mary for his wife, even though she was pregnant before they wed. It was unthinkable in those days for a man to do that. Mary was a young girl who love the Lord with a pure heart. She was especially chosen by God to be His mother, who would love and care for Him until He reached manhood. She was glad to receive the honor and also willingly gave up her reputation.

Then God gave up His Son for the sake of redeeming us. In a humble state, born as a helpless baby, Jesus came into this sinful, evil world and gave up His glory and majesty to become our Savior.

So Christmas is a time of giving. It is a time of being with family and celebrating, but for believers it is also a time to think about the real message of love and sacrifice behind the Christmas season. There are many people who don't know Jesus as their Lord and Savior, and this time of the year is a wonderful opportunity to convey the love, peace, and blessedness of our almighty God to those around us.

PRAYER: God, thank You for the unfathomable gift you've given us in your Son. Help me to offer myself sacrificially as a gift to others this season.

December 26

THE MAGI

NOW AFTER JESUS WAS BORN IN BETHLEHEM OF JUDEA IN THE DAYS OF HEROD
THE KING, BEHOLD, WISE MEN FROM THE EAST CAME TO JERUSALEM . . . THEN,
BEING DIVINELY WARNED IN A DREAM THAT THEY SHOULD NOT RETURN
TO HEROD, THEY DEPARTED FOR THEIR OWN COUNTRY ANOTHER WAY.
MATTHEW 2:1, 12

THE VISIT of the Magi to Bethlehem is one of the greatest miracles of faith in the New Testament. These three wise men came from another country in search of the Son of God. What information, mapped routes, or contacts did they have? They had no contact at all with anyone in Israel, but it was a supernatural star in the sky that led them to find the "The King of the Jews."

The more I read about the holy nativity, the more my faith grows, and the more encouraged I am that, for my God, absolutely nothing is impossible. As a farmer I am a practical man. But what practicalities must the wise men have overlooked to go and seek the young Savior? How impossible must it have seemed that they could find Him—and escape the wrath of Herod at the same time?

As improbable as it may seem, these wise men were led by a star to the very spot where they found the Boy and His earthly mother and father. The Bible tells us that they literally fell down on the ground with joy and worshiped Him. And with a final miracle, the three wise men were divinely warned in a dream not to go back to King Herod, for he meant harm to the Child. So again, on faith, they departed back to their own country another way.

This beautiful Christmas story highlights yet again that our God will lead us and take care of our every need, if we would just follow Him.

PRAYER: Dear Lord Jesus, thank You for taking care of all our needs.
Please continue to teach us to listen to Your voice. Amen.

December 27

ONLY BELIEVE

[JESUS] SAID TO THEM, "BUT WHO DO YOU SAY THAT I
AM?" SIMON PETER ANSWERED AND SAID, "YOU ARE
THE CHRIST, THE SON OF THE LIVING GOD."
MATTHEW 16:15–16

WHO DO you say Jesus Christ is? If you say that He was a good man, you would be correct; He *was* a good man, and we know that because He never harmed a single person. He never took advantage of a woman, He never stole, and He never murdered. But that is not good enough, because others are also good men.

Who do you say that Jesus is? I say that He is the living God, the Maker of heaven and earth. And He is living in my heart though the power of His Holy Spirit.

As you are reading this, you might say, "I just lost my loved one and I am so lonely," or you might be in jail, saying, "I made a terrible mistake." Maybe you are in the hospital and you've been told there is no hope for you. Perhaps your heart is aching and you feel as though you will never recover.

I want to tell you that Jesus Christ is the Son of the living God, that He is alive and with you at this very moment. I am praying that the Lord will meet you where you are and that He will undertake for you. He will lift you out of the pit, set your foot on a rock, and give you another chance. All you have to do is get on your knees and say, "Lord, help me," and God will forgive you.

The Lord is not dead. He is alive and He is coming back soon to take us home. What does He require of us? To believe; only believe.

PRAYER: Jesus, I confess that You are the Son of God.
Please lift me up in ways that only You can. Amen.

December 28
PRAY AND READ THE WORD

FOR THERE ARE THREE THAT BEAR WITNESS IN
HEAVEN: THE FATHER, THE WORD, AND THE HOLY
SPIRIT; AND THESE THREE ARE ONE.
1 JOHN 5:7

PRAISE GOD that we have an opportunity to start fresh every new day, and every New Year. Let us allow the Bible to renew our minds as well, dedicating ourselves to deeper study.

There are many men and women who are professors of religion and know the Bible inside and out, but they have not met its Author. The reality is that the Christian faith is all about a Man, not an organization, and this Man's name is Jesus Christ.

When we read the Word and God starts to speak to us through it, then we can find true intimacy. God will reassure us and give us direction. We will begin to notice His influence in matters such as when to buy, when to sell, whether to change jobs, how to take care of our families, and so on. There's an immense peace that comes upon a person who prays and reads the Word.

In Acts 4:13 we read, "Now when they saw the boldness of Peter and John, and perceived that they were uneducated and untrained men, they marveled. And they realized that they had been with Jesus." That is the bottom line.

What the world is looking for is not you and me, but Jesus Christ. The degree to which Jesus is involved in your life determines how effective you will be in kingdom work. Spend time with God. Have intimate times with the Lord, and watch your life change.

PRAYER: God, please bless the time I spend with You, and
open my eyes to the meaning of the Bible. Amen.

December 29
THE STRENGTH OF A NATION

"MY SERVANT CALEB, BECAUSE HE HAS A DIFFERENT SPIRIT IN
HIM AND HAS FOLLOWED ME FULLY, I WILL BRING INTO THE LAND
WHERE HE WENT, AND HIS DESCENDANTS SHALL INHERIT IT."
NUMBERS 14:24

WHEN SOUTH Africa was fighting the war in Angola, north of their borders, they were fighting against the Cubans. Fidel Castro had sent his army to help the Angolans. The South African soldiers came back with reports that the Cubans were easily defeated, and couldn't fight for toffee.

The problem was that the Cubans were not at home. They were in a foreign land, their wives and children were not there, and they had no desire to fight. Try and fight the Cubans in Cuba and you would have a different story. Just think of John F. Kennedy. When the Americans tried to invade Cuba at the Bay of Pigs, the Cubans repelled the might of the American army because they were fighting for their families.

The family unit is absolutely crucial if a country is to succeed. You can get the economy, the politics, and everything else right, but if there is no unity in the family, everything falls apart. For the good of our churches, armed forces, government, and society, let us pray for the health of the family. If ever we needed that prayer, it is now.

PRAYER: Dear God, please bless and strengthen the families of my nation. Amen.

December 30

THE OXYGEN OF THE SOUL

MERCY, PEACE, AND LOVE BE MULTIPLIED TO YOU.
JUDE V. 2

I RECALL an elderly farmer telling me that if my employees are happy and encouraged, they will enjoy going to work and will participate fully in the business operations. That is worth more than anything, he said, because they will work hard and do their best.

There is not one of us who doesn't need to hear the words, "Well done!" or "Great job!" In our current economy, when costs are rising and profit margins need to be carefully watched, we have to seriously cut back. However, there is one thing we cannot afford to do, and that is cut back on encouraging one another. This applies to our friends and family as well. All of us come under the whip at one time or another, and we need to know that there is always a kind word of encouragement or a hug to be found.

Even heaven can hear our words of encouragement to one another. When we give others our approval, we know that God approves of our desire to encourage and build people up.

Someone once said that "a compliment is verbal sunshine." To correct someone can help, but to encourage someone helps a lot more. In fact, encouragement after correction is like sunshine after a shower of rain.

I have a friend who believes that we should not complain to young people for behaving badly, but rather teach them how we would like them to behave. That takes a bit more effort, but most of us appreciate a chat and a word of encouragement. Let's take the time to encourage and build others up at every opportunity.

PRAYER: God, please help me to be a solid source of
encouragement for those around me. Amen.

December 31
COMING ON THE CLOUDS

BEHOLD, HE IS COMING WITH CLOUDS, AND EVERY EYE
WILL SEE HIM, EVEN THEY WHO PIERCED HIM.
REVELATION 1:7

I AM a cloud watcher. When I wake up in the morning and open the curtains, I look out and ask the Lord, "Is it today? Are You coming on the clouds today?" The Lord will come on the clouds to fetch us, bringing all His children with Him. What a day of rejoicing that will be. Those of us who believe will meet Him in the air.

First Thessalonians 4:16–18 reads:

> For the Lord Himself will descend from heaven with a shout, with the voice of an archangel, and with the trumpet of God. And the dead in Christ will rise first. Then we who are alive and remain shall be caught up together with them in the clouds to meet the Lord in the air. And thus we shall always be with the Lord. Therefore comfort one another with these words.

No one knows when the Lord is coming, so we need to prepare ourselves. In the coming new year, let us spend more time with God, and encourage each other just like it says in 1 Thessalonians 4:18—especially those who have lost a loved one. It is a terrible thing to be separated from someone we love, but we do not need to mourn for too long because we will see our loved ones again on the day the Lord comes for us. In the meantime, let us continue to walk the way of Jesus—keeping our eyes on the clouds.

PRAYER: God, please let me live today as if it is my last
on earth, looking forward to Your coming. Amen.

NOTES

JANUARY

January 5.
Based on Abraham Lincoln's letter to his son's teacher, as quoted in K. L. Bhatia, *Textbook on Legal Language and Legal Writing* (New Delhi: Universal Law Publishing Co, 2010), 37.

January 11.
L. B. Cowman, *Streams in the Desert* (Grand Rapids: Zondervan, 1997), 139.

FEBRUARY

February 14.
E. M. Bounds, *The Complete Works of E. M. Bounds* (Radford, VA: Wilder, 2008), 199.

February 25.
Oswald Chambers, quoted in Bruce Wilkinson, ed., *Closer Walk: 365 Daily Devotions That Nurture a Heart for God* (Grand Rapids, MI: Zondervan, 1992), 176; Charles H. Spurgeon, as quoted in Ron Rhodes, *1001 Unforgettable Quotes About God, Faith, and the Bible* (Eugene: Harvest House, 2011), 42.

February 29.
Quoted in C. Silverster Horne, *David Livingstone: Man of Prayer and Action* (Arlington Heights, IL: Christian Liberty Press, 2002), iii.

MARCH

March 19.

Oswald Chambers, quoted in Harold Myra, ed., *The One-Year Book of Encouragement* (Carol Stream, IL: Tyndale, 2010), 129.

March 23.

A. W. Williams, *The Life and Work of Dwight L. Moody* (New York: Cosimo, 1900, 2007), 105.

March 28.

Quoted in Roland H. Bainton, *Here I Stand: A Life of Martin Luther* (Nashville: Abingdon, 1978), 50–51.

APRIL

April 7.

Quoted in *John Fitzgerald Kennedy Jr.: Memorial Tributes in the One Hundred Sixth Congress of the United States* (Washington DC, US Government Printing Office, 1999), 56.

April 25.

This saying is often attributed to Luther but cannot be found among his writings.

MAY

May 3.

Adapted from accounts in Mary C. Crowley, *You Can Too* (Grand Rapids: Revell, 1980), 35, 138.

May 6.

Julia Savacool, "Usain Bolt: Training Secrets of the World's Fastest Man," *Details*, March 1, 2013, http://www.details.com/body-health/fitness-plans/201303/runner-usain-bolt-training-secrets-and-diet.

May 18.

Jerry Bridges, *The Practice of Godliness* (Colorado Springs: NavPress, 1996), 177.

JUNE

June 4.

Quoted in Isabella D. Bunn, *444 Surprising Quotes About Jesus* (Grand Rapids: Bethany House, 2012).

June 5.

Elisabeth Elliot, *Shadow of the Almighty: The Life and Testament of Jim Elliot* (Peabody, MA: Hendrickson, 1958).

June 15.

John Bunyan, *The Complete Works of John Bunyan* (Philadelphia: Bradley, Garretson, & Co., 1872), 79.

June 16.

Quoted in E. T. Horn and A. G. Voigt, eds., *Annotations on the Epistles of Paul* (New York: Charles Scribner's Sons, 1911), 184.

June 21.

Andrew Alexander Bonar, *Memoir and Remains of the Rev. Mac-Cheyne* (Dundee: William Middleton, 1850), 22.

June 22.

Jim Webb, *Born Fighting: How the Scots-Irish Shaped America* (New York: Broadway, 2005), 84.

June 26.

George Washington, *Rules of Civility and Decent Behavior* (New York: Cosimo, 2010), 20.

June 28.

C. T. Studd, *The Chocolate Soldier* (West Palm Beach, FL: Rejoice Publishing, 2012), 5.

JULY

July 3.

Quoted in John H. Armstrong, *True Revival* (Eugene, OR: Harvest House, 2001), 93.

July 5.

Augustine, "Letter 118," in *Letters 1–155*, trans. Roland Teske, part 2, vol. 2 of *The Works of Saint Augustine: A Translation for the 21st Century* (Hyde Park, NY: New City Press, 2003), 116–117.

July 10.

David Wilkerson, *The Cross and the Switchblade* (New York: Jove Books, 1962), 61.

July 17.

Rick Warren, *The Purpose Driven Life* (Grand Rapids: Zondervan, 2012), 63; Eliza E. Hewitt, "When We All Get to Heaven," 1989, public domain.

AUGUST

August 9.

Quoted in Michael Catt, *Upgrade: From Adequacy to Abundance* (Fort Washington, PA: CLC Publications, 2012), 158.

August 16.

Quoted in David J. Phillips, *Peoples on the Move: Introducing the Nomads of the World* (Pasadena, CA: William Carey, 2001), xiii.

SEPTEMBER

September 8.

John Bunyan, *The Holy War* (New Kensington, PA: 1985), 36.

September 23.

Oswald Chambers, "The Purpose of Prayer," *My Utmost for His Highest*, http://utmost.org/the-purpose-of-prayer/.

OCTOBER

October 17.

The film was directed by David L. Cunningham, the son of Loren Cunningham, who is the founder of the missionary organization YWAM (Youth With A Mission).

NOVEMBER

November 3.

Charles H. Spurgeon, *Faith's Checkbook: Daily Devotions to Treasure* (Issaquah, WA: Made for Success, 2014), January 5 entry.

November 5.

Quoted in Martin H. Manser (ed.), *The Westminster Collection of Christian Quotations* (Louisville, KY: Westminster John Knox, 2001), 165.

November 9.

Thomas à Kempis, *The Imitation of Christ: Four Books*, trans. W. Benham (London: John C. Nimmo, 1886), 203.

November 20.

Quoted in Leonard Allen, ed., *The Contemporaries Meet the Classics on Prayer* (West Monroe, LA: Howard, 2003), 195.

November 26.

Quoted in Roger Lipp and Kathi Lipp, *Happy Habits for Every Couple* (Eugene, OR: Harvest House, 2009), 21.

About the Author

ANGUS BUCHAN is a farmer turned evangelist whose life story was captured in the film *Faith Like Potatoes*. Angus is married to Jill and has five children and ten grandchildren. The founder of Shalom Ministries, the Beth-Hatlaim home for orphaned children, and Mighty Men Conferences, Buchan is recognized for his straightforward preaching and has spoken to hundreds of thousands of people around the globe.